THE SAN FRANCISCO 49ERS
TEAM
OF THE
DECADE

How to Order:

Quantity discounts are available from the publisher, Prima Publishing & Communications, P.O. Box 1260JMB, Rocklin, CA 95677; telephone (916) 624-5718. On your letterhead include information concerning the intended use of the books and the number of books you wish to purchase.

U.S. Bookstores and Libraries: Please submit all orders to St. Martin's Press, 175 Fifth Avenue, New York, NY 10010; telephone (212) 674-5151.

THE SAN FRANCISCO 49ERS
TEAM OF THE DECADE

Revised to Include the 1989-1990
Championship Season

Michael W. Tuckman

Jeff Schultz

Prima Publishing & Communications
P.O. Box 1260JMB
Rocklin, CA 95677
(916) 624-5718

Copy editing by Steve Hornbostel
Typography by Howarth & Smith Ltd.
Production by Carol Dondrea, Bookman Productions
Interior design by Judith Levinson
Cover design by The Dunlavey Studio
Cover photo by Michael Rondon, *San Jose Mercury News*
Color separations by Monarch Color Service

Prima Publishing & Communications
Rocklin, CA

Library of Congress Cataloging-in-Publication Data

Tuckman, Michael.
    San Francisco 49ers, team of the decade/by Michael Tuckman, Jeff Schultz.
    p.   cm.
    Includes index.
    ISBN 1-55958-053-4
    1. San Francisco 49ers (Football team)—History. I. Schultz, Jeff. II. Title.
GV956.5.S3T83   1990
796.332'64'0979461—dc20   90-8736
                                        CIP

90 91 92 — 10 9 8 7 6 5 4 3 2 1

Printed in the United States of America

Acknowledgments

The authors would like to express their appreciation for the valuable assistance provided by the following people:

Eddie DeBartolo, Carmen Policy, John McVay, Bill Walsh, George Seifert, Mike Holmgren, Bill McPherson, Tony Razzano, Jerry Walker, Joe Montana, Ronnie Lott, Dwight Clark, Randy Cross, Roger Craig, Harris Barton, Dan Bunz, Fred Dean, Riki Ellison, Keith Fahnhorst, Jeff Fuller, Pierce Holt, Guy McIntyre, William "Bubba" Paris, Tom Rathman, Jerry Rice, Bill Ring, Bill Romanowski, Mike Shumann, Dan Stubbs, John Taylor, Keena Turner, Wendell Tyler, Steve Wallace, Wesley Walls, Michael Walter, Mike Wilson, Eric Wright, Steve Young, John Ralston, Dave Rahn, Rodney Knox, Al Barba, R.C. Owens, Robin Lockwood, Gregg Houts, Nicole Langerak, Darla Maeda, Angi Repetto, Frank Cooney, Dan Hruby, Garry Nivers, Ron Thomas, Mike Silver, Mike Weaver, and the summer staff at Sierra College.

Leonard M. Apcar, Daniel Bardol, Jeff Bayer, Alan Benjamin, Newell C. Bossart, Michael Britton, Susan K. Bryant, Jim Carkonen, Gary O. Concoff, Peter M. Feibleman, Bob Griffith, Michael C. Harris, Howard Huff, Kristen Hutchinson, Hank Janpol, Jamie Kaufmann, Jill Kinersly, Michael Lewis, Stacey Mahlstedt, The Mahlstedt Family, Mark A. McClure, Paula Morgan, Charles "Butch" Nemec, Gilbert C. Powers,

Donald W. Steele, Scott Stover, Mike Strohmaier, and Tim Radi for providing the tools.

Special Acknowledgment

The authors wish to express their grateful appreciation to prominent Bay Area sports attorney William H. Hedden for his valuable contribution to this book.

Contents

x

Foreword

NFL pundits declared that the San Francisco 49ers dominated the '80s by virtue of their style of play and record. Regardless of whether this position is accepted as fact, there is no doubt that the team dominated my life during this period. It's as though an entire life experience was encapsulated and compressed into one decade.

Owning an NFL franchise is similar to being a parent. One day your child will come through the door with a straight-A report card and three community service awards. The next week you'll receive a call advising you that he or she just wrecked your new automobile after attending a wild party. The wins are exhilarating, but the losses can be incredibly depressing to an owner who has made a strong commitment to winning. I lived through all these peaks and valleys with a good deal of confusion and frustration. The learning process has reacquainted me with the virtue of balance, which is a basic principle that has been preached to me since childhood. Organizations of any kind require a proper alignment of resources and the right mixture of management and capital to guarantee their smooth and efficient operation. I feel that the 49ers have substantially reached this state of equilibrium.

I developed several "love affairs" during my thirteen years of involvement with the team. The liaison I enjoyed with my players has been invigorating and unique. Some of these men were older than me when I first purchased the team, and most were not much younger when the fortunes of the franchise started looking good. I have a special feeling for each and every athlete who has worn or does wear the 49er uniform, and I honestly believe that no matter how long I remain in the NFL I will never reach the point of viewing them as an economic commodity that is a necessary ingredient in the business of professional sport.

My relationship with the coaching staff personnel has been extremely rewarding and interesting. Bill Walsh and I experienced emotions in our years together that can be characterized as warm, affectionate and dedicated, and yet at times hostile, strident and adversarial. George Seifert has displayed a unique talent not only in his coaching abilities, but also in the quality of his leadership, which is very effective without displaying flair or a high profiled approach.

My front office executives have been a source of continuing pride for me and the rest of the team. Our organization has been characterized by many, both within and outside the NFL, as the best run entity in professional sport. We have been criticized by several factions for ignoring the traditional bottom line and thereby placing an emphasis on winning alone. These criticisms are somewhat exaggerated and have a tendency to ignore the realities of economic life connected with professional football, especially realities that develop with four world championships. The criticisms also ignore a basic philosophy that has guided my family in the operation of the Edward J. DeBartolo Corporation for 50 years. That philosophy simply holds to the tenet that good business is measured by many more factors than red or black ink at the bottom of a financial report. It is my personal belief that winning with style and dignity in the competitive and public world of the NFL amounts to good business.

The '80s provided me the opportunity to mature, to operate in a unique arena, to have some fun, and to provide the leadership and support that was necessary to bring four world championships to the City by the Bay. The enchantment and attraction that will never wane, whether or not I remain with the 49ers, is that special affection that I have developed for the San Francisco Bay Area. The team and the community now have four fantastic trophies that represent numerous memories and a legacy that can never be denied. I have realized even more.

Eddie DeBartolo

THE SAN FRANCISCO 49ERS
TEAM OF THE DECADE

Introduction

*I*n the annals of modern American sports history, two things—like death and taxes—are for certain. 1) Dynasties never last forever; and 2) Great players never play forever. Consider the Green Bay Packers, Dallas Cowboys and Pittsburgh Steelers of the National Football League.

Under legendary head coach Vince Lombardi, and with such great players as Bart Starr, Jim Taylor, Paul Hornung, Jerry Kramer and Ray Nitschke, the Packers dominated the NFL for years, winning five league championships from 1961 to 1967, including the first two Super Bowls. And with a total of 11, they garnered more championships than any other team in NFL history.

When the Dallas Cowboys joined the NFL as an expansion team in 1960, head coach Tom Landry began a 29-year reign that would include an unprecedented 20 straight winning seasons, 18 playoff berths and five Super Bowl appearances. Along the way the team's roster would boast such greats as Roger Staubach, Don Meredith, Bob Lilly, Dan Reeves and Mel Renfro. In addition, "America's Team" created one of the most envied operations in the history of professional sports.

Longtime Pittsburgh Steelers owner, Art Rooney, struggled through many losing seasons while setting new standards for futility. But with the hiring of head coach Chuck Noll in 1969, Rooney was rewarded with an unequaled four Super Bowl titles, from 1974 to 1979. With the likes of "Mean" Joe Greene, Jack Lambert and Mel Blount on defense, and an offense that included Terry Bradshaw, Franco Harris and Lynn Swann, Rooney's "Steel Curtain" teams of the 1970s were among the most feared and respected.

But while the noble Packers, Cowboys, and Steelers have together accounted for over one-third of all Super Bowl victories, they have recently fallen on very hard times. In fact, in 1988, the San Francisco 49ers won more games than these once-great teams combined.

The San Francisco 49ers were not among the NFL's strongest teams in the years immediately following the NFL-AFL merger. The team struggled to a 58-79-1 regular season record from 1971–79 and qualified for the playoffs only once. The change in ownership following the 1976 season—Edward J. DeBartolo Jr. bought 90 percent of the 49ers' stock from Jean and Josephine Morabito and Golden State Warriors owner Franklin Mieuli—had done little to improve the situation as the team went 5–9 and 2–14 in 1977 and 1978.

But the history of the franchise took a dramatic turn the following year when DeBartolo chose Stanford head coach Bill Walsh to guide the 49ers into the 1980s.

Pressure to win runs high for an NFL head coach. Even after achieving the Super Bowl, pro football's crowning glory, things hardly get easier. John Madden learned the hard way. He related this story after winning Super Bowl XI in Pasadena.

"Our team charter had just landed at the airport and a huge crowd was there to greet us. We just won the Super Bowl, right? So I walk off the plane and people start yelling and cheering. I'm smiling and waving and just starting to enjoy it, when this guy in the crowd yells, 'Hey coach, we're gonna win again next year, right?' I couldn't believe it. We hadn't even celebrated that one yet!"

Bill Walsh inherited a team that was the NFL's worst. To make his job even more difficult, the 49ers also finished dead last in total offense in 1978 and next-to-last in defense. The situation seemed hopeless for the veteran coach. But just two years after joining the Niners, Walsh took his team to the Super Bowl and won a convincing 26–21 victory over the Cincinnati Bengals, the first of four NFL championships in the 1980s. It was the fastest turnaround in NFL history.

Chapter 1

A TALE OF TWO SEASONS
The Third Championship

"Compared to the other two Super Bowls, this one will be remembered the most because of the way we came back from all of the adversity and criticism."
—*Bill Walsh after Super Bowl XXIII*

One on top of another, the improbabilities piled up, as if the season had been scripted by some demented Hollywood screenwriter.

Imagine. The quarterback, who had evolved into one of the most revered athletes in the history of professional football, was doubting from week to week whether he had a starting job. Imagine. The head coach, who used to devour Civil War battle accounts and probably dominated the neighborhood kids years before in summer battles with toy soldiers, was being second-guessed as a strategist. Imagine. A football team that had prided itself, even built a tradition, on comeback victories, had allowed one of the NFL's mediocre entries, Phoenix, to come back from a 23-

point deficit in perhaps the most humiliating loss in franchise history.

Imagine, that after a 16-week emotional roller coaster, this team would land in the Super Bowl. And win. With a quarterback who hyperventilated on the winning drive.

"It had never happened to me before," San Francisco quarterback Joe Montana said moments after Super Bowl XXIII. "I thought I was yelling as loud as I could, but nobody could hear me."

Neither Montana's teammates nor the opponent, the Cincinnati Bengals, nor any of the 75,000 fans on that warm January evening at Joe Robbie Stadium in Miami were aware the quarterback was struggling to inhale and exhale at a normal pace. What they knew was that he had just badly overthrown wide receiver Jerry Rice near the left sideline and that the 49ers still trailed the Bengals by three points with one minute and 22 seconds left in the championship game. They knew that 35 yards still separated San Francisco from the Cincinnati goal line and at least 10 yards separated the team from comfortable range for attempting a game-tying field goal.

On the sideline, San Francisco kicker Mike Cofer was loosening up. Head coach Bill Walsh was thinking field goal, too, at that point. He could not understand why, after the overthrow, Montana appeared dazed and confused, why he was twirling his right hand and seemingly pointing at himself. His lips were moving, sort of, but it was difficult to tell if they were forming words.

"He looked at me, and I thought he wanted a time-out," Walsh said, "I said, 'No. No timeout.' I had no idea that he was suffering. It was not worth a timeout even if he threw an incomplete pass again because we had to have the timeout in case of a field goal, in case we got down close enough where we wanted to run one play without the clock running out on us. I didn't think he was hyperventilating."

No matter. Montana's breathing soon returned to normal, and the stadium stopped spinning inside his head. He resumed being Joe Montana, resumed an opportunity to magnify his reputation as the greatest clutch quarterback in NFL history. He did. A few tosses and 48 seconds after nearly overdosing on huffing and puffing, Montana threw a winning touchdown pass to wide receiver John Taylor—which made for another unlikely subplot. It was Taylor who had been shackled the first four weeks of the season by a suspension.

It was one final twist of fate, even twist of logic, in San Francisco's 1988 season, a year that started with controversy and whispers but ended with a 20–16 championship victory over Cincinnati. Still, there was nothing confusing about the result of this roller coaster experience. It gave the 49ers their third Super Bowl of the 1980s—remarkably, their third championship with three unique teams in a span of eight seasons—and stamped them with a label that, until that evening in Miami, had been the subject of a lingering, coast-to-coast debate: "Team of the Decade."

Only one thing could make the Niners' third championship seem secondary in importance: closing the decade with another title and becoming the first team since the Pittsburgh Steelers of 1978 and 1979 to win back-to-back championships. Under new head coach George Seifert, who stepped up from defensive coordinator when Walsh stepped out of football and into the television booth as a commentator, the 49ers won 17 of 19 games in 1989, capping the season with a 55-10 dismantling of Denver in Super Bowl XXIV in New Orleans.

It was such a dominating season that even Walsh labeled the fourth championship team as the strongest ever in San Francisco. But for him, the third title team will go down as the most memorable, and that is no small statement. The 1981 team made a strong impression because its championship was the first in franchise history and followed a string of eight consecutive non-playoff seasons, and because its Super Bowl victory came against the Cincinnati Bengals, the team owned by Paul Brown, who had in 1974 refused to promote then-assistant Walsh to head coach. It was a season that caught everybody by surprise, even the players. "I think we were all too young and too stupid to realize what was going on that year," mused Mike Shumann, a wide receiver on that team.

Three years later, when the 49ers took their second title, they left no hint that it might have been a fluke, winning a league record 18 games and dismembering the Miami Dolphins in Super Bowl XIX at Stanford Stadium. It was such a dominating team, a lopsided season, according to wide receiver Dwight Clark, "From the first game, there was no doubt we would go all the way, even though we didn't make a video with six weeks to go, like the Bears, called, 'The Super Bowl Shuffle.' "

But San Francisco's third championship season would best be filmed as a two-part mini-series, with horror movie moderator Elvira as narrator for part one. There were the highs of winning consecutive road games in the loud and unfriendly confines of the New Orleans Superdome, Giants Stadium in East Rutherford, N.J., and the Seattle Kingdome . . . but the low of a 17-point loss in the home opener to the lightly regarded Atlanta Falcons. There were the highs of running back Roger Craig's 190-yard rushing day against the Los Angeles Rams, of quarterback Steve Young's last-minute 49-yard touchdown run against Minnesota . . . but the lows of blowing that huge second-half lead in Phoenix and an uninspired loss the following week to the L.A. Raiders.

The 49ers had fallen to 6–5, and suddenly it seemed

as though their multi-million dollar, gold-plated head-quarters in Santa Clara had been turned into a chamber of horrors. They were in danger of not making the playoffs for the first time in six years. Last rites were being read to them in Bay Area newspapers, and rumors began swirling that major changes in the organization could be coming, in the front office and on the field.

"We didn't know what was going on," guard Guy McIntyre recalled. "All of a sudden, everything was going wrong. We were getting all of these penalties on the offensive line, and we didn't think they were justified. I remember one day, Bill came in and really screamed at us—I mean he really screamed. He said we weren't getting the job done, made it seem like it was our fault. We didn't know what was happening."

It was at this point that the 49ers convened a players-only meeting. It was not the kind of session you hear about where team members curse and rip off locker doors and question one another's gender, all in the name of "clearing the air." This was a genuine, slightly more subdued therapy session, and, in the words of 13-year veteran Randy Cross, "not a pep talk."

Cross, who directed the meeting, told his teammates: "It's not the end of the world, but you had better realize the coaches are under a lot more pressure than you guys are. Coaches have a lot of things to worry about."

Whether it was that dose of reality or divine intervention or some cosmic fluke, a metamorphosis began that was as astounding as it was mysterious. In the following game against the defending champion Washington Redskins, Montana began to find his throwing touch, Rice, who had been bothered by nagging injuries, rediscovered the end zone for the first time in four weeks, and San Francisco pounded the Redskins on national television.

The 49ers went on to win seven of their final eight games, the only setback coming in a meaningless regular-season finale against the Rams. The seven victories came by a combined score of 210–79.

This was not an expected turnaround, not even by Cross, the team's resident therapist and master of perspective, who remarked before the Super Bowl, "I'm not going to lie to you and tell you I was planning on this." Even Walsh, who had survived his most emotionally draining regular season since 1982 (when he came close to resigning) had difficulty comprehending what he called, "one of the strangest seasons I've seen." From the early volatility, he saw his team come back to score one-sided playoff victories over Minnesota and Chicago, which, he says, are the two greatest games he has seen his team play.

Free safety Ronnie Lott, one of a handful of 49ers to play on all three championship teams, said the difference was in attitude as much as anything.

"When you start losing, you start doubting your skills," Lott said. "You doubt what you're about, and you start measuring yourself against other people. We're a good football team. We won the Super Bowl. But . . . we lost to Phoenix on some fluke. Those things are going to happen. We were looking to each opponent, going up and down, up and down. And that's how we played—up and down, up and down. We never really set that standard.

"There is one common denominator in all three championship teams we had. We set a standard. We all thought we could win. We don't worry and play to other people's standards. That's the main reason we won last year. We said, 'Look, let's play 49ers football. Let's play to our standards.' You maximize your skills, now you have a chance to win."

At the outset, the 49ers showed little difficulty doing that. In the season opener at New Orleans, the Niners faced a team that had been gearing up for them since the previous year, when the Saints finished second to

San Francisco in the NFC West Division. A lot of good it did them. Despite an injured elbow that would force him to leave the game in the fourth quarter, Montana threw three touchdown passes in the third quarter, two to tight end John Frank and one to split end Mike Wilson, to lead the 49ers to a 34–33 victory.

From New Orleans, the 49ers headed to another visitors' nightmare, Giants Stadium. Excluding a strike game in 1987, San Francisco had been outscored 66–6 in its last two visits to the New Jersey swamp. "We wanted to overcome whatever impression people had that the Giants had our number," Walsh said.

But there was a problem. Montana's elbow had swelled to the size of a grapefruit after the Saints game and, even though he proclaimed that he would be ready by the following Sunday, Walsh started Steve Young at quarterback. But by halftime, the Niners were struggling offensively, tied 10–10, and Walsh was upset about two Young fumbles, one of which helped set up a New York touchdown. As Walsh and Montana were walking off the field, the coach turned to his quarterback and said, "Be ready to go in."

Montana was startled. "I didn't know if he was kidding or not," he said.

Sure enough, when the 49ers' offense came onto the field in the third quarter, Montana had his helmet on and Young stayed behind to signal plays. Montana showed only moderate success against the Giants' renowned defense, but with 42 seconds left, he accounted for the biggest play to that point in the NFL season. Catching New York with single coverage on Rice, who had dropped two passes that day, Montana threw a 78-yard touchdown pass to his wide receiver to secure a 20–17 win.

The following day, a New York tabloid showed a picture of Giants cornerback Mark Collins sitting, dejected, on the sideline, with the headline, "BURNED," blazing across the top of the page.

If things were looking bad for the Giants, the 49ers were at the other end of the spectrum. They had two cardiac wins, and one of the few perceived "easy" dates on the schedule was coming up—the home opener against the Atlanta Falcons. The Niners had not lost to Atlanta in their previous eight meetings, and the Falcons were in one of those protracted rebuilding processes. But this game was one reason so many coaches leave the profession with a screwed-up pH level in their digestive systems. The Falcons won 34–17—their only victory in the first eight weeks of the season. Little did Walsh realize when he woke up that morning that his defense would crumble and that the Niners' offensive highlight would be a touchdown pass to McIntyre, who had lined up as a tight end.

It also had become apparent that the Niners had some growing up to do. Although the team was sprinkled with veterans, the influx of rookies and young free agents the previous few years had made San Francisco one of the youngest teams in the NFL. That youth showed under pressure. As nose tackle Michael Carter recalled a few days after the loss, "The worst thing about the Atlanta game was the way guys were shouting at each other. Really. Plays were coming in late and guys were yelling at each other in the huddle instead of worrying about their jobs. Atlanta players were laughing at us. Laughing."

Cross proved to be prophetic after the defeat, however. "Hopefully, in December and January, we'll be able to look back on this game as just a speed bump."

The smooth road was still miles away. After the loss, Montana, who had started but thrown three interceptions, intimated that his coach's quarterback rotation was making him uneasy. During the ensuing week, he and Walsh met to discuss the situation, after which both indicated everything had been smoothed over. For one more week, peace reigned. In fact, the Niners played their best game of the regular season, dismantling the Seattle Seahawks 38–7 behind Montana's four touchdown passes (three to Rice) and a defense that limited Seattle to 164 yards in offense.

"We were Atlanta today, and they were the 49ers," veteran cornerback Eric Wright cracked.

But more of those speed bumps were approaching. The Niners' offense struggled again in week five against Detroit, but the 49ers beat the Lions 20–13, thanks to strong play by the defense and a punt return for a touchdown by the just-activated John Taylor. However, tight end John Frank suffered a broken hand and was sidelined for six weeks.

The roller coaster continued. San Francisco lost the following week to Denver in overtime but defeated the Rams by a field goal in Anaheim. Uncharacteristically, any success on offense at this time wasn't because of the controlled passing game, which had been a 49ers trademark since Walsh drove up the peninsula from Stanford. Neither Montana, partly because of his health, nor Young had done much to distinguish himself in the coach's eyes. The most successful play was for either to turn around and hand the ball to running back Roger Craig.

Craig rushed for a career-high 190 yards and three touchdowns against the Rams, one of seven times he would bust 100 yards in the season. But despite the victory over a division rival and a 5–2 record, Walsh was disturbed. He never had been enamored with run-dominated offenses.

"You get trapped into something, and then you depend on those 5-yard gains," he once said. "Soon, 5-yard gains become 4-yard gains and 3-yard gains. Soon, you find yourself designing plays for 5-yard gains."

In Walsh's way of thinking, the 49ers had become

trapped in a one-dimensional, low-yield offense—and they didn't soon break free. Defensive coordinator George Seifert saw his unit come up with one of its best performances of the season at Chicago, but the Niners lost to the Bears 10–9. If that wasn't enough, Walsh was second-guessed in the media for his handling of the quarterback situation. In the Bears game, he pulled Montana before the last possession, hoping the more mobile Young could maneuver the team into field goal range. It didn't work, and Walsh was left with two confused quarterbacks—Montana because he had been pulled, Young because he had been asked to enter the game cold and move the team in a difficult situation.

Walsh said Montana was "fatigued" and rested him the next two weeks against Minnesota and Phoenix. Montana, not surprisingly, said he felt fine and expressed to the media his feelings of insecurity. Walsh, while not saying he would have pulled the strings differently, nonetheless began to admit that dealing with his two-headed quarterback was much more difficult than he had imagined.

"In the middle of the season, just absolutely zany things started to happen," Walsh said. "The Montana thing was part of it, the loss to the Bears. Any given play could have changed the outcome of that game. But as it turned out, it was the best thing that could have happened to us, just to set up how we felt and they felt psychologically before we played them again later. At the time, it wasn't devastating to me, but it was to others in the organization. A 10–9 game between two of the top teams in football is just a part of football. Ironically, we'd play there again with all of the chips on the line in the NFC title game, and they went into the game rather smug about how their defense could take us apart."

Forty-Niners owner Edward DeBartolo Jr., who has rarely been shy with the media, went out on a limb after the loss to the Bears and predicted the two teams would meet again in the conference title game. But he added in the next breath, smiling, "If I'm wrong, I'll just say I lied." The Niners needed to hear a good joke at the time. They were 5–3, and if the playoffs had opened then, the players and coaches would have been free to reserve tee times at their local golf courses.

It was clear that San Francisco was going to keep even the most adept prognosticators guessing. Minnesota, which had stunned the 49ers in the first round of the playoffs the previous season, appeared to be on the way to another win at Candlestick Park in week nine. Then came the Scramble of the Decade, ugly as it was. With less than two minutes remaining and the 49ers trailing by four points, Young was chased out of the pocket by Viking behemoths on a third-down play and took off toward the goal line . . . or at least in that general direction. His path was more like the infamous road to Hana. He ran, he broke tackles, he stumbled, he broke tackles, he went left, he went right—at times it seemed he went backward. Finally, when he reached the 5-yard line, he ran out of breath, but lunged and barely made it into the end zone to give San Francisco a 24–21 win.

In the locker room afterward, teammate Harry Sydney turned to Young: "A hell of a run, Steve. Next time, open your eyes."

"He won't get many points for style," Cross said, "but the final spasm got him in."

The fun lasted until the third quarter of the next week's game in the Arizona desert. After building a 23–0 lead over the Phoenix Cardinals, the 49ers wilted. Phoenix scored 24 unanswered points, the winning touchdown coming with three seconds left. Seifert walked off the field in a daze. Walsh walked off fuming and took those feelings with him into the locker room. His comments to the media were brief; his comments to his assistants weren't. The sounds of obscenities filtered through the walls and under the door of the coaches' dressing room. Not a prime-time word could be heard, and it was clear that the only things redder than Walsh's face were his assistants' ears.

"The first half of the Phoenix game may have been the best defensive game we've played since I've been here," Seifert said. "It was one of those games where everything was going right. But that last drive where they got into position to win the game was the worst defense we've played since I've been here. We were in a trance on the field. We kid the players about being the wildebeest. You know how just before the lion catches the wildebeest, it goes into a trance so it doesn't suffer when it gets killed? We were the wildebeest."

Walsh wasn't in a trance so much as he felt everything he had built was crumbling. For a man who has admitted to being too sensitive and taking things too personally, this was not an uncommon reaction. Still, he had not been this low since his defending champions went 3–6 in the 1982 strike-condensed season, leading him to borrow from Hamlet's soliloquy and ponder retirement.

"The Phoenix game was an absolute downer for me because we had always taken pride in beating people that way," he said. "It was just one of those things that hurt deeply. Your pride, your self-esteem was really hurt and it was terribly humiliating. Any play, any decision I could have made in the last drive could easily have won the game in retrospect. It was an utterly embarrassing game for all of us. But even worse was the next one."

Walsh's worst fears—residual effect from the loss to the Cardinals—were realized the following week when the Niners lost 9–3 to the Raiders at home to fall to 6–5. "I've seen this organization at the top, and I've seen it at rock bottom" free safety Ronnie Lott said in a quiet locker room. "Right now it's at rock bottom."

"Maybe," linebacker Riki Ellison said, "it's our turn to be behind the eight ball."

There was more lying around the locker room than spare parts and broken hearts, to borrow from a song. There was broken glass. Somebody had taken out his frustrations on a drink cooler, shattering the glass door. So much for the pause that refreshes. Everybody claimed innocence, even the owner, DeBartolo, who had been one of the first into the locker room. Who was the culprit? "Somebody with a lot at stake," a team spokesman said.

With Walsh taking heat for his play-calling and Montana and Young taking heat for their lack of play-production, there wasn't much reason for optimism. The only thing heating up was the rumor mill. An NFL gossip newsletter passed the word that unless there were dramatic changes on the field, DeBartolo would fire Walsh. There were other whispers that Walsh might head down to San Diego for employment, or to Detroit, or simply into hibernation for a year or so until an expansion franchise came along.

Super Bowl? This season? You had to be kidding. There were no such claims from this organization. Such a prediction would have wiped the three-headed Elvis impersonator off the cover of the *National Enquirer*.

Curiously, there was only one player in the 49ers' locker room after the loss to the Raiders who expressed even a hint of optimism heading into the final five weeks of the season. His name: Joseph C. Montana. "We have to be optimistic," the maligned quarterback said. "We'll probably be the only ones who will be."

Appropriately, it was Montana who rejuvenated the 49ers and slapped them out of their state of rigor mortis. Looking fresher and certainly performing more effectively, he threw for two touchdowns in a 37–21 Monday night victory over the Redskins. There were other signs the team's fortunes might be changing.

Taylor erred in catching a punt at his 5-yard line, but he broke two tackles and blazed 95 yards for a score. And Rice, who had been slowed most of the year by injuries, most recently a badly sprained ankle, caught a touchdown pass that was tipped by a Redskins defender.

"Maybe this is what I needed to turn things around," he said, and, indeed, the victory turned around the 49ers' season.

"We began to jell as a team," Walsh said, "and we could see our opposition fading." The Niners won their next three games—over San Diego, Atlanta and New Orleans—by a composite score of 91–30 and had clinched the NFC West Division title by the time they took the field for their regular-season finale against the Rams.

The players' meeting that followed the loss to the Raiders and preceded the winning streak apparently did more than any other team meeting in franchise history. Why? According to McIntyre, "We started playing with more enthusiasm. We knew we were good, we knew we could play, but we weren't going out there and having any fun. We weren't showing any of that high school type emotion, guys piling on top of each other after touchdowns. That's what was missing. I think you saw a few piles in that Washington game."

"We were 6–5, so obviously we had some problems," Cross said. "But people had played back to us before, and we thought they still could. You're more embarrassed than anything else, especially after a loss like that Phoenix game. You're getting flak from the press, you're getting flak from the fans, you're getting talk and comments from friends and family, and the coaches are working up a serious pucker, because that can be a tough, tough situation. Those are the kinds of losing streaks and games that can lead to job changes, both for assistants and head coaches."

Guard Jesse Sapolu thinks the team actually started feeling less pressure at mid-season. "When we were 6–5, everybody had us in the dump. Nobody thought we had a chance anymore, and that kinda took the pressure off. Expectations weren't so high, so we just went out and had fun. It all started with the Washington game."

The biggest factor was Montana's improved play. His previous ailments—bruised ribs, sore-shoulder, swollen elbow, sprained knee, sore back, even the flu—no longer appeared debilitating. At 32, perhaps he wasn't the same physically as he had been 10 years earlier, but he was moving well and throwing accurately and making few poor decisions.

"He was hurting in the middle of the season," Walsh said. "He wasn't performing to his full potential, but it was easily explainable. He wasn't moving as well and didn't have as much zip on the ball, and we were at a semi-crossroad because we knew from experience that the stretch run would be the most important, that in a sense it would be up to our opposition to fade and for us to come on strong, which we had been doing every year. So we knew the final five or six games would be the key to the season."

In the first four weeks of the season, the 49ers (4–0) had so far outplayed division rivals New Orleans (1–3) and Los Angeles (2–2) that it didn't matter that they turned into their mid-season evil twin in the finale against the Rams. L.A. won 38–16 and although it gave the 49ers a chance to munch on some humble pie, nobody seemed too upset about it. At least not in the Bay Area. The result put the Rams in the playoffs as a wild-card entry and knocked the New York Giants out of the box and into the Club Med season. When a New York reporter phoned Giants quarterback Phil Simms in the late stages of the 49ers-Rams game, Simms said,

"I'm just sitting here, staring now, watching the 49ers lie down like dogs."

How appropriate it was that a 49ers player named Bruce Collie issued this response: "At least we're still in the kennel."

Despite the loss to the Rams, it was obvious the 49ers' dog days were long over. Montana and Rice were back at the top of their game, and the defense had long since recovered from the Phoenix disaster. Even the drink cooler in the Candlestick Park locker room was repaired.

The team also had the previous season's playoff loss to the Vikings as motivation. As Walsh said going into the playoffs, "last year we were on such a big roll and the atmosphere was so positive, nobody seemed to be able to stay with us. This time, we're really sober, and that's probably the best state of mind to be in."

In the next two weeks, the Niners body-slammed the Vikings and Bears to earn a trip to Miami. Each win held special significance. Before the Minnesota game, Montana had not directed a post-season touchdown drive in the previous three years and Rice had never scored a playoff touchdown. Against the Vikings, the two hooked up for three scoring passes. Said Lott, "Jerry had to learn how to play in the playoffs."

San Francisco dominated both sides of the line of scrimmage. The offensive line smothered Minnesota's vaunted pass rush and paved the way for Craig to rush for 135 yards and two touchdowns. The defense held the Vikings to one touchdown and to 54 yards rushing and applied constant pressure on quarterback Wade Wilson. The result even gave the appearance that there had never been a problem between Walsh and Montana. The two posed for pictures together before walking off the field, and Montana presented the coach with the game ball for his 100th win with the 49ers.

There was another twist a few minutes later.

Although Montana told the media that the win "relieved a little pressure" the team had felt because of three previous playoff flops, he hardly expressed complete satisfaction during the locker room celebration. Not usually one to make speeches, Montana told his teammates, "Teams that have beaten other teams by big margins have come back the next week and played terrible, and that is not going to happen to this ballclub. I ain't bullshittin'. We've opened the door, we're gonna go through it next week, and we're gonna kick ass and take no prisoners the week after."

Indeed, the 49ers hardly played like a satisfied team against Chicago. They beat the Bears 28–3 in what Walsh called "the greatest road victory" since his arrival. San Francisco had no trouble acclimatizing itself to the meat-locker conditions of Soldier Field on the shore of Lake Michigan, where the temperature had dropped to 17 degrees—minus-26 with the windchill. Instead, they played as if it were 78 degrees with a breeze in Malibu.

"I remember their players staring at us in the pregame," Charles Haley recalled. "They didn't think we could take the cold. Well, my mama didn't raise no chump."

With the victory, the 49ers earned the right to defrost in Miami, earned their third trip to the Super Bowl in the 1980s and earned a shot at having their names surgically attached to a decade, much in the same way the Pittsburgh Steelers will forever be attached to the 1970s and the Green Bay Packers to the 1960s.

Suddenly, there wasn't a discontented player in the lot. There was no better example of this than offensive tackle Bubba Paris. Before the season, Paris had lost a battle for a starting job to Steve Wallace, and the team, unhappy with Paris' continued weight problems, entertained trade talks involving him. But going into the Super Bowl, Paris, who had been a starter on the 1984 title team, felt he would make a major contribution in the final game.

"In the last two weeks or so leading up to the Super Bowl, I had two premonitions," Paris recalled. "I knew we would beat Chicago by 20 points. It turned out I was a little off because we beat them by 25. Then on the way home from that game on the plane, I had a strong premonition I would start the Super Bowl. I'm a religious person so I really believed what I was feeling and I had to tell someone. I turned around and told Keena Turner. He looked at me like I was crazy. I told Wallace, 'Hey, Steve, I'm gonna start the Super Bowl,' and you can imagine what he thought. I told Guy McIntyre. I told half my teammates. Even in warmups before the game, I felt I was going to play, even though I hadn't practiced all week as the starter."

What happened? Three plays into Super Bowl XXIII, Wallace suffered a broken leg and was wheeled off the field. Although he didn't start, Paris played the rest of the game. Wallace's mishap typified the early stages of the game. Through the first half, the 49ers and Bengals were tied on the scoreboard (only 3–3) and in the trainer's room (Cincinnati nose tackle Tim Krumrie also suffered a broken leg early in the game). Nobody could foresee the drama of the second half, the drama of what then-Commissioner Pete Rozelle would call, "the most exciting Super Bowl ever."

Each team added a field goal in the third quarter, but the Bengals took a 13–6 lead on a 93-yard kickoff return by Stanford Jennings. San Francisco tied it on a 14-yard touchdown pass from Montana to Rice, who before the night was over would catch 11 passes and earn the game's Most Valuable Player Award. But with three minutes and 20 seconds left in the season, Cincinnati kicker Jim Breech nailed a 40-yard field goal to make it 16–13.

The 49ers were forced to start their final possession at their 8-yard line because of a holding penalty on the kickoff return, and logic said the Bengals were headed for their first championship. In one of Miami's luxury suites, even Montana's best friend was having his doubts San Francisco could come back. "I knew anything could happen, but it had been such a screwball day," said Dwight Clark, who seven seasons earlier had accounted for the most famous play in franchise history, the winning touchdown catch against Dallas in the NFC title game.

Clark's fear of something going wrong was not without base. San Francisco had amassed 362 yards in offense against the Bengals but only 13 points. But in the huddle, Montana and Co. were not thinking of vacation just yet.

"To look at everyone's face, it was almost like we were getting ready to face a war, like we were going to Vietnam, like life or death circumstances," Paris said. "We knew if we did everything we had to, we could rebound, we couldn't lose. It was unbelievable to see. It was beyond sport. At that point, the mind doesn't know the difference between being killed and losing a game. The mind tells you, 'Win. We're the best." Psychologically, you change into a different being. Winning becomes almost as essential as eating."

The drive was a microcosm of the 49ers' season. Success, obstacle, success and so on. In nine plays, Montana moved the team 57 yards from its 8 to the Cincinnati 35. Boom. The 49ers then were penalized 10 yards for having an illegal man downfield, Cross. Walsh accepts blame for the play, saying he had called a fake screen pass, a low-percentage play. The pass to Roger Craig had been completed, but it was too slow in developing. But the penalty preceded the biggest play in the drive. On second down and 20, Montana completed a pass to

Rice over the middle, and Rice wasn't stopped until he reached the Bengals' 18.

An 8-yard pass to Craig moved the ball to the 10, but then came another pothole. From the sideline, Walsh called "20 Halfback Curl, X Up," which calls for Taylor to line up on the left side, Rice to go in motion from right to left and Craig to line up behind Montana on the left side. But Craig, who was to be the primary receiver, lined up on the right side. Walsh's jaw dropped momentarily, but in the end it didn't matter. Taylor ran straight into the end zone, cutting inside Bengals cornerback Eric Thomas, found an opening, and then Montana found him for the winning score with 34 seconds left.

"All of a sudden, things were just happening," Guy McIntyre recalled on what forever will be known as The Drive. "Nobody panicked. Everything was so calm. It was almost like not being there. It was like looking down on everything that was happening. Before you knew it, we had scored."

On the sideline, everyone celebrated except the typically reserved Walsh. "You condition yourself over a period of time not to do any premature celebrating," he said. "Just think of the Cincinnati sideline of that game two years before when we came back or even the New York Giants the second week of the season. They were celebrating, high-fiving, doing gyrations and Phil Simms was going through his routine for the crowd, and as he was doing it, we were scoring."

On this day, there would be no Cincinnati comeback. On this day, the biggest comeback in Super Bowl history already was in the books.

"This game was so much like the season, with all of our ups and downs," DeBartolo said between swigs of champagne. "This is the greatest victory I've had as owner of the 49ers. We are the team of the '80s."

Chapter 2

ARCHITECT OF VICTORY
Bill Walsh

*"It has really been the strength of Bill's person-
ality, his demands and his intelligence, and the
structure that he has established and people he
has hired that have enabled us to do all of this.
Granted, you like to feel a part of it. But you have
to be realistic about it, too."*
— *New Head Coach George Seifert*

*E*ven in victory, Bill Walsh, at least momentarily, appeared safely and typically detached from the
frenzied celebration that had engulfed the 49ers' locker
room. A few feet from the television platform on which
he stood, his players were drenching one another in
domestic champagne. Some were even managing a
taste. There were handshakes and high-fives, hugs and
smiles, frequent shouts of "World Champions!" and
constant thuds of fists joyously denting lockers.

It was against this backdrop that Walsh stood,
quietly, next to his son Craig and CBS broadcaster
Brent Musburger. The seeming absence of emotion on
Walsh's face was not uncommon. After all, Walsh
himself had mused how people likened him to a

mannequin. In public, he often appeared as unimpressed in victory as he was cool in defeat. This time, however, it became apparent that William Ernest Walsh, the man most responsible for the 49ers' three Super Bowl victories in the 1980s, would be unable to mask his feelings.

"This is a tough moment, in a way," Musburger said to Walsh, forming the question that had been on everyone's mind since the moment San Francisco had put the finishing touches on its dramatic championship victory over the Cincinnati Bengals in Super Bowl XXIII. "Was this the final game on the sideline for a great coach, Bill Walsh?"

This time, there could be no immediate pat answer. This time, the coach of the decade could not respond to a question about his future in the same casual manner that he might respond to a waitress's question, "Will that be blue cheese or Italian?" This time, he turned away from the television cameras, broke down in tears and embraced his son. This time, Walsh's silence, amid the sounds of celebration, revealed far more than words could have.

Bill Walsh had coached his last game, and though he would later say that he had been preparing for this moment for two months, the reality of the sudden change in his life could not be absorbed without displaying some vulnerability. It was over.

"It had hit me," Walsh said in reflection. "When you know you are going to end your life's work, your career, it's a very emotional thing because it's so final."

It took Walsh 19 years to secure a head-coaching position, a wait that would persuade most to look for another line of work. But when Youngstown, Ohio, businessman Edward DeBartolo Jr., who knew far more about the ABC's of erecting shopping malls than the X's and O's of a football playbook, hired Walsh to run the 49ers in 1979, an evolution began that would account for the most dramatic turnaround of a franchise in NFL history.

The 49ers had never won a league championship and had suffered through losing seasons in five of the previous six years. Remarkably, it took merely three years before Walsh, whose offensive wizardry gave credence to the theory that he had plays stored on a microchip in his mind, crafted a world champion. San Francisco won its first NFL title in the 1981 season, winning more games that season (16) than in the previous four years combined. The 49ers won the coveted Vince Lombardi Trophy again in the 1984 and 1988 seasons, giving them an unprecedented three titles in the decade, as well as six division titles and seven playoff berths.

Walsh joined the Miami Dolphins' Don Shula and the Oakland Raiders' John Madden as the only NFL coaches to win 100 games in their first 10 seasons—which will serve as one more stamp on his passport into the Pro Football Hall of Fame in Canton, Ohio.

To quote DeBartolo, even before the 49ers' victory in Super Bowl XXIII in Miami: "Bill is the coach of the '80s. Whether we are the team of the '80s doesn't matter."

What a long, strange trip it has been.

It wouldn't seem that Walsh stepped into an enviable situation in 1979, inheriting a team that had lost 14 of 16 games the previous season and was the target of lampoons from coast to coast. But he had overcome obstacles before. In his sophomore year of high school in Inglewood, Calif., quarterback Bill Walsh was overshadowed by a running back named Hugh McElhenny—who later played for the 49ers and now resides in the Hall of Fame. Walsh's family moved to Oregon for a year, then to Hayward, just across the bay from San Francisco. After two years at San Mateo Junior College, Walsh transferred to San Jose State, where then-coach

Bill Bronzan, who would become a long-time friend, shifted him to tight end.

Regardless of the position change, it was apparent Walsh would not find his way into the NFL as a player. He wasn't very fast, he wasn't very big, he wasn't very strong. After college, he served two years in the Army at Fort Ord and returned to San Jose State to obtain his master's degree in education. To realize what direction this man was heading, you need only to know the subject of Walsh's thesis: "Defending the Pro Spread."

But although he established himself early as Mr. Goodwrench for football teams, Walsh's climb up the coaching ladder was far more protracted than he could have imagined. At Washington Union High School in Fremont, Calif., in 1957, Walsh inherited a team that had combined for three wins and 24 losses the previous three seasons. Two years later, he guided the school to an 8–1 record. Next came three years as defensive coordinator at the University of California-Berkeley, then three years across the bay at Stanford as a defensive-backfield coach. Off a recommendation from Bronzan to Oakland Coach Al Davis, Walsh landed his first pro job as offensive-backfield coach for the Raiders in 1966.

Davis concluded that any coach who had a thorough understanding of defenses must have some idea how to attack them. Indeed, Walsh began exploring new ways to dissect opponents—a pursuit that would punctuate his career—by sending multitudes of players out on pass routes. It was an offense inspired by one of Walsh's idols, Sid Gillman. Just over a year later, Walsh went to work for another great, Paul Brown, with the Cincinnati Bengals.

By now, Walsh was establishing himself as one of the most innovative coaches in football, but with success came frustration. Twice he was bypassed for the head-coaching job at San Jose State. The most devastating blow, however, came in 1975, Brown's final year as coach. Walsh, who coached the Bengals' quarterbacks and receivers, was certain he would be promoted to head coach, but Brown instead elevated offensive-line coach Bill Johnson. Brown explained that both assistants were qualified for the job but that he feared Walsh, a Los Angeles native, might soon get the urge to return to California.

Indeed, Walsh left for California, but it was because he felt snubbed in Cincinnati, where he had worked for eight years. Neither party realized it at the time, but it was the worst decision Brown ever made and the best thing that could have happened to Walsh. Brown has been reminded of his mistake twice—in Super Bowls XVI and XXIII.

Walsh did not have to wait long after the Cincinnati disappointment for a head-coaching position. After one year as offensive coordinator for the San Diego Chargers, Walsh was hired in 1977 as head coach at Stanford and directed the school to a two-year record of 17–7 and berths in the Bluebonnet and Sun bowls.

The success at Stanford did not go unnoticed by DeBartolo, whose first two seasons as owner of the 49ers were marked by three coaches (Ken Meyer, Pete McCulley and Fred O'Connor), four wins, 28 losses and a world of embarrassment. On January 9, 1979, DeBartolo made a move that he only prayed would make his team competitive but never dreamed would have such an impact. He hired Walsh, now 47 years old, to become San Francisco's 11th head coach and general manager. Before announcing his retirement 10 years later, Walsh would coach longer (10 years) and win more games (102) than any of his predecessors in the 49ers' organization. He would win three Super Bowls, a feat surpassed only by Pittsburgh Coach Chuck Noll, who has won four.

No DeBartolo shopping mall could claim such a staggering turnaround.

"I had been watching Bill Walsh, following his career, and a friend of mind told me he was at Stanford but he might be interested," the 49ers' owner recalled. "After their bowl game that year, I set up a meeting with him in downtown San Francisco at the Fairmont Hotel. It was just he and I, and I knew in two minutes that he was the type of man I wanted to run the franchise."

Walsh set rather modest goals at the outset. He wanted opponents and fans to stop laughing at the 49ers, which in truth was no small feat.

"To build the team to credibility was my goal initially," he said. "Thinking of Super Bowls was such a far-reaching long-range goal—a goal you would arrive upon when you went to the Super Bowl. We had people even in the organization early on who would keep approaching me, asking, 'Bill, what are our goals? You've got to set our goals. You've got to talk about where we're going and put it in print.' Our goal was to get credibility. We had so far to go. It's like saying our goal was to get to New York City, but we hadn't gone through Donner Pass yet. First let's get to Donner Pass and get through it and then we'll talk about something else."

Before getting to that something else, the first championship in January 1982, Walsh suffered through a 2–14 rookie season and a 6–10 second year, which might not seem so ulcer-inducing until you realize the 49ers lost eight straight games at mid-season.

Nonetheless, players who were with San Francisco before and after Walsh's arrival sensed an immediate metamorphosis in the organization. Randy Cross, who spent 13 seasons with the team as a guard and center before retiring after the 1988 season, called the pre-Walsh days, "pretty bad. It was like not being professional at what you did. It was like, 'Gee, wouldn't it be nice to play for a real good football team sometime in your career?'

"From the time Bill got here, you could tell it was going to be different. We knew as soon as we started playing the game we were going to move the ball and score points. But we knew we had to score 45 every week because everyone else was scoring 42—we didn't have any defense."

That changed in 1981. Sparked by a draft that included three members of the starting secondary— Ronnie Lott, Eric Wright and Carlton Williamson—the 49ers' defense started keeping opponents out of the end zone, while the offense continued to penetrate it.

As a San Francisco native and long-time 49ers fan, George Seifert, who succeeded Walsh as head coach after stints as defensive-backs coach and defensive coordinator, can appreciate the team's turnaround under Walsh.

"It's miraculous what Bill has done, to take this team from where it was," Seifert said. "I'm really kind of awed by it."

That the 49ers' first league championship should come at the expense of the Cincinnati Bengals and their owner, Paul Brown, was a scenario that had all of the makings of a Hollywood screenplay. "It was ironic to play the Bengals and beat them in the Super Bowl," Walsh said. "It was almost like a storybook chapter in a person's career. But going into the Super Bowl, the concentration and satisfaction would have been the same for anybody."

Others, however, could not help but feel that the 26–21 victory over Cincinnati in Pontiac, Michigan, was something special for Walsh. "In Bill's mind, something that he had created finally took off for him," said former wide receiver Mike Shumann, a member of that first championship team. "Here's a guy who was shunned for the Cincinnati job, determined to show the

NFL he could be a head coach. He carried a grudge with him for years."

The success of 1981 proved to be a mixed blessing for Walsh. On the up side, he had completely revamped a losing franchise and almost instantly established himself as one of the finest coaches in professional football. On the down side, the Super Bowl win created annual high expectations for a previously struggling franchise, and Walsh became widely known as "The Genius," a title that made him understandably uncomfortable.

"The term itself you can't relate to football unless somebody has long departed this earth," Walsh said. "The word 'genius' wouldn't be accurate, but the offense had been very effective and had reached notoriety over the years. Genius obviously is overstating it."

When the 49ers slipped to 3–6 in the strike-abbreviated 1982 season, it did not surprise Walsh that critics used the genius tag, as he said, "in a ridiculing way."

"Bill was a very personable person early on—in 1979, '80, '81," Cross said. "I think that whole experience in '82, between the strike and losing like we did, sort of affected his relationship with the players. There were some rough things for him to carry around, too. Who would ever like to be called a genius? Geniuses are dead people. Einstein was a genius. Mozart was a genius. I'm sorry, football doesn't take anything to be a genius at. Football is just a dumb game. We're not talking about chess."

As a result of the 1982 experience, Walsh doubted that he still could make all of the right coaching moves, and he was bothered by unsubstantiated but rampant rumors of drug use among his players and throughout the NFL. Here he was, one year after celebrating a championship and being named NFL Coach of the Year, and suddenly he was visiting the other end of the emotional spectrum.

It was such a traumatic year for Walsh that he went

into a deep depression and considered resigning as coach to step into a front-office position. After a year-ending loss to the Los Angeles Rams, he didn't speak to his players, nor did he appear for the customary team meeting the following day. The reason, he admits, was more a severe case of self-pity than it was "coaching burnout"—a condition that prompted Philadelphia's Dick Vermiel to resign after the 1982 season, two years after a Super Bowl appearance.

"The '82 season would have been about a low point in my career, and the frustration that went with it. I came very close to leaving," Walsh said. "I spoke with Mike White, I spoke with John Robinson, I spoke with Terry Donahue—all three about the possibility of taking the head-coaching job and my remaining as general manager. That was a difficult time because the problem that went with that season was that we had been through such trial and difficulty in 1979 and '80, and it appeared we had finally put it together in '81. Then in 1982, for things to cave in on us again was just disheartening, and I was sort of spent over the whole thing.

"Eddie DeBartolo was most helpful because he showed a lot of patience with me, and then good friends were most helpful in counseling and not overreacting to how I felt. There was just enough time that I began to resolve that I should remain as head coach. This all took place in a two-week period.

"Jim Finks and Jim Hanifan both really jumped me at the Senior Bowl. Both are very close friends, and both were very unhappy with the way I was responding to everything. They were beside themselves with the way I was handling it and flat out told me. Both of them individually reminded me of where I had come from and where I had been and what we had accomplished, and they just were not very understanding with me. I think I left Jim Finks one evening and he sort of shook me out of it a little bit. From that point on, I was working toward resolving it."

Finks, who then was the general manager of the Chicago Bears and later took the same position with the New Orleans Saints, remembered Walsh as "very depressed at that time. As I say, he had his sincere blue suit on. He looked more like a banker than a coach. He was down in the dumps, full of self-pity. I had no sympathy for him at all. I just told him I felt like he hadn't scratched the surface yet to what he could do. Each time he presented a problem to me, I responded with an answer. He is very sensitive to criticism. In this business, you're never as good as people say you are after a successful year, and you're not as bad as people say after a bad year. Of course, Bill wasn't under attack from the media at that time. It was all self-imposed criticism.

"More so than any coach I've ever known, Bill is very creative, and with creative people there is a tendency to be very sensitive. I mean, he can be super sensitive at times. I just felt like he was going through a period and he wasn't being very objective about things."

Once Walsh resolved matters in his own mind, he began refining and remolding the 49ers into a championship team. San Francisco reached the National Football Conference title game in 1983, losing 24–21 to the Washington Redskins in a controversial game. The Niners used that game as their primary motivational tool the following year, and it carried them to a league record 18 victories against only one loss.

Just two years after nearly quitting, Walsh answered his critics again, building what is still regarded as one of the most dominant teams in NFL history. The 1984 edition of the 49ers dismembered the American Football Conference champion Miami Dolphins 38–16 in Super Bowl XIX at Stanford Stadium on the campus where Walsh held his first head-coaching position. Walsh didn't create this team in a secret laboratory. He merely excelled in four specific areas that were trademarks of his coaching career: 1) Defining an opponent's primary weakness and attacking it as aggressively as humanly, or even inhumanly, possible; 2) Taking risks with roster moves and in the annual college draft; 3) Anticipating when a veteran player has reached the peak of his career and, subsequently, replacing him, not letting emotions get in the way of decisions; 4) Motivating players in any way possible.

What has made Walsh unique is that even many of the veteran players who have not been enamored with what they perceive to be a cold, calculating, heartless style of roster shuffling nonetheless have expressed a tremendous amount of respect for him. Consider the case of former offensive tackle Keith Fahnhorst, who once said, "All of the veterans have discussed it. There comes a time when Bill tries to phase you out." Fahnhorst found that out in 1987, his 14th and final season with the Niners, when he sensed constant hints from the coaching staff that he no longer was wanted or needed.

"In a lot of cases, he's the same old SOB he always was. In a lot of cases, he's the same good guy he always was," Fahnhorst said. "He's a demanding guy to work for. He didn't treat any two players the same on the whole team. He treated every guy a little different. But the way he did it, he brought the best out of that player. He'd baby a guy who needed to be pampered, but screw with the guys who probably should have been appreciated most, but he just wanted to keep them motivated. I'm talking about guys like Joe Montana, who probably should have gotten as much respect as anybody who ever played the game. But in a lot of cases, it seems Bill has been messing with him since the first Super Bowl. I don't know if it's a conscious effort on Bill's part, but he probably made Joe a better player because of it. He probably made a better player out of me because half the time I was pissed off at him. If he wasn't messing with me the way he did, I probably wouldn't have lasted 14 years."

Former 49ers wide receiver Dwight Clark, whose famous touchdown catch in the NFC title game against Dallas in the 1981 season was one of the most memorable plays in NFL history, paid Walsh a similar compliment when he related a story from training camp in his rookie season. "Bill motivates through fear. I remember my first training camp in Santa Clara, I was running as hard as I could on every play. I was even running back to the huddle. I was just trying to catch someone's eye. About three weeks into camp, Bill walked past me in the hallway and said, 'You're fading on me a little bit out there.' It crushed me. It was like, 'Oh my God, I'm going to be cut tomorrow.' But I guess it motivated me. I'll never forget that day.

"Even in my last year, when I was having problems with my knee and I was pretty down, he would come up to me and ask if maybe I had thought about retirement. That made me angry, but it motivated me to get back out there."

Of course, motivating employees through fear is not uncommon in any walk of life. But as Walsh has said, "If we motivated just through fear, we would not have the positive moments that we've had. But we do motivate through whatever humane method possible. And each player is somewhat different. We try to find whatever motivates his mind and work in that direction. I don't know if it's motivation through fear as much as it is motivation through competition."

Although Seifert was known to throw a tantrum or two during his years as defensive coordinator—once breaking his toe while kicking a chalkboard that just happened to be standing against a wall—even he marveled at Walsh's intrepidity in dealing with players in the locker room. "I've seen him stand up to players where I thought, 'Oh, my God, I don't think I can handle that.' To stand up to their challenges and confront them and move right through the thing is amazing."

Through the decade, Walsh also caught players off guard with his sense of humor. There was the time he greeted the players' bus at the team hotel before Super Bowl XVI dressed as a bellhop; the time during a losing streak in the early years when he dressed as a taxi driver, walked into a team meeting and asked, "Who ordered the cab?"; the time he strolled around the locker room in the days before a playoff game wearing flashy black and red running tights, an outfit that was punctuated with a few socks stuffed down in a strategic location.

"I remember those first meetings in training camp in 1979," Fahnhorst said. "It was like the Johnny Carson show. He always had something funny to say. He was a riot. He can be a real entertainer. Then we went out and got our asses kicked."

Not for long, though, which is the bottom line where coaching is concerned. "I remember as a player myself the way you talk about different coaches," Seifert said. "You say, 'This guy's an SOB. That guy's a good guy. He's a hell of a coach.' Well, that's the bottom line. When the players are all through, what do they say about you from that standpoint? I'd be surprised if any player or anybody who has worked for him said they didn't respect him. And if they say it, they're probably lying. Or, they were one of the first players cut in training camp."

That Walsh's three Super Bowl titles came over an eight-season span is, in itself, a remarkable achievement, for the three championship teams were decidedly unique. Although Montana was the quarterback at each juncture, the supporting cast on offense and many of the principal figures on defense changed. The roster was reshaped after the 1981 championship, and further retooling was needed after the dominant 1984 year, particularly after consecutive first-round playoff losses to the New York Giants in 1985 and 1986.

Explaining the 49ers' sustained success through the decade, Walsh said before Super Bowl XXIII, "There are a lot of risks to take in sports, related to personnel and planning for a game. We've been able to take those and then recover from our misfortune and miscalculations a lot better than other people. The reason is we have an excellent staff, but we don't have a committee form of decision-making. The bottom line is Ed DeBartolo has given me the responsibility to do it. We have super people. If we're wrong, we recover. A lot of other organizations stop and start pointing fingers at each other. Before long, no one will make a decision; no one will step forth. We have an atmosphere that's able to deal with adversity more than other teams."

Because of that, Walsh's greatest coaching season may have come in a non-championship year, in 1987. Even before training camp, he realized a players' strike was a strong possibility and prepared for that by keeping fringe players longer than usual in training camp. When the union walkout came two weeks into the season, Walsh was prepared with a well-tutored group of replacement players. The 49ers' strike team was the strongest in the NFL and went 3–0 during the four-week strike. After the strike, Walsh, fearing ramifications from some veterans crossing the picket line during the walkout, lectured his players on unity after the first practice.

"I think the biggest problem in a work stoppage is the paranoia and suspicion that develops through that period when you're out of your element," Walsh told the media after that pep talk. "You begin to magnify things or get the wrong impressions, and then they grow. I've seen it happen in my own life and in work stoppages."

Before the strike, the Niners lost their season opener at Pittsburgh and escaped with a narrow victory at Cincinnati, largely because of a last-second coaching pratfall by the Bengals' Sam Wyche. But after the strike, at least in part because of Walsh's handling of the sensitive post-strike situation, the 49ers appeared strong and united. They won nine of their last 10 regular-season games, and in the process, Walsh corrected a weak running attack when he shifted fullback Roger Craig to halfback and inserted Tom Rathman into the starting lineup.

Ironically, however, that amazing regular season erupted into a tidal wave of controversy when the 49ers dropped their opening playoff game to the Minnesota Vikings. The media put Walsh under the microscope again, first for pulling Montana in the second half of the Vikings game and later because of increasing rumors of a rift between Walsh and team owner Edward DeBartolo Jr. When the 49ers announced an organizational restructuring two months after the season, with DeBartolo assuming the title of team president from Walsh, there was further speculation that Walsh had been stripped of authority and was one step from unemployment.

"Never, believe me, never did I ever seriously consider letting him go," DeBartolo said.

As the 1988 season began, it became clear Walsh was still running the day-to-day operations of the football team—making the trades, coordinating the draft, cutting the roster and creating the game plan—even though his business card said only "Coach." This was still Bill Walsh's football team, and if the 49ers were to make another trip to the Super Bowl, it would be because of Bill Walsh. "The success of this football team will rest on me," he said before the 1988 season. "There is no way to deflect that or evade that or dilute that into

five or six different offices. If the team does poorly,
there's no reason to think of anyone else."

Walsh said DeBartolo "supported me in the toughest
times—that's 1979, 1980 and 1982. Coaches are often
only given two years. He was frustrated with the team
not making it past the first round of the playoffs for
three straight years. We didn't take it out on each other,
but we were both very frustrated. We didn't talk for up
to two months after the Minnesota game. But he went
his way and I went mine. We were both trying to
recoup. We knew the other person was there and we
were functioning normally. But that game was a
shocker, less of a shock to me than it was to Eddie.
Being a coach for so many years and knowing the
dynamics of the game, I understand a frustrating loss,
whereas a person who hasn't been in sports wouldn't
understand it.

"People considered us the best team in football.
After that game, people could still consider us the best
team in football, but because of the two previous years,
people took us to the depths. People said, 'Three playoff losses in a row; the 49ers can't win the big one; the
coach has lost his fastball; Montana can't play like he
once could.' During that period, it was difficult for
everybody. I felt strains from some people, and it wasn't
too hard to take shots at me personally at that time
because I wasn't the most popular coach in football.
That was a very difficult time for me during those
months."

At the outset, it didn't appear 1988 would ease
Walsh's mind. The 49ers started strong but lost four
out of six at mid-season to fall to 6–5, and playoff hopes
were dissipating. Rumors swirled again about a
Walsh–DeBartolo rift. But the 49ers won four straight
to clinch their sixth NFC West Division title under
Walsh and stormed through the playoffs, pounding the

Minnesota Vikings and Chicago Bears en route to their Second Super Bowl meeting with Cincinnati.

Walsh told close friends in the weeks before the championship game that Super Bowl XXIII would be his final time on the sideline, win or lose, although a public announcement was not made until a few days ater the game. Having commented earlier, "I'm not going to die with my cleats on," Walsh no longer relished the stressful nature of the job and had exhausted his list of coaching goals. Ten seasons, three Super Bowls and 102 victories was more than enough.

The man who once said, "I've never been able to sit back and feel totally satisfied," now felt he deserved the chance to enjoy what he had accomplished as coach and step into a role as the 49ers' executive vice president for football operations.

"Ed offered a sizable raise for me to remain as coach, and we spoke of it, but it was very brief because we both acknowledged that, sooner or later, I would leave," Walsh said. "The thing I didn't want was the experience of this being the coach's lame duck year. It was important that the team not be distracted where my career was going. So the less said the better about what my plans were."

As it turned out, even Walsh wasn't aware which direction he was heading. After six months in his front-office position, he became almost bored in his administrative duties and sought a new challenge. In July, just two weeks before the 49ers were scheduled to report to training camp, Walsh decided to leave the 49ers to become a football analyst for NBC Sports.

"I think I felt a loss on the field," he said. "It was as tough a loss as I ever anticipated, seeing the players on the field, even in mini-camp. As a coach, you like to feel, 'That's my team out there.' But with the passing of the torch, it became George Seifert's team. There was a real loss, and I'll feel that forever."

Although the abruptness of Walsh's departure surprised most, it did not surprise many that he moved
into the broadcast media. ABC sportscaster Al Michaels
said Walsh approached him shortly after the Niners
won their first Super Bowl in January 1982. "He spent a
lot of time asking me about the television business, how
he thought he would fare in this business and if I
thought there was an opening for him in this business—
meaning right away. Now. Next year. So there was a
part of him even then who was interested in TV."

Walsh's second career change in six months didn't
stop many from speculating that it would be only a matter of time before he returned to football, whether in a
coaching or front-office capacity. The only certainty is
that if Walsh does shift into another form of employment, this time he won't break down in tears.

Chapter 3

COTTON BOWL TO SUPER BOWL
Joe Montana

"Without Joe, we're not the Team of the Decade."
—Tony Razzano, 49ers' director of scouting

Mark Twain once wrote, "The next best thing to a good lie is a true story no one believes." Well, in the curious case of Joseph C. Montana, the top-rated quarterback in NFL history, the story he couldn't believe himself was that the San Francisco 49ers were actually having doubts about his ability to lead the football team in 1988.

It was as if he expected Allen Funt to burst on the scene at any minute and tell him it had all been a put-on, staged for the camera and the audience at home.

"What? I've lost the starting job? After the year I had?"

"Smile, Joe! It's just a joke. OK, here's your team back."

But it was no joke. And even harder to believe was that it occurred after Montana had put up such great numbers in just 13 games the previous season. Those incredible numbers, Hall-of-Fame caliber to be sure:

266 completions in 398 attempts for 3,054 yards, a 66.8 completion percentage, 31 touchdowns, just 13 interceptions, the top quarterback rating in professional football (102.1) and a 13–2 record in the strike-shortened 1987 NFL season. And that included three games in which he played only part time and was a combined 15 for 25 for 217 yards with 3 TDs.

Joe Montana was an unhappy 49er in 1988. He found himself splitting time with Steve Young in some kind of crazy platoon system at the position many fans and experts believed Montana had mastered. In nine seasons in San Francisco, the ruggedly handsome former Notre Dame star from Ringgold High in Monongahela, Pa., had re-defined the role of quarterback. He had brought the Bay Area two NFL championships and had been named MVP of both Super Bowl games. He had been named to the Pro Bowl five times and had made at least six All-Pro teams. Why, he was even named All-Madden by CBS' resident funny guy and bus enthusiast, John Madden.

He was "The Comeback Kid" after career-threatening back surgery in '86. "The Cardiac Kid" after last-second, come-from-behind wins in the 1979 Cotton Bowl, the 1981 season's NFC championship game and at least a dozen regular-season NFL games. "Cool Hand Joe" for his grace under pressure. Even "Big Sky" when a local newspaper decided Montana needed a worthy nickname and ran a contest.

Big Sky? Makes you wonder what names they had to choose from.

And yet, after leading a rag-tag group of veterans and highly rated rookies to a Super Bowl victory in the '81 season and duplicating the achievement in the '84 season with possibly the NFL's best team ever, Montana found himself in the middle of a genuine, bona fide, first-class quarterback controversy. And he simply could not understand the reason.

"I thought it was a puzzling situation to say the least," he said with more than a hint of hurt. "I probably had my best year in terms of numbers in '87, but before training camp even started in '88 there were rumors I might be traded. Then in camp I didn't get as much playing time as in the past. They said I didn't need it, that they wanted to give Steve Young more time to see what he could do. That was fine with me. But you know, you always wonder, 'Are they phasing me out?' "

If the San Francisco 49ers are the Team of the Decade, then Joe Montana is the Player of the Decade. The fact that he thought the 49ers might want to phase him out in '88 is an indication of how far the team had come since Eddie DeBartolo took over in 1977. In the years immediately following his purchase of the Bay Area's "other" professional football team, Eddie would have been thrilled just to make the playoffs. But winning two Super Bowls and five NFC West Division titles in seven years has a way of raising the standards for success to a level that may be just a little unrealistic.

The real reason for the uncertainty of Montana's future with the team in 1988 may actually have been two-fold. On one hand, DeBartolo and then-Coach Bill Walsh had those ominous medical reports from the back surgery in '86 and testimony from Joe's doctor that he might require major surgery again at any time. And on the other were Joe's horrible—for him—performances in the 49ers' three playoff losses in successive seasons since winning Super Bowl XIX. The losing streak featured humiliations at the hands of the New York Giants twice, and the Minnesota Vikings in a game in which he was replaced in the third quarter with the Niners trailing—a situation that called for the kind of comeback that had been his signature.

Under those circumstances, and with the yearly expectation of having an NFL contender, the 49ers' brain trust could not be blamed for trying to insure the future. Nevertheless, that didn't diminish their super-star's feeling of betrayal.

"What are you going to do about it?" he asked in reference to the trade talk. "Nobody wants to be traded. But I was at the point where I thought about it and said, 'So what? I could play wherever I would go.' If they didn't want me here, I didn't want to be here."

As strange as it would have seemed for Joe to wear anything other than the scarlet and gold of the 49ers, it was widely rumored that DeBartolo had come close to a deal with the San Diego Chargers. Reportedly, Montana would be traded for two first-round draft choices and a front-line player, the deal hinging on the identity of that other player. According to the story, the Chargers offered running back Gary Anderson, but the 49ers wanted linebacker Billy Ray Smith.

"Blown out of proportion," Eddie vehemently insisted. Completely blown out of proportion. "It was not our intention at all. They came to us. We never, ever went to anybody and said, 'Do you want Joe Montana?' That was the last thing in the world I would do."

Considering the intensely close relationship between the quarterback and the owner, and all they had achieved together, it is not hard to see Eddie's point of view. And yet, to some it smelled an awful lot like the trade the Niners made with the Buffalo Bills in 1978 to get O.J. Simpson: "Offense-poor doormat from opposing conference seeks legendary superstar to become legitimate. Willing to give up large chunk of immediate future. (Read: First-round draft picks.)"

As tempting as it may have been to wind up on the right side of one of those deals for a change (Simpson's immense talent had already been air-mailed to the Pro Football Hall of Fame in Canton, Ohio, by the time he joined the 49ers), Eddie's instinct was that Joe had plenty of championship football left in his skinny legs.

And if, as some suspected, the trade talk was one of

those crafty Bill Walsh ploys to motivate Joe into another super season, well, all the better. "We attempt as a
coaching staff to motivate—period," Walsh said about
the possibility, in his brief but to-the-point style. Joe just
shrugged his shoulders and responded, "Who knows
what Bill's thinking? I've reached the point where I
don't care."

What was this? Was this any way for two future Hall
of Famers to be talking about each other? Was this the
end result of ten years of championship professional
football together?

Walsh fueled the fire in training camp before the '88
season by saying, "We are not looking to change the
quarterback position and don't expect that the starting
quarterback position will be changed this year. But we
are looking at the alternative of playing Young more
than we'd ever consider playing a second quarterback.
And I suppose if Young is performing markedly better
than Montana, then naturally, like any other position in
this competitive game, we would make a change."

Of course, the focal point of the friction—although
both were loath to admit it—was the benching of Montana in the playoff loss to Minnesota. When Joe came
out, he had completed only 12 of 26 passes for 109
yards with one interception, and the Niners trailed
27–10, the lone San Francisco touchdown coming from
the defense. Steve Young, the BYU southpaw (yes, he's
really Brigham Young's great-great grandson), entered
and ran for one touchdown and threw for another,
although the Niners lost 36–24. Walsh had made the
change because Montana was having trouble eluding
Minnesota's heavy pass rush, as evidenced by four sacks
in less than three quarters. In fact, the Vikings' rush
had been so intense and Joe's mobility so limited, that it
actually looked as though he had sustained an injury—
which he had not.

"It was a very traumatic time for everybody," Walsh

said. "It was really my judgment as to whether we continue with Joe or make a change. It was not total desperation, but it was a matter of figuring Steve's running ability had to come into play. We were not moving the ball."

But Walsh's rationale for the substitution was not what was going through Montana's mind in the locker room after the game. "He felt bad—we all felt bad," said Mike Holmgren, the 49ers' quarterbacks coach. Former Niners wide receiver Dwight Clark, Joe's best friend, had a slightly stronger recollection. "He was angry," Clark said. "That's his thing. His whole life is bringing teams back from the depths. The greatest comeback kid of all time. But who knows if he could have done it that day? A lot more things went wrong than just the quarterback position."

Montana concurs with his friend. "Well, you're going to get criticism," he said later. "The quarterback's going to take most of it. But the thing is, you can go back and watch the game films and see that everybody really played poorly. I didn't exactly see him (Young) setting the world on fire, to make it that big of a deal."

In truth, the game was probably lost by the time Young came in, but Joe's point was well-taken. It had become widely known around the NFL that when a team was faced with a seemingly impossible comeback, the quarterback would be "pulling a Montana" if he could bring his team back into contention.

A six-month off-season did little to stem the controversy. In one of Walsh's first press conferences upon returning to the Niners' training camp at Sierra College in Rocklin, Calif., the enigmatic coach said, "I don't think there's any way I could downplay a controversy, minimize it or act as if it didn't exist. I don't believe that the press would not note that there was a competition at quarterback."

The tune was too familiar, and the lyrics were redundant.

For Joe's part, not much had changed. "I just didn't understand it," he said. "I knew Steve was a good quarterback. I knew he was highly touted coming out of college. But to all of a sudden be in a controversy for no reason . . . because I thought I had a pretty good year. I could understand it if I'd been the shits, but I didn't think I played that way. And for that to happen, I just didn't understand."

By the time the season started, the competiton had given way to a sort of platoon system that saw the players used almost according to who was hot and who was not. When it was suggested to Montana by John Madden that the cloudy quarterback picture might be shaking his confidence, Joe responded, "It's not so much my confidence. But I think it has to do with my decision making. Sometimes there are tight, close plays you have to make. The situation the way it is, I might think, 'Oh God, should I try to throw the ball? I may get pulled if it doesn't work. If I make a mistake, I might get pulled.' It's hard for any player to play under the assumption that if you make a mistake, you'll be on the bench."

All the while, throughout the controversy and the rumors, testimonials to Montana came rolling in from as far away as Atlanta, where Falcons cornerback Bobby Butler was quoted before the Niners played his team as saying, "I can't figure out why Young is playing at all. Young's a good quarterback, but Montana is in another class."

All-Pro center Randy Cross, an unabashed Joe Montana fan, said, "I think it's pretty obvious that Steve's a really good quarterback. But in this system, there's no comparison as far as who is more adept at running this offense."

That sentiment was echoed loudly by former offensive tackle Keith Fahnhorst, who retired following the

1987 season after 14 years as a 49er. He said of the trade talk: "All of the veterans have discussed it. There comes a time when Bill tries to phase you out. I think Joe felt that way for the past year or so, especially after the playoff loss to Minnesota. It's unfortunate that a guy of his caliber, and after everything he's done for Bill and the organization, has to go through all of that stuff. It's unfortunate he has to be treated like that."

Fahnhorst paused, and after pondering the San Diego rumor added, "I was thinking, 'God, I'd love to see it happen.' Then everyone would know what Joe means to (the 49ers') organization. It would have been total disaster."

Considering the way the 1988 season turned out, he certainly had a point.

All anyone really needs to know about Joe Montana is that he loves to play football. And basketball, too. Notre Dame almost lost him to North Carolina State on a basketball scholarship, but he decided the opportunity the Irish provided was too good to turn down and shuffled off to South Bend.

Oh sure, his wife, Jennifer, and daughters Alexandra and Elizabeth are way up there on his list of priorities. To realize how important that commitment is, one needs only to be reminded of that scene of Joe and Jennifer walking with the girls through the Magic Kingdom a few weeks after Super Bowl XXIII, when Joe made good on his post-game promise to "go to Disneyland." Or that he put off a scheduled interview session for a few days at summer training camp when his wife and daughters showed up to spend the afternoon with him.

But we're talking about a football man here. A man who lies in a hospital bed the day after major back surgery and plans his return to the game that put him there. A man who lives, breathes and even dreams— honest—the sport that has taken him from a blue collar

steel town of western Pennsylvania to the white wine so-
phistication of Northern California. A man who thrives
on winning. A man who thrives on pressure. A man
who no one thought would have a chance in the NFL,
where rifle-armed quarterbacks are the standard.

Funny how it all started . . .

"Say, do you want another 'Golden Domer'?" Bill
Walsh asked Eddie DeBartolo in the hallway outside the
49ers' "War Room" at their Redwood City facility on
the afternoon of May 3, 1979, when the NFL was con-
ducting its annual college draft via telephone from New
York.

The draft that year was more of a puzzlement than
most, with no clear "franchise" player on the board.
Buffalo selected first, ironically with the pick the 49ers
had traded to acquire O.J. Simpson the year before.
The Bills chose Tom Cousineau, a linebacker from
Ohio State who 49ers Director of Scouting Tony Razzano thought was extremely overrated.

Quarterbacks were in fairly short supply. Jack
Thompson, "The Throwin' Samoan" from Washington
State, was the first one taken—third overall—by Cincinnati. He was followed by Phil Simms—seventh—by the
New York Giants and Steve Fuller—23rd—by Kansas
City. No quarterback was taken in the second round,
and the 49ers actually traded down, sending their
third-round pick—57th overall—to Seattle for linebacker Bob Jury and the 27th pick in the third round.

It was that selection—the 82nd overall—that Walsh
and DeBartolo were discussing in the hallway.

All 28 teams had passed up Joe Montana that draft
day, most of them three times, before the 49ers claimed
him. And, according to Razzano, it was a good thing
they took him when they did. "I was very nervous," the
stocky, silver-haired scout said. "I had him as my number one all the way. Ahead of Thompson. Ahead of
Simms. Ahead of Fuller. Our first pick in that draft was

in the second round, and hell, I wanted to take him then. But the other coaches didn't agree. We were lucky to get him."

"I didn't really know Joe Montana that well," Eddie recalled. "Even though I went to Notre Dame, Coach (Dan) Devine was shuffling quarterbacks around that year. Bill said, 'Well, we're gonna take this kid Montana in the third round.' And I said, 'That's great by me. Anybody that went to Notre Dame can't be all bad.' And he turned out to be a Hall of Famer."

Joe and Eddie would become very close. When the quarterback wanted a pay increase in 1983 and team president Walsh wouldn't give it to him, Joe went straight to Eddie and got the raise, much to Walsh's consternation.

And although it didn't help him much in securing the starting quarterback job during that wacky 1988 season, Eddie rewarded Joe with a fat contract extension that could net him close to $10 million through 1992 and place him among the highest-paid athletes. The contract, which was originally signed in 1984 and scheduled to expire after the 1989 season, was extended by three years and included base salaries of $1.1 million for 1988 and $1.2 million in 1989. The additional three years called for base salaries of $2 million and reporting bonuses of $550,000 each season, for a total five-year value of $9.95 million. It is important to note, however, that none of the deal is guaranteed; Joe would have to make the club every year in order to be paid.

In apparent contradiction to his much-publicized "quarterback controversy," Walsh said about the contract: "Joe deserves the extension. He had an All-Pro season last year ('87), and we felt he would be at the top of his game for years to come. He's one of the top quarterbacks in football." Montana's agent, Boston-based attorney Bob Woolf, seemed quite pleased with the deal, saying: "The 49ers have shown me that they are very appreciative of Joe Montana's efforts."

Eddie's concern for Joe was most pronounced during the eight weeks in 1986 that Montana spent recovering from surgery on the herniated disc he suffered in the first week of the season.

"I thought he was done," the owner said. "Or at least facing a long road back. He's also got the intestinal fortitude like nobody I've ever seen. A lot of things went through my mind. I spent a lot of time with him in the hospital, and we talked quite a bit. What do you say to a guy? He was very, very depressed and down in the dumps. You see your franchise going up in smoke because he was really at the top of his game. But more importantly, you're just concerned for his health when you hear disc, and you hear back. You know, if you get 100 people who have problems with discs in their backs, probably 95 of them have problems the rest of their lives. And 99.9 percent of them don't play professional football."

Dr. Arthur White, who performed the operation in September 1986, told a local newspaper before Super Bowl XXIII: "It would not surprise me, after he played another season or two, that he would need additional surgery and would have to finish playing. I frankly felt he would have done himself in by now. It's amazing, simply amazing."

Well, that did not provide much comfort to the 49er Faithful, especially coming less than 10 days before the NFL championship game. But Joe, who had been defusing pessimism about his health almost since he first climbed out of his hospital bed, maintained his cheery outlook. "Not at all," he said when asked if he thought he was taking a risk by continuing to play. "We had talked a long time ago, right after the surgery. That's one of the major reasons I have CAT scans done every year." On the possibility of having surgery again,

Montana said, "Well, that's always been the talk. What Dr. White has told me was 70 percent of all back patients who have had operations usually require them again down the line. But there's no specific date."

There are probably safer professions in the world than NFL quarterback. Like many of his peers, Joe Montana has been battered and bruised regularly by the new generation of bigger, faster, stronger defensive players.

A partial list of his injuries and ailments during his career reads like a med student's textbook: strained ligament in his sternum after being hit in practice; concussion after suffering a massive hit against the Giants in the '86 playoffs; severe hamstring pull and minor knee strain when he stumbled over Roger Craig's foot in an '87 game against Chicago; inflamed bursa sac at the elbow of his throwing arm that required surgery in '88; arthroscopic surgery twice on his left knee, most recently in May 1989. Arthritis, tendinitis, broken fingers, sprained wrist, bruised shoulder, jammed thumb, twisted knee and, of course, the back.

The injury was suffered in the first game of the 1986 season against Tampa Bay on a pass play. Joe had scrambled to his left to avoid the rush and twisted his body back to the right to throw a pass. The awkward motion had caused a disc in the base of his spine to rupture, causing, naturally, severe pain. One week later, White, medical director of the Spine Care Medical Group in Daly City, Calif., removed the disc, creating an opening in the small of Montana's back to relieve the pressure.

Almost immediately, word spread that the prognosis was not good. "This is a very serious injury," White told the press. "But with proper rest and therapy, there's every chance that he could lead a normal life."

But did "a normal life" include professional football? "I think there's very little chance he'll play football again," the doctor said to the astonishment of those who had grown accustomed to seeing number 16 bending over centers Fred Quillan and Randy Cross to take snaps. All of a sudden, one of the most promising careers in NFL history seemed finished.

"I think he was just covering for me," Joe said three years later in his typically low-key style. "He told me he didn't think anything major could happen to me again. I probably will need surgery again because of the occupation I have chosen, but it could be 20 years down the road if I do things right." Team doctor Michael Dillingham was quoted as saying, "He knows more about taking care of his back than most back therapists."

But just being able to get up in the morning and bend over to pick the newspaper off the front porch is not all Joe had in mind. "I wanted to come back and play because I missed the game. I watched a game from the TV in the hospital, and it wasn't much fun."

But was that the right time to make that kind of decision?

"It was hard while I had the surgery and it was like, 'Oh God, I'm hooked up to a morphine machine, and the thing's making me crazy,'" he said. "So once I got off that, the next day I was thinking more clearly. Then at that point Jennifer and I actually discussed the fact of retiring. They'd start walking me around the hospital, and I got off the medication and the pain stuff because I wasn't dealing with it real well. I got off the morphine, and they put me on something else because they wanted me up and moving, and I had to have something so I could move. Once I got off of that, the second or third day, I said, for some reason: 'I'm not ready to quit.'"

It is hard to imagine that just three days after major back surgery Montana was planning his return to the NFL. Even more astounding was that he would be back in a 49ers uniform less than nine weeks later, and in just his second game would throw a career-high 60 passes against the Washington Redskins for 441 yards.

"Jennifer and I had a long talk with Dr. White, and we thought I could make it back," he recalled. "Not as fast as I did; he was a little worried I think. But it was a mutual decision."

And what if his wife had insisted he retire?

"I would have had to have substantial evidence that I couldn't make it, or that I was in danger," he said. "But we have two little girls and another on the way, and it's not worth risking the rest of your life for. I didn't have to worry about the money, so it wasn't that. It was just, she knew how much the game means to me. She was behind whatever she felt I could do safely."

"Safely," is a relative term if you are a professional football player. White said that the opening in Joe's spine is gradually closing because of the wear and tear of playing football. "As the hole closes off, the likelihood increases more and more that any single blow could close it off, and that would be it." But, he quickly added that Joe is not in any more danger of paralysis or other catastrophic injury than any other football player. "It's not as if he's throwing caution to the wind. Besides, if a million dollars was on the line, I'd probably play the next game too," he told the press before the Super Bowl.

* * *

Growing up in the western Pennsylvania steel town of Monongahela, 25 miles southeast of Pittsburgh along the river that gave the town its name, Montana was a three-sport star from 1972–74 at Ringgold High School. The proud and sturdy town of 5,900 lies in the heart of the "rust belt," the once-thriving area now dotted with the crumbling smokestacks of abandoned steel mills that reflect the country's shift to a high-tech economy.

In a way, Joe Montana represents that evolution as well.

To many in his hometown, Joe is a bit of an enigma, turning his back on the community that gave him up when he left to attend Notre Dame. A feature in a San Francisco newspaper quoted several townspeople who knew Joe from his childhood. As might be expected, the comments ranged from supportive to slightly indignant. "Either they love him or they hate him," said Joe's cousin, Paula Ludwick, who still lives in the town. "That's the way it is, and that's the way it's always been."

"I'm proud of him," said Gilbert Hardison, whose football career followed Montana's by six years. "I'm proud that somebody from this area succeeded in life."

"His dad was really his mentor," said Paul Zolak, an assistant coach during Joe's high school days. "A lot of people in town thought he pushed him too hard. I remember when Joe pitched American Legion (baseball) games, his dad would arrive about the eighth inning, and after all the others were gone, he would go out to the outfield and snap (footballs) so Joe could work on his drop-back."

Driving through the small town, it is hard to see even the slightest evidence that the two-time Super Bowl MVP lived there. The local sporting goods store does not carry 49ers jerseys. And in The Outhouse, a blue collar tavern that is the unofficial headquarters for the few Niners fans in Steelers territory, not one photo of the quarterback can be found.

"I've always liked Joe," said Brian Herman, the sports editor of the Valley Independent, who covered him in the earliest stages of his career. "But I think he's turned a lot of people off the way he's come across. Somebody said they'd seen him quoted as saying he was from Washington County. Not Monongahela, but Washington County. I guess he's too good for us now."

Another source of resentment may be his divorce

from the former Kim Moses, a local girl from nearby Donora who was his first wife.

Montana does not really have much reason to return. His parents, Joe Sr. and Theresa Montana, moved to the Bay Area in 1987 to be near their only child. And, after all, how much can he really be expected to have in common with the community anymore?

"A lot of people look down on him, but that's the general consensus of this type of town," said Ken (Chider) Baran, who played Little League baseball and football with Montana. "As soon as someone makes it big, everyone talks shit about him. But I've got to hand it to him. He worked hard and deserves everything he's got."

Jook Bartman, the owner of Angelo's restaurant in Monongahela, agrees. "The best part was when he went to Notre Dame and all these football experts said, 'He'll never make it,'" he said. "I said, 'Give him a chance.' Now look what he's done."

"Some people feel he owes Monongahela something," Brian Herman said. "But put yourself in his shoes. Monongahela didn't make him. In a way, he made Monongahela. Does he really owe them something?"

The rest of the country got its first glimpse of Montana at the 1979 Cotton Bowl when he was playing quarterback for Notre Dame. After a redshirt season in 1976, he led the Irish to the national college football championship the following year. But in his senior season, Joe got his first taste of a quarterback controversy when Coach Dan Devine platooned him with two other Irish players. Although receiving irregular playing time in '78, he made his mark in the bowl game at the end of the season.

In a foreshadowing of his future heroics in the NFL, he guided Notre Dame to one of the greatest comebacks in collegiate history against Houston in the Cotton Bowl. After the Cougars held a commanding 34–12 lead midway through the fourth quarter, Montana led the Irish to a 35–34 victory, the winning score coming with no time showing on the clock. As a quarterback, he had gone relatively unnoticed in college, but the '79 Cotton Bowl caught the attention of many scouts, including one Anthony Razzano, working for the San Francisco 49ers.

"Joe got my attention in a hurry when he was a junior," Razzano, the 49ers' director of college scouting, said. "Hell, Devine didn't know what he had. Joe has a feel, a second sense. He knows where everybody is around him. It's an uncanny ability that he has. The staff didn't have him rated as high as me. He was a projection (the coaches would have to project, or estimate, his NFL potential). Everybody noticed him after the Cotton Bowl, but there were question marks. His arm, his size, his strength. But somehow I just knew. I had him rated as my top guy."

"The first thing I noticed about Joe was his feet," Bill Walsh said. "He had very quick feet, and he could move real well. A lot of people said he didn't have an arm, but that didn't concern me. We didn't draft him because of his arm."

Wendell Tyler, the outstanding running back the 49ers acquired from the Rams in 1983, recalled meeting Joe in Los Angeles prior to the 1979 college draft. "I met Joe my second year with the Rams," he said. "He was down at our facility, and the Rams gave him a tryout. They said he was too short. Of all the quarterbacks I played with—Bert Jones, Joe Namath, Vince Ferragamo, Pat Haden—he was the best. He was the guy you'd want in a fight to watch your back. He's just one of the guys from the neighborhood. Just one of the guys."

Montana had a fight on his hands when he challenged Steve DeBerg for the starting job after joining the 49ers for his rookie season. DeBerg, who has had a star-crossed NFL career that also included competitions with John Elway in Denver and Vinny Testaverde in Tampa Bay, had won the top spot with the 49ers in '79 after beating out former Heisman Trophy winner Jim Plunkett. Montana started one game his first year and seven his next, before winning the job outright for the '81 season. The results were immediate. Montana led the team to a 13–3 record in the regular season and its first Super Bowl championship, over the Cincinnati Bengals.

Fred Dean, the ferocious pass rusher the Niners acquired from San Diego that year, was very impressed. "Joe gave us all a lot of confidence," he said. "He was a very different type of quarterback to me. He never got uptight; he was always cool. I called him 'Cool Hand Joe' because that's the type of person he is. He was real cool about it all and never let it bother him no matter how big the play."

"He is a great guy," Randy Cross said. "You knew his reputation in college as a comeback player. After those '77, '78, '79 seasons (when the Niners posted a 9–37 combined record), you'd love to see guys come in and play, but you didn't know if they could help you win. It would have been nice if O.J. (Simpson) could have still run when he came here. It would have been nice if Hollywood Henderson could have still played football when he played here. It was obvious Joe was good, but you didn't know how good he would get. It was made very clear to John (Ayers), Fred (Quillan), Keith (Fahnhorst) and me (the starting offensive line) that we would have a real big part in how he was going to do and how healthy he would stay."

Montana was not getting rave reviews from the rest of the league. In spite of his clutch performances in the 1981 regular season and the spectacular drive he engineered to beat Dallas in the NFC championship game, he was criticized for not being an overpowering passer.

Mike Shumann, an outgoing wide receiver who was on the '81 championship team, said about Joe: "I used to love to tease him. We'd tell him he threw a 'tight wobble.' He was so shy and quiet, we didn't know if he'd ever develop. He was raw, which is what Bill (Walsh) looked for. He liked someone he could develop. He developed Greg Cook and Ken Anderson when he was with Cincinnati, and he developed Joe Montana."

If Montana had doubters after the '81 season, most of them were gone by the end of the next year. Although 1982 was a miserable season for players and fans because of a strike that canceled seven weeks of the season, Joe set an NFL record by throwing for at least 300 yards in five consecutive games.

Other records would follow in succeeding years, including the NFL record for most consecutive pass completions, which came in 1987. After finishing a 38–24 victory over Cleveland that year with five straight completions, Joe connected on his first 17 passes the following week against Green Bay for a record 22 in a row—to seven different receivers.

Aside from the well-chronicled battles Montana and Walsh waged over the years, which Dwight Clark described as a love-hate relationship, Joe got his strongest criticism during the strike-plagued 1987 season from an unusual source: his teammates. The walkout, which bitterly divided the players, occurred after the second week of the regular season and prompted the owners to stage games with non-professional replacements. After two weeks of relative solidarity with the union membership, Montana led a group of 11 players back to camp and was derided by a few hard-liners, who charged him with betrayal.

"This isn't going to affect how I think of Joe as a player," guard Guy McIntyre said at the time. "But it might with regard to respect. When you have people play as a team, you don't expect them to just play one half. And it's the same way in a strike. You have to ask yourself, 'Can you trust a man in the trenches?' We'll have to see."

Although McIntyre regrets the comments now, as do most of the others, they were fairly typical of the feelings during the emotionally charged work stoppage. Even his close friends Randy Cross and Keith Fahnhorst questioned Joe's move. "It's got to affect some people," Cross said. "Not on my part. But there is bound to be some feelings on the part of some people." And union representative Fahnhorst admitted there was "some bitterness" among strikers toward teammates who broke ranks.

"To say it won't have an effect would be real hard," linebacker Milt McColl said. "I'll try not to hold anything against Joe or anyone else."

Fellow linebacker Riki Ellison was similarly disposed. "I was a friend of his before the strike, and I'll be a friend of his after the strike," he said. "I'm just disappointed. It wasn't that hard to miss one week, one paycheck. It's not like we're all on skid row."

If it seems hard to believe that the man who had been the heart and soul of the 49ers was the target of malice, it is a good indication of how strongly some players felt about the issue. Maybe it should have occurred to them that Joe just wanted to play football. After all, in the two regular-season games prior to the strike, Montana was off to a pretty good start. He was 61 for 87 passing, a 70 percent completion average, for 566 yards and five touchdowns. And after the return of the rest of the players for game six of the season, Montana threw for more than 250 yards in seven of the next eight games, passing for 23 touchdowns, and the 49ers won seven of the contests. One of his most effective pass blockers was Guy McIntyre.

Apparently, winning football games heals even the deepest wounds.

The Super Bowl has been the scene of Montana's most famous victories. He has set or tied at least seven Super Bowl records in his three appearances and is the NFL's all-time leader in completions in post-season games. He was named Most Valuable Player of the 1982 game in beating the Cincinnati Bengals 26–20 and again in 1985 when the Niners defeated the Miami Dolphins 38–16. He has never suffered an interception in a Super Bowl game despite throwing more than 90 passes.

Ironically, his best performance statistically came in Super Bowl XXIII but failed to win him a third MVP award. He completed 23 of 36 passes for 357 yards and two touchdowns, including the game-winner to John Taylor with 34 seconds to play. But the MVP voters felt Jerry Rice's record-breaking receiving performance was more deserving. After the game, Bengals receiver Cris Collinsworth said: "Joe Montana is not human. I don't want to call him a god, but he's definitely somewhere in between."

Said Randy Cross: "He's as cool and composed and handles situations like the last drive better than anyone who plays this game. Those who think he might have a peer might have to reconsider." Ronnie Lott said: "I've seen him do this time and time and time again. It's sad that people have questioned his ability, but you can't question his heart. You can't question his desire to be the best."

Again, Randy Cross: "How many quarterbacks have done what Joe's done? How many have come back from the odds he's been against at Notre Dame, early in his career, with his bad back and this year ('88) with the Steve Young thing? Joe is the classiest football player I've ever been associated with. He is the winningest individual I've ever known. You have to credit the organization for building a great team, but you take Joe Montana out of the formula and this is not the same team."

It has been said that the best measure of an athlete is what opposing players say about him. After Super Bowl XXIII, Norman "Boomer" Esiason, the starting quarterback for the Bengals, said of Montana: "He's somebody who's not only a professional on the field, but he's a professional off the field as well. Everything that was necessary for his team to win this football game, he did. That's an indication of why he'll go down as one of the greats of all-time, why he will be in the Hall of Fame when his career is over.

"I heard earlier in the season how the 49ers were losing and Montana was going to be benched, and I couldn't believe it. Here he comes and plays probably three of the best games of his life, and now everybody is ready to put him back on the pedestal where he belongs in the first place. He's been around the league about eight or nine years; he's been through it all; he's been through the ups and the downs. He's been able to handle it all, and he's always stayed on an even keel. He is definitely a role model."

Collinsworth was also quoted after Super Bowl XXIII as saying about Montana: "I have never seen a guy—and I'm sure he did it in college, high school and pee wee football, and now in professional football—that every single time he's had the chips down and people are counting him out, he's come back.

"We had them first down on their 10-yard line with three minutes to go, and somebody came up to me and said, 'We got 'em now.' I said, 'Have you taken a look at who's quarterbacking the San Francisco 49ers?' And that's what it comes down to. He's maybe the greatest player who's ever played the game. I don't know what else Joe Montana has to do to prove that he's the greatest player to ever play this game."

Keith Fahnhorst, the 49ers' All-Pro offensive tackle, retired after the 1987 season and moved home to Minnesota, where he went to work as a stockbroker for a regional firm based in Minneapolis. When asked for his thoughts on the essential ingredients of a championship football team, he paused momentarily, then smiled.

"You don't win championships without a quarterback," he said. "It's funny. Right before the last Super Bowl, there were some guys arguing in the office here. One guy was comparing Fran Tarkenton to Joe Montana. They turned to me, the so-called 'expert,' for my opinion and asked me what makes a great quarterback. I said, 'The one who wins the big one.' That pretty much quieted everyone down."

As far as Joe is concerned, the accolades are flattering, but he is just doing what makes him happy. As he looks back on a successful and fulfilling career, the question is asked, "What is left to accomplish?" He smiles that boyish grin, uncrosses the leg that rested casually on his knee and leans forward in his chair.

"You know," he begins, "last year, after the party we had for Super Bowl XXIII, I was lying in bed trying to sleep. I couldn't stop thinking about the touchdown pass to John Taylor that won the game. My mind kept replaying the pass over and over. I could see my linemen opening the passing lane so I could see him, and then I could see myself throwing the pass. Then I was throwing my arms up and jumping around like a little kid. I had that tremendous feeling of satisfaction all over again.

"Just as I began to fall asleep, I thought, 'What an incredible feeling. What could possibly be better than winning three Super Bowls?' I heard myself say, 'Four!'"

The folks in Monongahela—well, some of them anyway—could not be prouder.

Chapter 4

THE SUPPORTING CAST
The Offense

"The offense has done well because of its adaptability. If you compare how this offense operated before the 1988 season to the way it operated before the 1981 season, you wouldn't even recognize it. It was completely different."
—**Retired center Randy Cross**

Until their first Super Bowl, when the 49ers won a world championship despite one of the worst rushing attacks in professional football, some perceived this business of a "controlled passing game" as a contradiction in terms. The adage was that when you put the ball in the air, three things could happen and two of them were bad: 1) Incompletion; 2) Interception; 3) Completion.

Controlled passing? How, skeptics wondered, could you pass and still be in control? This was the National Footall League, home to the former champions of Green Bay and Chicago and Pittsburgh, teams whose offenses did not rely on X's and O's so much as they did on knocking opponents into Silly Putty. There was no room for finesse, no room for pretty little patterns—no matter if the receivers appeared as in sync as the Blue Angels.

But Bill Walsh, who learned from passing-game guru Sid Gillman but seemed to have his offense designed at the Rand Corporation, was convinced the key to a championship was not merely running over right tackle. Indeed, when the 49ers won their first championship in January 1982, they did it with an offense that averaged 3.5 yards per running attempt, which ranked last in the NFL. They did it with their running backs flaring out for dinky little passes and the tight end floating over the middle and wide receivers running down-and-out patterns, thereby leaving defenders down and out in the ozone.

They did it with a playbook that at least doubled the size of any playbook that the team's players had seen before at any level of competition.

"I ran a veer and wishbone offense in college," said Cross, a graduate of UCLA. "Then I came here and we went from Monte Clark's offense to Ken Meyer's offense to God knows what we ran in 1978. In Bill's offense, we were like Sugar Ray Leonard fighting Mike Tyson every week. We weren't gonna knock anybody out. We had to keep moving and jabbing. We didn't have any kind of a running game until Roger Craig and Wendell Tyler got here."

Without question, the 49ers struggled for a number of years to gain credibility in the running game. In the five seasons from 1978 to 1982, San Francisco had five different leading rushers—O.J. Simpson (who bore little resemblance to the younger O.J. of the Buffalo Bills*), Paul Hofer, Earl Cooper, Ricky Patton and Jeff

*Simpson, one of the greatest running backs in NFL history, was the first NFL player to rush for over 2,000 yards in a season when he amassed 2,003 in 1973, and he totaled 10,183 in nine years with Buffalo. By the time he was traded to the 49ers in 1978, Simpson was a shadow of his former self, running for 1,053 yards in two seasons.

Moore. Tyler, who was acquired from the Los Angeles Rams for pocket change, led the Niners' ground game in 1983 and the championship 1984 season, and Craig has led in the four seasons since.

But it has long been Walsh's philosophy that although a running game is important, an offense cannot thrive on churning legs alone. An offense needs movement; it needs to keep defensive players running in circles and defensive coaches reaching for the antacid. It needs an efficient quarterback—a position with which Walsh has long been associated in creating excellence, from Greg Cook to Ken Anderson to Dan Fouts to Joe Montana.

From the time Walsh arrived in San Francisco, he said, "I felt very positive the offense would be one of the best in football, and soon that would be the case when we finally put together the personnel. It had been very successful at San Diego and Stanford and Cincinnati. It had its own style to it. The fact I would be orchestrating it and directing it, I felt very confident."

If that statement seems flavored with just a touch of arrogance, it is no wonder. Perhaps Walsh was not thrilled with the genius tag, but he has said on many occasions, "Coaching the quarterback position is what I know best."

Although the 49ers lost with regularity (14 of 16) in Walsh's first season in 1979, the Niners went from ranking among the dregs of professional football in offense to first in passing in the National Football Conference and sixth in total offense in the NFL. Quarterback Steve DeBerg threw an NFL record 347 completions for 3,652 yards. Compare those totals to the year before, when he completed 137 passes and threw for 1,570 yards.

Montana has thrived in the Walsh offense, too. In 1980, when he started only seven games and rotated with DeBerg, he still managed to throw for 1,795 yards and established a club completion-percentage record of 64.5. In 1981, the 49ers' first Super Bowl season and Montana's first full year as a starter, he threw for 3,565 yards with a completion percentage of 63.7.

"The system has been successful because it's a good system," said 49ers' offensive coordinator Mike Holmgren, who coached the team's quarterbacks from 1986 to 1988. "It is a system that allows the quarterback to be as successful as he can possibly be. Some people may not think it's as spectacular as others, but it works. Why change it?"

The system worked in 1981. When the Niners were devoid of a fearsome rushing attack, Montana's accurate arm and Walsh's high percentage plays carried them. It worked in 1988. When injuries and inadequacies wrecked the passing game, Craig high-stepped his way to a career-best season and kept the 49ers in the heart of a playoff race. Seldom have both ends of the offense failed simultaneously.

Sid Gillman, a former coach of the Los Angeles Rams, Los Angeles Chargers, San Diego Chargers and Houston Oilers and long considered the father of the modern passing game, says Walsh's system is flawless. "No. 1, his passing concept is as good as there has been in the business. Nobody has a better one. And his running game in the last Super Bowl looked like the San Diego Chargers' in 1961. They ran those sweeps, and the Walsh sweep says, 'You get your ass around that end as fast as you can,' but you reserve the right to change your mind and cut back to the middle when you get in the area of the tight end.

"Technically, the system is so good; everybody is so well-coached. When Roger Craig runs that short little angle pass, he's going to go places. The son of a bitch is going to carry the ball 20 times and catch that angle pass 10 times until he finally wears you out. I think the key to the whole thing is, technically everybody is as sound as hell. Their execution and techniques are superb. They look good. They just look good in their uniforms. And the fact that Walsh is going to utilize his productive people is key. So many coaches have great players and don't use them enough. That always gets me."

Craig, who played on two championship teams and is well-acquainted with the developments of the 1981 title season, agrees that the Niners' offense has proven to have few, if any, weaknesses. "That's what has been so great about our championship teams. Every team has been different. A different mixture of guys, different things that worked. Bill did an excellent job of finding talent and fitting it into certain areas, molding the team together. The three different teams had three different personalities."

Though the 49ers' offense most often has been associated with Walsh's choreography and Montana's precision passing, the team's running game has been as good as any in football in recent seasons. Just as the team's defense unjustly has been stamped with the "finesse" label in seemingly indelible ink, the offensive line rarely has been mentioned in the same breath as the famous mammoth blockers of the Chicago Bears, Washington Redskins and Los Angeles Rams.

Consider this evolution: In 1986, the 49ers finished 10th in the league in rushing and second in passing; in 1987, they were first in rushing and second in passing; in 1988, second in rushing and 10th in passing. Does this sound like a team that cannot defeat opponents physically?

"Look at the last two years, how many yards we rushed for, and compare that to some of the teams like the Bears and the Redskins, teams that people perceive have great running games, teams with great offensive lines like the Los Angeles Rams," Cross said. "Let's see who has rushed for the most yards in the last two or three years. That is the metamorphosis of this offense. Now we have a guy like Jerry Rice. We no longer have possession receivers."

In Roger Craig and Jerry Rice, the 49ers have, as Cross puts it, "lightning from two positions."

When Craig was drafted in the second round out of Nebraska in 1983, the 49ers had already acquired an effective halfback, Wendell Tyler, by trade. Craig always considered halfback a more natural position for him than fullback, which requires more blocking and garners less yardage and, subsequently, less glory. But he was not about to complain when Walsh asked him to split his time between carrying the ball and knocking linebackers out of Tyler's way.

"I didn't know what to expect when I got there," he said. "I was fresh out of college, and I just wanted to make an impact. I wanted to show that I was worthy of being an early draft pick. I listened and learned and watched the veteran guys and tried to become the mode of running back they wanted. I thought I did an excellent job as fullback for five years. I knew what my role was. I didn't expect to do any more. I was Wendell Tyler's blocking back. When I was called upon to do more, whether it was to catch the ball or take some pressure off of Wendell, I was ready. I put pressure on myself not to let my teammates down."

Ever the team player, Craig has not let anybody down since draft day '83. He rushed for 725 yards in his rookie season, only 131 fewer than Tyler, the team leader, and added 48 receptions; and in 1984, Craig led the team with 71 catches while maintaining his effectiveness as a runner. But his breakthrough season arrived the following year, when this former Cornhusker (who spent most of his college career as a backup to Jarvis Redwine and Heisman Trophy winner Mike Rozier) became the first NFL player to break the thousand-thousand barrier. Elevating himself to one of the greatest all-purpose backs of all time, Craig rushed for 1,050 yards and added 1,016 on 92 receptions.

Although it was a record-setting season for Craig, it took some time before he gained national recognition that the statistics screamed he deserved. There was no doubting his athletic skills, his tireless work ethic, his devotion to the team. But with the presence of Walsh and Montana, some perceived that Craig, although a marvelous athlete, was largely a product of the 49ers' system. It followed that the Niners' running game rarely inspired fear, regardless of what the statistics sheet said after the game.

"People just won't label us as one of the great threats in running the ball," he said. "They still call us a finesse team. But as far as I'm concerned, they can keep calling us finesse as long as we have the Super Bowl rings to show for it. Let them call us a pass-dominated team."

That was not the case in 1988, one of the strangest championship seasons in the annals of the NFL. For much of the year, it seemed as if somebody had stuffed a sock in the muffler of the team's passing attack. Nobody was quite certain whether Montana was as banged up physically as Walsh kept saying he was, or if opposing defenses had caught up to Walsh's offense after all these years, or if the attention given to a perceived quarterback controversy had left both Montana and Steve Young dizzy. All that was certain was that Craig was doing his best to keep the team afloat.

Week two: Craig runs for 110 yards against the vaunted New York Giants' defense. Week six: Craig rambles for 143 more yards, giving him 574 for the year. Week seven: Wow. Craig leaves clete marks all over the Rams, rushing for a career-high 190 yards and three touchdowns, including one of 46 yards. By the time the regular season ended, Craig had rushed for a team record 1,502 yards, third best in the league behind Eric Dickerson and Herschel Walker; he had busted 100 yards seven times, eclipsing his previous season high of two; he had firmly established himself as one of the greatest running backs of all time and had moved closer to the access road to the Hall of Fame.

Part of the reason for Craig's bonanza season was a move Walsh made midway through the 1987 season, when he shifted Craig to halfback and inserted Tom Rathman at fullback for improved blocking. After the year, Craig adjusted his training schedule and committed himself to losing about 15 pounds to become quicker and gain more endurance for the halfback position. Of course, this meant something far more painful than any tackle or six-mile run.

"I had to give up oatmeal raisin cookies and French vanilla ice cream," he said. "That was the toughest thing of all."

To truly appreciate Craig's accomplishment, one has to comprehend the punishment he absorbed each week. Though he has managed to escape a major injury, his body is constantly covered with welts and scratches, his joints ache, his bones creak, and everything down to his eyelids seems to throb. He can deal with the pain, he says, because he puts himself through pain to prepare for the season. Even teammates refuse to join Craig in his off-season workouts, which include torturous runs up steep horse trails in the Bay Area.

"I condition my mind as well as my body," he said. "I mean, I beat myself up in the off-season. The pain I go through during the season is nothing compared to what I put myself through in the off-season."

Furthermore, the pain he goes through now is preferable to the pain he went through as a blocking back. "I still take hits, believe me. But it's not like I'm in contact all the time. Tom is taking the inside linebackers, which I don't have to now, and that's a lot of punishment—240 to 250 pounds coming at you all the time. When I was blocking for Wendell all of those years, I took a pounding."

Craig's work ethic and good fortune have blended nicely. Excluding one game he missed during the NFL players' strike in 1987, he has not missed one outing since he was drafted—a span of 105 games (playoffs included) in his first six seasons. "Roger has improved as a runner," Walsh said. "You know backs tend to lose something as the years pass. Roger has gotten better. He's dealing with tackles better. He's getting his pads lower when he's making contact. He's spinning off people."

Jerry Rice, the Niners' other lightning bolt, figures to be spinning away from cornerbacks and dancing in the end zone for years to come. Named the Most Valuable Player of the 1987 season and MVP of Super Bowl XXIII, Rice had amazing totals of 264 catches and 49 touchdowns in his first four seasons and was on a pace to become the greatest wide receiver in NFL history. His 22 touchdown catches in 1987 shattered the old league mark of 18, and the feat was particularly remarkable when you consider he played only 12 games, because he sat out during the players' strike that season.

About the only knock ever placed on Rice was that he seemed to disappear when the post-season rolled around, but his performance on the road to Super Bowl XXIII was unparalleled. He had five catches and three touchdowns in a first-round playoff victory over Minnesota, five catches and two touchdowns in the NFC championship game against Chicago and 11 catches for a playoff record 215 yards and one touchdown in the 20–16 Super Bowl win over Cincinnati at Miami's Joe Robbie Stadium.

"I had to prove something to myself," Rice said. "Everyone was saying, 'Jerry can't perform in the playoffs,' I had to prove to myself that I could get the job done. I just wanted to concentrate on my job and not be distracted by anybody."

The Super Bowl win and the MVP honor may have removed that proverbial monkey from Rice's back, but his celebration was rather low key. How low key? "I went back to the hotel after the game to help my wife pack her bags. I couldn't get to sleep that night. I stayed up all night. I felt really good. I felt like I had achieved a lot. My goal was to participate in the Super Bowl, and just to win the game meant a lot to me. Also, I had a little input."

The fact Rice made such an enormous contribution in the game led to a little controversy. He discovered in the days after the Super Bowl that he remained only the third most important story in the Bay Area sports pages, behind Bill Walsh's imminent departure as coach and lingering reaction to Joe Montana's leadership on the winning drive in the final minutes of the game. When Rice realized that he was not going to be flooded by endorsement opportunities in the off-season, he complained that he was being slighted by the media and intimated racism was involved. Predictably, reporters hounded Rice at every off-season function and asked him to expound on his comments, and it got to the point that he finally called one reporter "dickhead" at a 49ers' mini-camp.

But when Rice reported for training camp in July 1989, it was apparent that he had done some growing, some thinking. "I'm a totally different guy now. A serious guy," he said. "I understand things a lot more than I did. I guess you could say I'm just more mature. I think some of the things I said about not getting enough recognition were blown out of proportion. I'm not going to say I'm sorry I said it, but I did learn from the experience."

When Rice reported to camp at Sierra College, in Rocklin, his attitude was not the only thing that had changed. Endless wind sprints in the off-season had dropped his weight to 192 pounds, roughly a dozen below his usual reporting weight. He said he wanted to get faster, to get quicker, to gain more endurance. All this from somebody who already was the best wide receiver in the league. "That's why he's so great," Gillman said. "Here's a guy who's an All-Pro and he's trying to get better."

"He's the best wide receiver in football right now, and if he stays healthy he could be the greatest of all time," said former 49ers receiver Billy Wilson, now a scout with the team. "All he has to do is keep doing what he's doing."

The 49ers had to do some maneuvering to get Rice in 1985. They went into the draft with the 28th and final pick of the first round as a result of their Super Bowl win the season before, but packaged the selection with second- and third-round picks and sent them to New England for the Patriots' picks in the first round (16th overall) and third round. When the Niners made the deal and drafted Rice, no team was more infuriated than the Dallas Cowboys, who were set to take him with the next selection in the 17th spot. In retrospect, it is amazing that Rice lasted as long as he did and that he was the third wide receiver taken, behind Wisconsin's Al Toon (10th by the New York Jets) and Miami of Florida's Eddie Brown (13th by the Cincinnati Bengals).

Rice, quiet by nature, was shy and slightly overwhelmed when he arrived from Mississippi Valley State. He once recalled that when he stepped into the terminal at San Francisco International Airport, "I saw all of those cameras, and I was shocked. I had never been exposed to that kind of attention."

He adjusted, first to his surroundings, then to NFL defenses, which were significantly more sophisticated than the ones he had faced in division I–AA college ball. From the outset of his workouts with the Niners, he impressed coaches and teammates with his natural ability. He impressed one player in particular: Dwight Clark.

Unlike Rice, Clark, as a 10th-round draft choice out of Clemson, came to the Niners with little fanfare. The Niners knew of him only because their scouts had gone to the Clemson campus in South Carolina to work out quarterback Steve Fuller. But Clark rapidly became a vital gear in Walsh's offensive machine, leading the team in receptions in 1981, '82 and '83, accounting for the most famous play in club history—the Catch in the 1981 seasons' NFC title game—and completing his career as the 49ers' all-time leading receiver with 506 catches for 6,750 yeards.

Clark realizes that Rice, barring a catastrophe, eventually will dominate the team's record book. In 1987, Clark realized something else as well. After Rice scored three touchdowns against the Cleveland Browns, giving him 14 in his first eight games of the season, Clark told him: "I used to think you were the best receiver I had ever seen. Now I think you're probably the best football player I've ever seen."

Wilson said that if you put Rice on a track with other wide receivers, chances are he would lose in a sprint. "I think his fastest time coming out of college was 4.55" for the 40-yard dash, he said. "But if the ball is in the air, he'll get under it." It is the extra gear he has after the ball is thrown that separates Rice from other receivers and surely separates him from opposing defensive backs. Add to this the superb manner in which he runs pass routes and the strength of his hands, which was developed at an early age when he caught bricks for his father, the bricklayer, in Mississippi, and it is easy to see why he is destined for the Hall of Fame.

Clark's credentials also are worthy of consideration for the lads in Canton, Ohio. When he caught the 500th pass of his career, in 1987, he became the 20th NFL player to achieve that feat. Not bad for a guy who once recalled, "Even after I made the team, after the final cut, they were still bringing in guys for tryouts."

The Catch, the 6-yard touchdown pass from Montana to Clark that put the Niners in their first Super Bowl, had such an impact that a commemorative cancellation stamp, picturing the play, was issued. Clark's No. 87 jersey is one of only 81 retired in the NFL, seven by the Niners. The others whose numbers were retired by San Francisco are quarterback John Brodie (12), running back Joe Perry (34), defensive back Jimmy Johnson (37), running back Hugh McElhenny (39), defensive tackle Charlie Krueger (70) and defensive tackle Leo Nomellini (73). Perry, McElhenny and Nomellini have been inducted into the Hall of Fame.

Clark's final season in 1987 was not a joyous experience. He was plagued by injuries and played sparingly, catching only 24 passes. By the time the season had ended, with the surprising first-round playoff loss to Minnesota, he realized it was time to devote his full attention to his Redwood City restaurant, *Clark's by the Bay*, his insurance business and his family.

"It's not that tough for me to watch games," he said. "The first home exhibition game against the Raiders (in 1988) was tough. But in my mind and my heart and the way my body felt, I knew it was time for me to leave; there was a lot less pressure on me. When the team was 6–5, I really didn't miss it. I'd be lying if I said I didn't want to be in the Super Bowl and catch the pass that John Taylor caught. But then I thought, 'How can a guy with two Super Bowl rings feel sorry for himself?' Just because I wasn't one of the six or seven guys who played on all three?"

In all, seven players were on the 49ers' roster for all three championship teams: from the offense, quarterback Joe Montana, center-guard Randy Cross and wide receiver Mike Wilson; from the defense, defensive backs Ronnie Lott, Carlton Williamson and Eric Wright and linebacker Keena Turner. Montana, Cross and Wilson represent only a fraction of the players who enabled the Walsh offense to work in the decade. It all starts up front with . . .

[The offensive line:] Long one of the most underrated blocking units in the NFL, the 49ers' offensive line has included such players as Cross, Keith Fahnhorst, John Ayers, Fred Quillan, Dan Audick, Bubba Paris, Guy McIntyre, Jesse Sapolu, Steve Wallace, Harris Barton, Jeff Bregel and Bruce Collie. Through the years, they have protected Montana from on rushing masses of thundering blubber and opened holes for Craig, Tyler and other backs.

Given much of the credit for the line's development is assistant coach Bobb McKittrick, who left the San Diego Chargers after the 1978 season to join Walsh's new staff. "I remember when I came here, some members of the media said, 'McKittrick, you've got the worst part of a very sad 49er team.' It would have been nice if every player was a first- or second-round draft choice, but that wasn't the case."

Because the Niners' line has generally been a solid unit but lacked a dominant player, say along the lines of Cincinnati's Anthony Munoz, the group has not been showered with honors. Cross was voted to play in the Pro Bowl three times, Quillan twice, Fahnhorst once. That's it. Despite the success of the offense in 1986, '87 and '88, no 49ers offensive lineman played in the postseason all-star game.

The voting by the league's players and coaches has not gone over well in San Francisco. Sapolu said, "If you lead the league in offense, it's not just because Joe made a good pass or Roger made a nice run." Collie chimed in, "I think the reason we play so well as a unit is because any of us could start on another team. If we're No. 1 in the league in rushing, that should be enough.

If we're near the bottom of the league in allowing sacks, that should say it also."

Rather than shift blame to the Pro Bowl voters, Cross put the onus on the 49ers. "We're not perceived as being intimidating or great. We're not touted by the organization as a whole. What I mean is, Rams Coach John Robinson goes out of his way to compliment his offensive line. New York Giants Coach Bill Parcells talks about his linebackers. Here, the offensive line doesn't figure into that."

[The running backs:] Rumors were flying before the 1983 draft that the Los Angeles Rams were going to draft running back Eric Dickerson of Southern Methodist University. That might have initially seemed like tragic news for the 49ers, but it actually helped San Francisco build its running game. How so? To make room for Dickerson, the Rams traded Tyler, defensive end Cody Jones and a No. 3 pick to the Niners for second- and fourth-round picks. Tyler played four seasons for the Niners and led them in rushing twice.

"I had heard rumors the Niners were trying to trade for me," Tyler said. "All I knew was they needed a running back, and then they drafted Roger. . . . In the past with their offense, just the passing game was effective. But when I came and Roger came, Coach Walsh got comfortable running the ball more, and the line got better and better."

Until the arrival of Craig and Tyler, 49ers running backs had been mostly role players, doing certain things well but nothing spectacularly. The list included Paul Hofer, Bill Ring, Ricky Patton, Earl Cooper and Carl Monroe.

[The tight ends:] The Niners' three championship teams had three different starting tight ends—Charle Young in 1981, Russ Francis in 1984 and John Frank in 1988. The next one will have a different starter as well, because Frank retired after the season to devote all of his time to finishing medical school. A broken hand during the year convinced him that extending his football career and exposing himself to further injury would endanger his chances of becoming a surgeon.

"My body is sort of thanking me for the decision," he said. "You know, you only get one body. I don't know if you could say the hand was the only factor, but it made me realize what a sacrifice it is to play football. Every time I saw someone get hurt bad, it reminded you these things (can be) lifelong catastrophes. I have other things I want to do."

Frank, a second-round draft pick out of Ohio State in 1984, spent most of his first four seasons as a backup to Francis, and though he became a full-time starter in 1988, he missed half the season with the hand and injuries. When he played, the Niners were a different team: They were 10-1 during the regular season and playoffs with him playing. To look at it another way, they lost five of eight without him. His retirement, combined with the departure of free-agent tight end Ron Heller to Altanta, was a concern for the Niners heading into the 1989 season, but the team felt the position could be filled by returning veteran Brent Jones, free-agent acquisition Jamie Williams from Houston and rookie Wesley Walls.

Francis and Young, neither of whom began or finished his career with the 49ers, were acquired through trades not only to fill the role of starting tight end but also to provide a steadying influence over the team's younger players. Not that Francis has ever really been known as a steadying influence. As Walsh recalls, "About all you can say is he was a real free spirit." Picked up from New England in a draft day trade in 1982, Francis proved to be a consistent receiver, his best year coming in 1985, when he had a career-high 44 catches. He also had five receptions in Super Bowl XIX against Miami.

Young, acquired from the Rams in 1980, also proved to be a valuable pickup by Walsh. He played in every game in his three seasons with San Francisco and had 37 catches and five touchdowns in the championship '81 season. Then there was his other, more subtle contribution: "My role was to bring the elements together, inspire and encourage players, tell them that despite the odds, "We can win let's do it.' But you couldn't just do it with lip service. You had to do it with action."

[The wide receivers:] Clark dominated the first half of the decade and Rice the second half. But in a Bill Walsh offense, wide receivers are not starved for attention. Freddie Solomon started the first two Super Bowls at flanker opposite Clark, and he remains fifth on the team's all-time reception list with 310 in eight seasons; Mike Wilson has played on all three championship teams, has been a part-time starter and overcame a serious neck injury in 1986; Mike Shumann started the 1981 season's NFC title game and likes to point out that he made the first catch of the game for the Niners (Clark, of course, made the final catch); Renaldo Nehamiah gave the team a speed threat as a third wide receiver, although he never quite developed as Walsh hoped; Terry Greer proved to be an effective backup in 1988 with some big catches; and John Taylor entered the '89 season as the team's starting split end after catching the winning touchdown in Super Bowl XXIII.

Taylor's last-minute heroics may not soon be forgotten, except maybe by him. "I try not to think about it anymore," he said. "I talked to my brother, and he said, 'Imagine how you would have felt if you had missed it. The loneliest person in the world.' "

He undoubtedly would have felt like Jackie Smith, who dropped a sure touchdown pass from Roger Staubach in the Dallas Cowboys' 35–31 loss to Pittsburgh in Super Bowl XIII in January 1979. As Smith said after that game, "I've dropped passes before but never any that was that important."

Chapter 5

THE HIT PARADE
The Defense

"Defense is the most important part of the game, because if your opponents can't score—you can't lose."

— *An old coaching adage*

*F*inesse. In the world of professional football, the word may prompt titters and cause eyes to roll, but in the '80s, it accurately described both the offense and the defense of the San Francisco 49ers.

In the honor roll of all-time NFL defenses, a handful of great ones stand out. The "Doomsday" defense of the Dallas Cowboys; the "Steel Curtain" of the Pittsburgh Steelers; the "46" defense of the Chicago Bears; the "Purple People Eaters" of the Minnesota Vikings; the "Fearsome Foursome" of the Los Angeles Rams; and George Seifert's "finesse defense" of the San Francisco 49ers.

George Seifert's finesse defense? Well, it should be.

When Bill Walsh took the reigns of the 49ers in 1979 he really had only two major problems: 1) the offense, and 2) the defense. The special teams were managing fairly well on their own. Since it was Walsh's specialty, anyone who knew the team—Eddie DeBartolo in particular—felt it would only be a matter of time before he turned the offense around. The defense, however, would require some special attention.

How bad were the 49ers at the time Walsh took over?

George Seifert left his position as defensive backfield coach at Stanford to join Walsh's 49er staff in the same capacity in 1980. Seifert's coaching career had included stops as a graduate assistant at his alma mater—the University of Utah—and as an assistant at the University of Iowa, the University of Oregon, Stanford, and as head coach at Cornell, before rejoining Walsh at Stanford in 1977. When Walsh went to the 49ers in '79, Seifert stayed for one more season, then moved to the pros as Walsh's assistant the following year.

"I remember going up to Candlestick to watch a 49ers game after one of our Stanford games was over," Seifert recalled. "It was Bill's first year there and it was pretty bleak. We could sit anywhere we wanted. The stadium was practically empty, there were no parking problems, no lines for anything."

But even after Seifert made the short drive up the Bayshore Freeway to become a 49ers coach, the team's improvement was not immediate. And neither was the respect of the fans.

An avid yachtsman, Seifert was leaving to go away on vacation soon after joining the 49ers' staff . . . "So I called some guy up north who I knew a little bit because I wanted to try and get a berth for my boat up along the coast. I said something along the lines of, 'I hope you can find one for me. You know, I'm coaching with the 49ers now.' I don't usually do that, but I threw it out to the guy anyway. And he said, 'Well, that's your problem.' That's how far down the 49ers were."

Everyone with a pennant and a beer mug knew the 49ers were weak on offense. But the defense needed a major overhaul as well. In the four seasons prior to Seifert's arrival, the 49ers had only one player elected to the Pro Bowl—defensive tackle Cleveland Elam in 1977. By 1979, they ranked 27th in the NFL in total defense. About the only way to go was up.

To the veterans, the initial efforts to improve the defense were an indication of how far they had to go. Veteran linebacker Dan Bunz, a first round draft choice in '78, recalled his teammates feelings as Walsh made wholesale changes. "The first year Bill was here everyone said, 'Well, it can't get any worse.' But it did. We went 2–14 for the second year in a row and everybody got cut. They brought in new guys all the time trying to find the right combination. We had the 'defensive back of the week.' They'd bring a guy in on Wednesday, work him out in a couple of practices and he'd be starting on Sunday." Not exactly the trademark of a championship team. But the team's deficiencies on defense soon went from the ridiculous to the sublime.

"I remember one time Cedric Hardman and I were talking together in the huddle," Bunz continued. "Nobody could keep track of the defensive backs they were bringing in—no one knew their names. One guy had come to practice earlier in the week and he was starting in the game that Sunday. He made a real nice play over in the left flat and Cedric said to me, 'Hey, that was a nice play, who is that guy?' I said, 'I don't know. Check out the name on the back of his jersey when he comes back to the huddle.' Here it is the NFL and we don't even know the name of the guy playing next to us. That really cracked me up."

After drafting offense in '79, Walsh and Seifert focused on the defense in '80 and '81 and came up with tremendous talent—especially at linebacker and defensive back. The 1980 draft yielded defensive end Jim Stuckey and linebackers Keena Turner, Craig Puki and Bobby Leopold. But the Niners hit the mother lode the following year when they drafted defensive backs Ronnie Lott, Eric Wright and Carlton Williamson and acquired veterans Jack "Hacksaw" Reynolds and Fred Dean.

Bunz would no longer have to wonder about the name of the guy playing next to him.

No one appreciated the change of scenery more than Fred Dean. A second round draft choice of the San Diego Chargers out of Louisiana Tech in 1975, Dean was an All-Pro defensive end in '79 and fearsome pass rusher who was skilled in getting to the quarterback. A 30-day salary holdout in 1980 soured his taste for the Chargers, so he welcomed the trade to the 49ers in '81 as a breath of fresh air. And with the group Seifert and Walsh had assembled, it was like a dream come true for the man who would become one of the football's finest pass rushers.

"Coming to the 49ers was really the ideal situation for me," Dean said. "With the type of personnel we had, with the new DBs and linebackers—Ronnie Lott, Hacksaw—I could just pin back my ears and go after the passer. With those guys behind me, there was no doubt I could go out and make things happen."

Things definitely happened that season. With Joe Montana guiding the offense, the addition of the seven or eight defensive starters enabled the Niners to actually stop some people on defense. The team went 13–2 in the regular season and won Super Bowl XVI against Cincinnati the following January.

But Walsh and Seifert still needed to do some convincing. Unfortunately, even with some of their own players.

"The defense was always overlooked," said Bunz. "If anything was ever talked about it was the offense. It was Walsh's whole emphasis. We didn't even see Bill in a defensive meeting unless he was mad about something."

In the early years of Walsh's tenure it was easy to understand his offensive focus. After all, he had labored dutifully in the coaching ranks to earn the opportunity of becoming an NFL head coach. He had so much he wanted to show the football world, and the 49ers were so pathetic. When he adopted his wide-open passing offense, a sportswriter asked Walsh why he favored such an attack over the more conventional and less risky style of run-oriented offenses so popular with his opposition. "Our turnovers are downfield, theirs are at the line of scrimmage," he replied.

Still, many players felt the pass-happy coach spent too much time on his intricate offensive game plans. Including Dan Bunz.

"His first year, he spent all his time on offense," the linebacker said. "When the offense would do something wrong they'd go over and over it. But when the defense did something wrong, it was, 'Well, we gotta get out of here.'"

That emphasis showed up on the scoreboard. But ironically it soon paid real dividends in terms of the evolution of the defense.

"One thing I saw was that the offense was really complicated," said Bunz. "It was much more elaborate than anything else we'd ever seen, and that helped us a lot defensively. I mean in practice we'd see nine million formations and even then he was always trying to adjust something. You started to get the feeling that whatever the other teams would try and do against us with their offense, there was no way it could be tougher than what we saw every day in practice. So, by the end of the first Super Bowl year ('81), we gained a tremendous amount of confidence in the defense because we faced the league's best offense every day."

The 1981 season was a watershed year for many reasons. Joe Montana had assumed the leadership role for the offense, and the team had begun to gel defensively. Young players like Ronnie Lott and Keena Turner learned from the veterans Walsh brought in that year; especially Hacksaw Reynolds.

"It was the addition of Hacksaw and the new secondary that really began to establish us in a certain way," said Turner. "Hacksaw had been through so much in his career with the Rams and he gave us a lot of leadership that everyone listened to. I was one of those guys who thought I just had to be an athlete and that was pretty much all it took to succeed in football. But with Hacksaw, I learned that there was a lot more to it than just being a good athlete. He was real dedicated. All football. A real role model for the younger players. A little crazy, but hey, this wasn't a CPA firm."

"Hacksaw was a real piece of work," recalled Seifert. "But he was an incredible influence on the younger players. He had a work ethic that I wish more players had. But he sure was eccentric. He always brought a bunch of spiral notebooks and a couple of dozen pencils with him to every meeting. As soon as a coach started talking he would start scribbling furiously in his notebook, like he was writing down every word. The guy was very intense, and very committed to the game."

Some thought Hacksaw should have been committed to another sort of institution—one with rubber walls—but his impact on the 49ers' younger players was undeniable.

"At meetings," Seifert continued, "he'd sit down at a desk and he had this big old box crammed full of his pencils and a pencil sharpener, and he'd just go through 'em. I kind of had the reputation for holding long meetings and talking quite a bit. He would sit there and write down everything I said. If you said something in a meeting and he wrote it down and two or three days later you contradicted yourself, you would be reminded of it even to the point of him showing you the notes where you said to do something one way and later said to do it another way.

"From the standpoint of study habits, coaches naturally try to advise and encourage players to look at a lot of film, study, and take good notes just like any teacher would. But here was a person that was basically doing what coaches always said . . . and that had a profound effect upon the players."

Ronnie Lott was no exception. "Hacksaw did a lot for this team," he said. "He created a lot of good habits for this organization. He taught a lot of people how to win. He even taught some of the coaches how to win. He did a lot more for this organization than most people know."

One thing Seifert did for the organization was preside over the emergence of the defense. The restructuring included a change of philosophy to maximize the skills of the personnel.

"Going back to the start when Chuck Studley was Bill's first defensive coordinator, they were primarily a 4-3 philosophy," Seifert began. "Norb Hecker had the linebackers and I had the secondary. We had drafted Keena Turner and Bobby Leopold and we ended up with an abundance of linebackers. We began to think in terms of going to a 3-4 to create more confusion and have more blitzing as opposed to being set. Pressure was something that was important. In reality, now that I think of it, as a defensive back coach I was probably thinking, 'Hey, I can get more guys into coverage.' There'd only be three guys rushing. I think we just saw greater flexibility overall."

In addition to the veterans who came along in '81, the defense was blessed by a sensational college draft that year. It is rare for a team to get more than a couple of starters from the same draft, but in '81, the 49ers acquired their entire defensive secondary for the decade in one afternoon.

Forty Niners director of college scouting Tony Razzano credits Walsh and Seifert and a strong scouting staff.

"Bill wanted a defensive draft in '81," he said. There was a lot of talent we were watching, but we knew we needed defensive help. I love scouting. I like to prepare for the draft. The process is very democratic and it takes input from everyone involved with the organization. All our coaches are involved. We don't have one guy who ultimately has to make a decision, although Bill usually did."

The '81 draft was symbolic of what the 49ers' organization was able to do year-in and year-out in the '80s: Take raw football talent and mold it into a winning combination. George Seifert dealt with the problem of drafting players like Lott, Wright and Williamson out of their normal positions. It was a nice problem to have.

"They were all safeties," the defensive coordinator said. "Dwight Hicks was a college safety. Carlton Williamson was a college safety. Ronnie Lott was a college safety and Eric Wright was a college safety. We wound up with maybe the biggest defensive secondary in football. We found it to be an advantage in playing against the big offensive backs that came into the league. When you have small defensive backs trying to tackle these big guys—and I don't care how good they are—eventually the big back's going to pop through. With our guys, they could come up and take these guys on and usually win. It was evident in this last Super Bowl with Ronnie Lott's tackles against Ickey Woods. That was an important factor in that ballgame."

With all due respect to All-Pros Hicks and Wright and Pro Bowler Williamson, the heart and soul of the 49ers' defense in the '80s was former Southern Cal strongman Ronnie Lott. The eighth player taken overall, and the second defensive back (Kenny Easley was selected fourth by Seattle) in the '81 draft, Lott terrorized Pac-10 offenses for two All-Conference seasons before joining Seifert's forces in one of the NFL's most underrated defenses.

"Playing for this defense has been tough," said Lott. "It's tough because you want your own identity. And compared to our offense, we have almost gone unnoticed."

Which seems unfair, because without a strong defense the Niners would have just been . . . oh, maybe the Chargers. And according to Lott, they might have been lighter by about three Super Bowl rings.

"Without question," Lott began, "throughout the years I've been in San Francisco we never would have won any of these championships. We never would have won in '81. We never would have won in '84. We never would have won this past year if it wasn't for the defense.

"The reason I can say and believe it is because the defense helped make the offense successful. The defense initiated turnovers and often gave the offense great field position. And we prevented the opposition from controlling the game. Otherwise, it would have been similar to the '79 team when they scored a lot of points but didn't win. You have to have defense to win championships. No Super Bowl champion has ever won without a strong defense. And in the '80s, we were the embodiment of a strong, but underrated defense."

And just who were these non-stars who combined to become one of the league's best defenses? And what was the secret of their success? The defensive backs, especially Lott.

Lott became an immediate starter at cornerback as a rookie and was runner-up to Lawrence Taylor of the New York Giants for NFL Rookie-of-the-Year. The superstar has been named to the Pro Bowl seven times —a 49ers' record—and has made All-Pro five times. He is second to Jimmy Johnson in career interceptions on the 49ers' all-time list and has scored a team record five touchdowns off interceptions. He earned his reputation as a hard hitter in college and has maintained his status through nine seasons in the professional ranks. But like the other 49ers, Ronnie Lott is much more than just statistics.

"Like Hacksaw and Fred Dean, Ronnie has tremendous inner confidence," said Seifert. "It's not demonstrated in terms of outer emotion like some other players who may bang lockers or punch walls. He's very quiet and to himself on gamedays, almost sullen. But you can just sense that something is going on inside. You can see it in Ronnie when he's sitting at his locker before a game almost in a trance. You learn to leave those guys alone."

But Lott is not just a bomb waiting to detonate according to Seifert.

"Something that's been important on our defense is that the coaches do not feel threatened by players who present their opinions and make suggestions to improve the team. Ronnie Lott's the main example of a guy who has a feel or a sense for what's going on in the game."

The arrival of Lott also signalled an end to the revolving door in the 49ers' secondary. "I knew I could make a difference," said Lott. "I knew I could do better than what they had here before. Whatever they had here, they wouldn't have to worry about rotating 30 DBs in like they did that one year."

And what does he think of his reputation as one of the NFL's hardest hitters?

"I don't think about it much," he said, with a trace of a smile. "It's funny, in basketball you know you're on the money with your jumper when you get in a groove and everything just flows. It's the same in football when you crack somebody and you know you've hit him right below those numbers—you know he's going to be out.

It's like hitting the 'sweet spot' in baseball. You know when you've put on a great hit."

With all that ferocity, how about pain?

"You learn about pain when you're a little kid," he said. "Some kids don't like getting beat up, others don't mind. We all learn how to deal with it. I was so intent on doing my job that pain never entered my mind.

"I can remember growing up and watching guys like Larry Brown, Ray Nitschke, Sam Huff, Chris Hanberger, or Pat Fischer or Charley Taylor. I used to think that if I was playing on the pavement and I'd run into a wall, that I'd always get up because I saw them get up. Pros have a strong influence on kids—it's something I never forget."

Lott's running mates in the defensive secondary have been very impressive as a supporting cast. Dwight Hicks, who came to the Niners in '79 and suffered through those first two losing seasons, started at safety and had four straight Pro Bowl years between '81 and '84 along with an All-Pro season in '81. Carlton Williamson and Eric Wright were also added to the defensive secondary along with Lott in the '81 draft and joined forces to comprise the youngest starting line-up in the NFL. The duo of Williamson and Wright, who played safety and cornerback respectively, combined for four Pro Bowl and two All-Pro seasons and shared a total of six Super Bowl rings.

To underscore the effectiveness of the 49ers' secondary, all four players—Lott, Hicks, Williamson and Wright—were named to the 1985 Pro Bowl, the only time in NFL history an entire defensive backfield received the honor.

But even the best teams cannot play together forever. Dwight Hicks went to the Colts after the '85 season when Jeff Fuller, who was a fifth-round choice as a linebacker out of Texas A&M in '84, developed into a major force at strong safety. Lott moved to free safety in '86 when the 49ers drafted another dynamic defensive secondary duo in Tim McKyer and Don Griffin.

To Ronnie's credit, he was also named to the Pro Bowl twice as a safety in '87 and '88 to go along with his five other such honors at the corner. Griffin and McKyer, dubbed the "Holdout Twins" for their contract disputes in '88 and '89 (they have the same agent), developed into one of the league's finest cornerback tandems and seemed poised to continue the team's Pro Bowl and All-Pro tradition.

Jeff Fuller—who may be the finest athlete on the team and has followed in Lott's footsteps as a ferocious hitter—is also capable of All-Pro seasons according to Walsh and Seifert. But Fuller's finest accomplishment to date may have been his inclusion on the coveted "All-Madden" team for the '87 and '88 seasons. The brainchild of former NFL coach and CBS football analyst John Madden, the all-star team is comprised annually of the NFL players who most exemplify its creator's idea of a traditional football player. In layman's terms, someone who gets his jersey dirty and exhibits spirited (read: physical) play.

The linebackers. If the Pro Bowl is the measure of individual exellence in the NFL, the 49ers must have had a weak decade. Only Keena Turner was named to the post-season all-star game at this position until the versatile Charles Haley—who played both linebacker and defensive end—received the honor after the '88 season. But the Pro Bowl is not a true indication of the contribution made by these outstanding athletes.

Beginning with the '80 draft, the 49ers were strengthened by a linebacking corps that included Craig Puki, Bobby Leopold, Riki Ellison, Todd Shell, Jim Fahnhorst, Michael Walter, Bill Romanowski, and in the '89 draft, top draft pick Keith DeLong. But somehow the NFL honors routinely passed by the Niners.

"The best example of our defense's lack of respect is

with our linebackers," said George Seifert. "When most people think of linebackers, the Giants, Bears, Rams, Cowboys, Redskins and Vikings have gotten more attention than us, at least in the NFC. And that's not a good indication of how important the position has been to our defense. But we're not looking for recognition. Results are of greater importance to us, and we've had plenty of those."

The evolution of the defense included a changing role for the linebackers thanks to the influence of the strong defensive secondary. Dan Bunz noticed the difference as soon as Lott and Company arrived.

"I remember my first and even second year, the coaches would tell you to get 18 yards deep on your pass drop because we needed the help in coverage. Then all of a sudden we get Lott and Wright and the coaches say, 'Just drop 12 yards and that's it. If you get back any farther you're gonna get in their way. Damn these guys are good, so stay out of their way.' So talent wise, when you start surrounding yourself with good people on defense—which we didn't have at first by the way—it makes your job a lot easier."

After Hacksaw Reynolds and Fred Dean retired in '85 the void was filled by Keena Turner—a 1980 draftee from Purdue and Riki Ellison—a 1983 draftee from Southern Cal. Jim Fahnhorst—a free agent signed in '84 out of Minnesota and brother to 49er veteran offensive lineman Keith Fahnhorst—also joined the crew to give the team a dependable force inside. Seifert's linebacking ranks were really strengthened with the acquisition of former University of Oregon standout Michael Walter.

Walter became one of the symbols of Seifert's adaptability on defense. A defensive end in college, Walter was a second round draft choice of the Dallas Cowboys in '83 but Tom Landry made the mistake of playing him at outside linebacker, a position he was ill-suited for due to his size. The 49ers claimed him in '84 off waivers and immediately moved him to the inside linebacker spot in tandem with Ellison. Walter excelled in Seifert's system and led the team in tackles in '87 and '88.

"Dallas misused me," Walter said. "I knew I could play in the NFL, but I never felt I got a good shot to play with the Cowboys. I'm just real grateful for the opportunity the 49ers provided."

Walter thrived in the post-season. He led the 49ers in tackles in the playoffs against the Vikings and Bears and has solidified a group that was so versatile that many of them were interchanged. For his size, Walter is very fast and covers a lot of ground, which was the signpost of Seifert's defense.

"You have to know what your talent is and you have to be able to work with it," said Lott. "George does a great job of improvising and putting guys in the right positions."

Seifert further demonstrated his eye for talent with the acquisition of Charles Haley in the fourth round of the '86 draft. The 6-foot-5, 230-pound team leader in sacks, Haley became a Pro Bowl selection in his third NFL season and could prove to be one of the league's dominant defensive performers for years to come. His quickness and tenacity are typical of the skills Seifert requires in his defensive strategy that stresses speed in getting to the quarterback in combination with blanket coverage in the secondary.

The 49ers' linebacking ranks swelled in the college drafts of '88 and '89 with the acquisitions of Bill Romanowski from Boston College and Tennessee's Keith DeLong respectively. Romanowski distinguished himself in Super Bowl XXIII with a clutch interception of a Boomer Esiason pass in the second half that set up a key field goal. He credits Seifert and the 49ers' coaching staff with top-notch preparation.

"The 49ers get you ready to play," he said. "I've heard a lot of horror stories about training camp—that it's all out every day. But the 49ers take a civilized approach to it. They get you ready for the long haul of the season. Training camp wasn't as hard physically as I thought it would be, but it was real tough mentally. We don't get beaten up all day in practice. We have real long days but a lot of it is mental, the coaches really teach us well."

And according to Romanowski, the Niners' system produced a winning environment.

"The team has developed a winning attitude that includes everyone," he said. "We're expected to win and that's fine with me because I hate to lose. I was psyched to come to the 49ers because I knew they won just about every year."

The defensive line. The honor roll of 49ers defensive linemen in the '80s has included veterans Dwaine Board, Archie Reese, Fred Dean, John Harty, Gary "Big Hands" Johnson, Louie Kelcher, Pete Kugler, Lawrence Pillers, Jeff Stover, Jim Stuckey and Manu Tuiasosopo. Each one contributed his special skills to the Niners' success in the decade and was rewarded with at least one Super Bowl ring.

The honor roll swelled in the second half of the decade with the acquisition through the draft of starters Larry Roberts and Kevin Fagan in '86, and Danny Stubbs and Pierce Holt in '88. The four became the cornerstone of the defensive foundation as the 49ers moved into the '90s.

But by far, the superstar of the Team of the Decade's defensive line was All-Pro nose tackle Michael Carter.

A fifth round selection in the 1984 college draft from Southern Methodist University, the 6-foot-2, 285-pound Carter's arrival in the NFL was postponed by a few weeks while he competed for the United States in the Los Angeles Olympics. Carter won the silver medal in the shotput and did not report to the team until the fifth week of training camp.

As far as George Seifert and the rest of the 49ers were concerned, it was worth the wait.

Like Lott, Carter was the heart and soul of the defense and he drew the most attention from opponents. Sandwiched between Roberts and Fagan in the Niners' 3-4 defensive alignment, Carter led the linemen in tackles three straight years despite being double-teamed on almost every play. His unique blend of quickness and size created many problems for other teams and often afforded his teammates—like Haley and Walter—an unimpaired path to the quarterback or ball carrier. His efforts were rewarded with three Pro Bowl appearances and four straight All-Pro designations beginning in '85, his first full season as a starter.

"Michael Carter is the anchor of our defense," said Seifert. "He causes unique problems for the opposition because he's obviously very imposing physically, but also because of his tenacity. His presence is pivotal to the success of the defense."

"We've had a lot of good defensive linemen in here over the years," said Ronnie Lott. "Fred Dean, 'Big Hands' Johnson, Pillers, Dwaine Board. But Michael adds another dimension to what those guys were capable of. He makes our defense a homogenous unit, front to back."

"We had a couple of great players in that position," said Fred Dean. "Lawrence Pillers and Dwaine Board for example. But coach Seifert could take guys with a little talent and make them superstars in his system. Michael Carter really excelled. His quickness was a tremendous asset and with the amount of attention the offense had to pay to him, I could really pin back my ears and go after the quarterback."

Carter's character also plays a role in his effectiveness. In 1988 his teammates voted him co-recipient, with Roger Craig, of the Len Eshmont Award given annually to the player who best exemplifies the inspirational and courageous play of former 49er Len Eshmont who died in 1957.

"Michael is the best," said his college roommate. "He's a great athlete. I think all that track stuff helped his quickness and I know he presents a world of trouble to the offense. The 49ers were smart to draft him."

Why should anyone care what Michael Carter's college roommate has to say about him? Because Carter's former roommate just happens to be the man to reach 10,000 career rushing yards faster than any player in NFL history—Eric Dickerson.

The man who designed and implemented the 49ers' defensive system and is most responsible for its success is self-effacing about his achievements. "You really don't have to be defensive in your thinking," said George Seifert. "You can be offensive in your thinking and start putting in specialized types of defenses to attack the offense before they have a chance to attack you."

To a man, the Niners' defensive players credit Seifert with their accomplishments in the '80s. And most feel Eddie DeBartolo chose the right person to succeed Bill Walsh as head coach—including scouting director Tony Razzano. "I think he's being rewarded for his many years of running a very underrated defense," he said. "He's done a remarkable job with this team and he'll be a very good head coach."

Many players cite one particular incident when they try to explain the effect Seifert has had on them. It occurred at halftime of a Monday Night game against the Chicago Bears during the 1987 season. In the locker room at the break, he felt his players were losing their focus so he decided to take drastic action. He kicked his foot wildly at a chalkboard to try and get their attention, but ended up breaking his toe instead.

"That all stemmed from the New York Giants game the year before," he explained. "We were ahead something like 17–0 at halftime, but went ahead to lose the game 21–17. As I looked at the group of defensive players in that locker room I saw the exact same look I saw the year before. We call it the 'fish-eye look'—you're kind of just dazed. Players go through such an emotional charge in these games, by halftime they can be drained—if you're not careful. Sometimes they need a shock—boom!—to get them out of it."

While breaking his toe was not part of the original plan, it had the desired effect.

"The impression that had on me was his commitment to the game," said Ronnie Lott. "If George was big enough or fast enough, he'd love to strap it on (a helmet). He has that kind of heart to play the game. He'd be like a Rick Gervais or a Billy Ring—everything it takes to win football games."

The 49ers won the most football games of any NFL team in the 1980s and the three most important were Super Bowls XVI, XIX and XXIII. True to championship form, the defense was the key to victory. An old football adage goes: Entertain on offense and win on defense. The 49ers took the saying to heart in their Super Bowl appearances. The turning point was 1981.

"The feeling in '81 was that we were all trying to push each other," said Lott. "We knew as individuals that we could do the job, but it was important to believe in ourselves as a team. Lots of teams have great players as individuals, but they don't win championships because they don't play well as a team.

"We didn't worry about who we were playing, we just concentrated on getting better each week. We beat one team, I think it was Houston, but we had played terrible. I came into the locker room and nobody was jumping up and down and celebrating the victory, they were upset because we had played poorly. We had set a standard for ourselves and on that day we had underachieved. More than any other sport, championship football is all about working as a team. With the mix of rookies and veterans that year we learned that lesson well."

In many ways, the unit Walsh and Seifert molded in the 1981 championship season came of age with the sensational goal-line stand the defense contributed against the Cincinnati Bengals in their first Super Bowl. In the second half and with the 49ers' lead in jeopardy, the Bengals had a first and goal at the San Francisco three-yard line. But Cincinnati failed to score on four successive plays including three plunges by massive fullback Pete Johnson. The highlight for the 49ers was a clutch tackle of a screen pass just inches from the goal-line by Dan Bunz.

"We knew it was do or die," said Lott. "We also knew they were going to give it to Pete Johnson. Everybody on our team knew we could stop him. That's why Danny Bunz' play was so significant, so great, because it was the only play they thought they could score on. It was the biggest moment in the team's history to that point."

The tradition continued in Super Bowl XIX. The 49ers stifled the high-powered offense of the Dan Marino-led Miami Dolphins and held the AFC champs to just 16 points. Even though the Niners offense scored 38 points, Walsh credited the defense.

"This was a great overall effort," he said after the game. "Obviously Joe (Montana) and the offense played well to score as many points as we did, but the defense deserves recognition for stopping a very highly-rated opponent."

George Seifert concurs with the head man. "The high points for me with the 49ers—aside from being named head coach—were limiting the scoring of teams in the last couple of Super Bowls. Obviously the game against Miami was big because they were *the* team."

To many, the effort put forth by the defense in the second Super Bowl encounter with the Bengals after the '88 season was vintage 49ers, and the decade's crowning achievement. Cincinnati was pro football's top-ranked offense during the regular season, but the Niners had their way with Sam Wyche's team in Super bowl XXIII limiting them to just 229 total yards. Boomer Esiason was held to just 11 completions for 144 yards on the day, and the high-scoring AFC champs were kept out of the end zone the entire game—their lone touchdown coming on a 93-yard kickoff return.

"That was very satisfying from a defensive stand-point," said Seifert. "To keep a high-powered offense like the Bengals from scoring a touchdown was all we could ask for from our players."

If Super Bowl XXIII was one of the decade's high points in terms of defensive accomplishment, the regular season loss that year to the Cardinals in Phoenix was the low point. Leading 23–0 in the second half, the 49ers let the Cards off the hook and lost the game 24–23 on a last-second touchdown pass from Neil Lomax to Roy Green.

"The Phoenix game was an absolute downer for me," said Walsh. "We had always taken pride in beating people that way and it was just one of those things that hurt very deeply. It was an utterly embarrassing thing for all of us."

Seifert was struck by the paradox of his team's performance.

"The first half of the game may have been the best defensive game we played since I've been here," he said. "But that last drive they had to get into position to win the game was the worst defense we've played since I've been here."

The Phoenix game notwithstanding, when Walsh retired after Super Bowl XXIII, Seifert was Eddie DeBartolo's choice to be Walsh's successor. "George is a qualified, high-caliber guy," the billionaire owner said. "He was the perfect choice to continue the 49ers' winning tradition."

Although Seifert may have been Eddie's choice all along, there were a few anxious moments for the defensive coordinator after Walsh announced his retirement as the Bay Area papers speculated on a replacement.

"Outwardly, I expressed doubts (about the promotion)," Seifert said. "But inwardly I knew I wanted to replace him all along. As soon as I realized it was available or that I would be offered the job, it was like that," he said, snapping his fingers for emphasis. "I can honestly say since the second Super Bowl that I wanted to be the head coach here."

Just a few days after the franchise's dramatic victory in Super Bowl XXIII, he finally got his chance.

As the decade came to a close, the 49ers' pre-eminent player, Ronnie Lott, reflected on the condition of the defense and how far it had travelled.

"George set the standards for the team," he said. "He challenged us to excell and we took pride in our evolution. He'll be a good head coach.

"The real challenge in sports is to exceed your expectations and the expectations of others," Lott continued. "To be on top—the favorite—and to win is not exciting. It can't be, our country is not based on that. From that regard, the '81 Super Bowl was the best. We set that standard in 1981 that this is 49er football. And the only way that tradition is going to carry on is to pass it on to younger people and hope that they can carry it on after I leave."

Considering the results the 49ers posted in the 1980s, the rest of the team must be listening.

Chapter 6

PANNING FOR GOLD
The Draft

"I don't think you find many people who say, "I worry about it." But I don't think you find many players who don't watch it with quite a bit of interest. They want to make sure the guy who's picked No. 1 doesn't play their position."
— *Randy Cross, 49ers' All-Pro center/guard and 2nd-round draft choice in 1976 (UCLA)*

Question: What do Frank Broyles, Ernie Stautner, Al DeRogatis, Y.A. Tittle, Earl Morrall, Monte Clark, Bronko Nagurski, Bernie Casey, Billy Kilmer, Lance Alworth, Steve Spurrier and, yes, John Lennon have in common?

Answer: They were all selected by the San Francisco 49ers in the college draft between 1947 and 1971. (With all due respect to the surviving Beatles, the John Lennon chosen in the 1971 draft was a 6-foot-3, 221-pound defensive end from Colgate taken in the 15th round, and sadly, he did not make the team. One can only reflect fondly on what could have been a P.R. person's dream come true: "Beatles break up. Niners draft Lennon!")

The draft. As a college senior, Bill Romanowski watched it on television with his family and friends in

'88. Dan Bunz went to the beach to break the tension in '78. Riki Ellison wore a 49ers T-shirt for two weeks straight after he got his call in '83. Keena Turner thought the Vikings would call, then didn't know who the 49ers' head coach was when they called instead in '80. Joe Montana went to lunch with his agent in Los Angeles and got his call between bites of fettuccine in '79.

Every year since 1936, college seniors across the country have waited patiently on "Draft Day" to get the phone calls that would change their lives. While most of their classmates were busy boxing up the refuse of a four-year assault on higher education, the cream of the college football crop was being poked and prodded and timed in 40-yard dashes as potential employers went shopping for that special someone to fill their special needs.

Need a defensive lineman who can bench-press the cheerleading squad and eat quarterbacks for breakfast? Try that kid from Nebraska who had five sacks in the Sugar Bowl. How about a receiver who can run a 4.2-second 40 and dance the lead in "Swan Lake"? That kid from UCLA ought to fit the bill. A 6-6, 300-pound offensive lineman who can play the violin? There's this guy we heard about from Ohio State . . .

It's very simple really. All you need to do is watch about 500 hours of film, visit a couple of dozen campuses, half as many scouting combines and spend about a million bucks, and you should be in perfect position to make that no-pressure choice that will determine whether you're talking to Brent Musburger about the Super Bowl or the sales manager of the local Chevy dealership about a job. And don't forget: Drafting them is not enough. You also have to sign them. But we're getting a little ahead of the story.

The college draft has been as much a part of professional sports as hot dogs and beer, and many teams have used the opportunity as a means of renewing a depleting human resource—which of course is the whole idea. But some franchises seem to have missed the point of the draft entirely and as a result have been mired in mediocrity, much to the disappointment of their fans.

Pro football's draft is arguably the most vital of all professional sports drafts because of the nature of the game. Unlike in baseball and basketball, where players can be somewhat interchanged to play different positions, football requires such specialization that virtually all 24 positions—including punter and place-kicker—carry different skills, and the players who fill them must be drafted accordingly. Football is also unique in that players usually perform on offense or defense only. Coupled with the shortness of the pro football career (4.2 years on average), it's easy to see why the draft becomes so critical to the composition of a winning program.

"Football is unlike baseball and basketball," Randy Cross says. "There are people who are stars on some NFL teams that would not be stars for other teams. You can take a baseball player, give him a different hat, the same bat, and he's still going to hit the ball. Same with basketball. Football is a game of systems and different situation type players. There have been a number of players with the 49ers, myself included, that if you put them in a different type of system on a different team in the NFL, they would not be stars. They wouldn't play for a long time."

With the importance of good drafting established, it should come as no surprise that the 28 NFL teams spend millions of dollars each year on the process.

From scouting combines and mini-camps, where each player is given closer physical examination than NASA gives its astronauts, to the detailed psychological testing that evaluates a player down to his favorite color, the teams leave no stone unturned. And yet, even with all the effort and money spent in this area, on draft day many clubs find themselves the objects of unkind jeers and impolite snickering when they choose unknown players from unheralded schools as their number one draft choices. Not that there's anything wrong with drafting a "sleeper," but by definition someone of such low profile should be available in a later round, and certainly one of the most disheartening things a general manager can hear on draft day after his top selection is announced is a resounding: "Who?"

Tampa Bay heard the snickers in 1986, when it made Heisman Trophy-winning running back Bo Jackson from Auburn the number one pick in the draft. In all fairness, the Bucs probably deserve only half the blame (well, maybe three-fourths) for the selection of Jackson. Hardly anyone believed him when he said he would forgo football for a career in professional baseball. And when the Kansas City Royals assigned him to their affiliate, the Memphis Chicks, the snickers could be heard all the way to Los Angeles as Bo brought new meaning to the term whiff, while striking out regularly in AA ball.

Of course, history will show that "Bo knows baseball" after all (and football, running, cycling, tennis, hockey, soccer and weightlifting, according to Nike). With his towering home runs and blazing speed, both on the bases and in left field, his legend continues to grow, more so after he was named MVP of the 1989 All-Star Game in Anaheim. The ultimate pie-in-the-face was given to Tampa Bay after failing to sign him, when he later signed with the Raiders, who took him in the seventh round of the next year's draft.

The blueprint of a championship team takes many forms. Ask former L.A. Rams and Washington Redskins head coach George Allen, and he surely will say there is no substitute for experience. With his "the future is now" philosophy, Allen rarely bothered with the college draft, preferring to wheel and deal for proven veterans to build his teams. The results were varied, and Allen ultimately retired from coaching without an NFL championship to his credit.

At the other end of the spectrum are the San Francisco 49ers. Of the 45 players on their roster in Super Bowl XXIII, 36 were obtained through the draft. And in 1986 alone, the Niners found eight starters in just six rounds. That kind of success comes very rarely in the NFL and is preceded by years of experience and preparation.

"1979," said Tony Razzano without hesitation. The 49ers' director of college scouting had been asked, in his opinion, which year's draft was the best for the 49ers.

1979? Really? What about '81, when you got those great defensive players: Ronnie Lott, John Harty, Eric Wright, Carlton Williamson, Lynn Thomas and Pete Kugler? Or '83, when Roger Craig came along, with Tom Holmoe, Riki Ellison and Jesse Sapolu? Surely '84 was better. You got Todd Shell, John Frank, Guy McIntyre, plus Michael Carter and Jeff Fuller both in the fifth round that year. And Derrick Harmon in the ninth. 1985 was not bad either. You got Jerry Rice that year, and Bruce Collie for good measure.

Wait a minute. No way was '79 better than '86. You did not even have a first-round pick, yet you drafted eight starters for Super Bowl XXIII: Larry Roberts, Tom Rathman, Tim McKyer, John Taylor, Charles Haley, Steve Wallace, Kevin Fagan and Don Griffin. '87 was pretty good too. Harris Barton, Terrence Flagler, Jeff Bregel and John Paye came along that year. And how about '88? Danny Stubbs, Pierce Holt, Bill Romanowski and Barry Helton all contributed strongly to a Super Bowl season. OK, it may be a little early to evaluate '89. Who knows whether Keith DeLong, Wesley Walls, Keith Henderson, Mike Barber, Johnny Jackson,

Steve Hendrickson, Rudy Harmon, Andy Sinclair, Jim Bell, Norm McGee or Antonio Goss will contribute?

"1979," the 49ers' director of college scouting repeated without changing expression.

But you got only two players that year really, not counting James Owens, who lasted two seasons.

Why 1979?

"Two reasons: Joe Montana and Dwight Clark," he said smugly.

OK. Sure. No question. But can it really compare to getting eight Super Bowl starters and two All-Pros in one year?

"If you can get a quarterback like Joe Montana who can play the way he has, and who can lead the way he has, for as long as he has, there is no limit to where you can go," Razzano said with conviction. "Joe has done more than (any other) one single person for this team, including coaches. Without Joe, we're not the Team of the Decade."

Oh, is that all?

"You don't coach Joe," he continued in earnest. "That is, you don't coach the things he's able to do. He's very coachable, and he's learned an awful lot. He's smart. What he does is uncoachable in the sense that he does so much on his own. And when you put him in combination with a receiver like Dwight Clark, who can catch just about anything thrown at him, well, let's just say it's a very, very valuable tandem to have. Leaders. Role models. We were fortunate to have two men of their caliber on this team."

Oddly enough, Steve Fuller was the quarterback the 49ers really had their eye on in 1979. Montana was almost third string his senior year at Notre Dame. Almost none of the scouts were impressed with the 6-foot-2, 190-pounder with skinny legs whose strongest moves were on the run. The NFL wanted sturdy, rugged, drop-back passers who could stand in the pocket

without fear and see above the linemen, then deliver a
shotgun blast to a guy streaking down the sideline. Dan
Fouts, Bert Jones, Terry Bradshaw, Jim Plunkett; those
were the guys the NFL wanted. After all, when you
were behind in a game, you needed a guy to wind up
and heave the ball downfield about 60 yards in the last
few seconds to win it for you.

What could this Montana guy do in the last two
minutes to win a football game for you? Run around in
the backfield and wear the defense out?

"Sometimes you have to look for things that are a little unconventional," Razzano said. "Something that
other scouts may have overlooked."

Well, if that is the case, then how about explaining
your draft philosophy? Assuming you have one.

"You always go defense," he began. "That's my philosophy anyway. You start at the nose. Well actually,
your first position, of course, is quarterback. But then
you go defensive line, even over other skill positions.
Assuming the quality is the same. That is, if you don't
have a superstar."

Like Joe?

"Like Joe.

"You would take a lineman over a linebacker or DB,"
he said, "given the same level of quality. Next is your
offensive line, again in your big-man category. And last
is your wide receiver, because there are so many of
them, and you only need a couple. A couple of good
ones anyway. Unless, of course, someone like Jerry Rice
comes along, an impact player of that level. You take
him first."

Glad we asked. Anything else?

"Of course, we spend a lot of time looking at film,"
he continued. "Scouting combines are helpful to a certain degree, but we really look mostly at film. We also
can't rely on a coach's opinion of his own player because
he has an interest. We only evaluate a kid in the spring

before his senior year. We don't project ahead two or three years because so much can change in that time. And the last thing you want to pay attention to is this All-American stuff because you're letting someone else do your evaluating for you."

Makes sense.

Sometimes a team will get lucky and find a solid player in one of the least likely places. In 1979, the 49ers sent a couple of scouts down to South Carolina to give Clemson quarterback Steve Fuller a workout. Giving a prospect a private workout is often the best way to determine if he will fit in with your system. And it gives your people a chance to see the player in an environment other than under the microscope of scouting combines. In the case of a quarterback, the workout usually includes a complete physical and some performance tests to gauge his strength under certain conditions. Weights, 40-yard dash, agility drills, that type of thing.

The real test is an on-the-field passing drill in shorts to see how well he can throw. Naturally, a quarterback needs someone to throw to, so Fuller persuaded one of his Clemson teammates to come out and run some routes so he could impress the scouts from the West Coast. Fuller did impress the 49ers with his quick release, smooth delivery, accuracy, velocity and arm strength. The scouts reported back to Bill Walsh, who was in his first season as head coach, that Fuller appeared to be everything they thought he was and would probably be a first-rounder. But they said, if he lasted into the second round, the Niners would be smart in taking him. The Kansas City Chiefs made Fuller the 23rd pick in the 1979 draft.

Oh, by the way, the scouts said, there was this receiver whom Fuller was throwing to who was not too bad. He probably would not be a superstar in the NFL —he was not really very fast—but if you get a chance with a late-round pick, he may be worth a look. His name was "something" Clark. Dwight Clark, we think.

"That's a true story," Razzano confirmed. "Kinda funny, huh?"

The 49ers' all-time leading receiver was taken in the tenth round of the 1979 college draft, the 253rd selection overall. "I didn't think I had a chance at all," he said recently from Clark's By the Bay, the restaurant he owns in Redwood City, Calif. "I thought it was a chance to see California. I brought my golf clubs and figured after I got cut, I'd head down the coast and play some golf. Then I'd go down to L.A. so I could say I saw Hollywood and go home. I had no idea I'd be out here this long. I was as surprised as anybody. Heck, even after I made the team, after the final cut, they were still bringing in guys for tryouts."

Nine NFL seasons later, after 506 receptions, 6,750 yards gained, 48 touchdowns, two Super Bowls, two Pro Bowls and some of the most memorable catches in the franchise's history—the NFL's, really—Clark saw his uniform jersey No. 87 retired in a special ceremony at Candlestick Park in 1988.

The importance of the 1979 draft for the Niners was felt almost immediately. Walsh had been hired to replace Fred O'Connor in January of that year. In less than four months he had to settle into his office, hire a staff, decide the 49ers' short- and long-term objectives, evaluate his players and determine the team's needs, review the pool of college talent and be ready on May 3 to start the road back to competitiveness. He had a long way to go. The team he inherited had won just 15 games in the previous three seasons combined. Two years later, the 49ers would win 16 games in one season. Walsh credits the draft.

The difficulty of the job was compounded by the absence of a first-round pick. The 49ers had traded it to Buffalo to get O.J. Simpson the previous season. The trade was understandable—at least in theory—because the Niners had one of the NFL's worst offenses in 1977, a distinction they exceeded the next year by being the absolute worst.

To underscore the ineptitude of the 1978 season and the dire need for offensive help, the club leaders in the major offensive categories—rushing, passing, receiving and scoring—that year were, respectively: O.J. Simpson (161 carries, 593 yards, one touchdown, 39th best in the NFL); Steve DeBerg (137 completions, 1,570 yards, eight touchdowns, 22 interceptions, 28th best in the NFL); Freddie Solomon (31 catches, 458 yards, two touchdowns, 83rd best in the NFL); and place-kicker Ray Wersching (15 field goals, 69 total points, 22nd best in the NFL).

By comparison, the 1987 club leaders were: Roger Craig (215 carries, 815 yards, three touchdowns, eighth best in the NFL); Joe Montana (266 completions, 3,054 yards, 31 touchdowns, 13 interceptions, first in the NFL); and Jerry Rice (65 catches, 1,078 yards, 22 touchdowns, first in the NFL). Rice was also the NFL's leader in scoring in 1987 with 23 touchdowns overall and the league's Most Valuable Player.

"We felt we needed to draft offense in 1979," Walsh said, in perhaps the understatement of his career.

At least he had a little bit of history on his side. In 1959, Vince Lombardi had been hired to coach the last-place Green Bay Packers. He later won two Super Bowls and a total of five NFL championships in six years. In 1969, Chuck Noll was hired to coach the last-place Pittsburgh Steelers. He won four Super Bowls in five years. In 1979, Walsh was being asked to perform similar magic with the last-place 49ers.

"In the final analysis," he said, "if you build a team from the depths, you get more satisfaction because you know you've started at ground zero. But most often a coach who's taken on a poor team gives a poor team to the next coach. He's not given enough time to develop the team properly. Ownership doesn't have the patience to do the job right. I'd rather start with what Pat Riley did than what Don Nelson did." His last comment is a reference to professional basketball. Riley inherited a world championship Los Angeles Lakers team when he took over as coach, and Don Nelson was saddled with a Golden State Warriors team that was the worst of the Western Conference of the NBA.

With the 49ers having had the NFL's worst rushing offense in 1978, Walsh felt the backfield was as good a place to start as any on a team that needed a lot of help. He used his second-round choice—the 29th selection overall—to acquire UCLA running back James Owens, an exceptional athlete who had excelled on the Bruin track team as well. The choice turned out to be a poor one though. The world-class track star proved to be injury prone, and his skills did not transfer well to football. He played two seasons with the Niners and was gone.

"You've got to get production out of your top three draft choices," Razzano said. "You cannot afford to have those guys be busts. Owens was one of those. But we got good value in the third and tenth rounds."

The 49ers' tradition of strong drafting continued in 1980, when Walsh shifted his focus to the defense. Six players were selected in rounds one through eight who would contribute strongly to the Super Bowl team the following season. Running back Earl Cooper and defensive end Jim Stuckey were taken in the first round, and linebacker Keena Turner was chosen in the second. The third round brought punter Jim Miller and linebacker Craig Puki. Bobby Leopold, also a linebacker, was picked up in the eighth.

Turner was a little surprised when the 49ers called. "Minnesota asked me to fly up from Chicago one night to meet Bud Grant. He seemed real easy-going, and I kind of liked him," the veteran recalled. "I had grown up listening to Vikings games, and the way they talked, I thought I was going there for sure. I really didn't know much about the 49ers. It was funny, Norb Hecker (49ers' linebacker coach) called me to tell me they'd picked me. I thought he was the head coach. I'd never heard of Bill Walsh."

Walsh and his staff hit their stride in 1981 and pulled off one of the greatest defensive drafts in NFL history. Selecting in the eighth position, the 49ers made Ronnie Lott their first-round choice. A hard-hitting safety from Southern Cal, Lott has become a fixture in the Niners' secondary and a perennial Pro Bowl player. He is also number two behind Jim Johnson on the 49ers' career interceptions list and is the heart and soul of a defense that has consistently ranked among the leaders in the NFC.

The bounty of '81 did not end with Lott. Defensive end John Harty was taken in the second round along with cornerback Eric Wright, and in the third and fifth rounds, the 49ers came up with a draft rarity: they took two defensive backs from the same college team. Carlton Williamson and Lynn Thomas, both from the University of Pittsburgh, were chosen, respectively. For good measure, defensive tackle Pete Kugler was taken in round six. All those members of the class of '81 received Super Bowl rings for their victory over Cincinnati the following January.

"That was a great draft," Razzano said. "We got our secondary for the whole decade in one afternoon. Now that's pretty good scouting." Lott, Wright and Williamson alone have made 11 Pro Bowl appearances. Not bad for an afternoon.

In the wake of an NFL championship, and after obtaining 15 roster players in just three years, the 49ers can be forgiven for a lapse in the draft of 1982. Of course, having just one pick in the first four rounds did not help matters, but they made the most of the situation—especially by weight—in taking mammoth offensive tackle William "Bubba" Paris in the second round. Good-natured and well-liked by his teammates, the 300-pound-plus lineman from Michigan has been an on-and-off starter throughout his career and has provided the team with one of the NFL's true characters. He is also one of the few players with a weight clause in his contract. "Sometimes we have to pry him away from the dinner table," said one of his teammates who requested anonymity. "I think he keeps a steak sandwich underneath his jersey for emergencies, like overtimes, for example. I would never want to be between him and the last item on the dessert tray."

The Niners got back on track in 1983. Without a first-round pick for the second straight year, they took a shot in the second round with an unheralded running back from Nebraska who spent most of his college career backing up Jarvis Redwine and Heisman Trophy winner Mike Rozier. Roger Craig was the 49th selection overall and the sixth running back taken in one of the NFL's strongest drafts in recent memory. In addition to quarterbacks John Elway and Dan Marino, the class of '83 also yielded running backs Eric Dickerson (second overall, to the Rams), Curt Warner (third, Seattle), Michael Haddix (eighth, Philadelphia), James Jones (13th, Detroit), and Gary Anderson (20th, San Diego). One of the most talented, durable running backs in the league, Craig has not missed a game because of injury during his entire career.

Joining Craig in San Francisco that year were defensive back Tom Holmoe, linebacker Riki Ellison and offensive lineman Jesse Sapolu in rounds four, five and ten, respectively.

"To tell you the truth, I wasn't supposed to get drafted," Ellison said. "That's what everybody told me anyway. I had four knee surgeries at USC, and no team took a look at me. The day before the draft (defensive coordinator George), Seifert (defensive-line coach Bill), McPherson and Norb Hecker flew down and worked me out. I had a knee brace on, and I was just so excited because they actually worked me out. They gave me a 49ers T-shirt, and I thought that was my consolation prize or something. Then, at the very end of the TV broadcast of the draft, I saw my name on the back of the screen going to San Francisco. I went totally crazy. I wore that T-shirt for about two weeks straight. I was so proud to be a 49er."

The 49ers are proud of him, too. Since joining the club, he has started all but five of the 89 games he has played, including the post-season, and was named All-Rookie in '83. Not bad for a fifth-round draft choice with bum knees.

The following year, 1984, brought a landmark harvest for the team. Six players taken in the draft would make the club and finish the season in the Super Bowl against Miami. Linebacker Todd Shell, tight end John Frank and guard Guy McIntyre were the 49ers' selections in rounds one, two and three, and running back Derrick Harmon was taken in the ninth. But the Niners hit paydirt in the fifth round by choosing two stalwart defensive players from prominent football programs in the state of Texas. Michael Carter, the massive two-time All-America nose tackle from Southern Methodist, was the 121st overall selection, and hard-hitting strong safety Jeff Fuller from Texas A&M was the 139th player chosen.

Although Carter missed the first four weeks of the 1984 season, he had a pretty good excuse: he was competing for the United States Olympic team in the shot put at the L.A. Games. The only four-time indoor, and three-time outdoor, NCAA champion, Carter won the silver medal in the Olympics and capped an incredible year with a Super Bowl ring. He has been named to the

Pro Bowl three times and made All-Pro four straight years ('85–'88). Fuller has teamed with Ronnie Lott in the defensive secondary to give the team a dynamic one-two punch.

According to veteran linebacker Keena Turner, Carter and Fuller made an immediate impact, but Fuller was really something else. "Jeff Fuller was my choice for best athlete on the championship team—hands down," he said. "He had the best body control for his speed and size that I have ever seen. My mouth hung open when I saw the things he could do on the field."

Although the 1985 draft was not a banner one in terms of quantity for the 49ers, it was very significant in terms of quality. Versatile offensive lineman Bruce Collie, who has started about a third of the 58 games he has played in, was taken in the fifth round from Texas Arlington. He was proven to be a rugged competitor at both guard and tackle and has given the team depth in a very talented offensive line.

The 49ers' first-round selection was a real bonanza. Every few years, with good scouting and a little bit of luck, a team finds a player who makes such an impact that he can dominate his position for several years. Joe Montana was such a player. Ronnie Lott, Michael Carter and Roger Craig are in that category as well. But when the Niners made wide receiver Jerry Rice the 16th pick in the 1985 draft, they acquired a player of such awesome talent that he is already being mentioned as one of the all-time greats.

In just four NFL seasons he has established himself as pro football's premier wide receiver and has earned three straight starting berths in the Pro Bowl. In addition, he has been named All-Pro three years in a row and was the NFL's Most Valuable Player after a sensational 1987 season that included a record 22 touchdown catches. He also shares the NFL record for touchdowns in a post-season and was named MVP of Super Bowl XXIII with a record-breaking performance.

According to Razzano, Rice was talented coming out of college, but not quite a sure thing. "J.R. had awesome stats in college," he said. "But he was from one of those small schools (Mississippi Valley State) that you just didn't know for sure. He had all the tools, but it's not like he played in the Big Ten. A player of his ability comes along very rarely. We had him very highly rated. He could be the very best at his position for many years to come."

If 1985 was a smashing success for the acquisition of one of the NFL's best players, 1986 was a masterpiece of team drafting. In just the first six rounds, and without a first-round pick for the third time in the '80s, the 49ers found eight players who ended up starting Super Bowl XXIII.

"We did our homework," Razzano said.

Drafting in the 18th position, San Francisco sent its first-round selection to Dallas, then took Alabama defensive lineman Larry Roberts in the second round with the 39th pick overall. Roberts has played in every game since joining the team, and in 1988 became a full-time starter.

The third round provided a real bounty. The Niners used the 56th pick in the draft to select 6-foot-1, 232-pound Nebraska fullback Tom Rathman. A back-up to Roger Craig his first year, Rathman teamed with his fellow Cornhusker in '87 and '88 after Craig was moved from fullback to tailback to make up one of the NFL's most devastating backfields. Just eight selections after Rathman, San Francisco picked cornerback Tim McKyer from Texas Arlington. The cocky McKyer, who has been a holdout from the team's last two training camps in contract disputes, has started every game since joining the team—44 of 44 contests, not counting '87 strike games, and all five postseason games. And just 12 picks later, the 49ers found wide receiver John Taylor from Delaware State.

Taylor, one of the heroes of Super Bowl XXIII for his winning touchdown catch in the final seconds, spent his first season on injured reserve, then started seven games during the 1988 season, including both playoff games and the Super Bowl. He was also selected to the 1989 Pro Bowl, one of two '86 draftees so honored.

The other Pro Bowler taken in the '86 draft, with the 12th pick in the fourth round—96th overall—was linebacker/defensive end Charles Haley from James Madison. The 6-foot-5, 230-pound Haley, who has led the team in sacks in each of his three seasons, is described in the 49ers' 1989 media guide as an "unyielding attacker" who is a "constant performer at getting to the quarterback." Although media guides are not generally considered a real reliable source for player descriptions (they are prepared by the P.R. department after all), in the case of Haley, the Niners may have understated his abilities. When team P.R. assistant Dave Rahn was approached with a request to interview Haley for this book, he said: "Charles is a pretty serious guy. He may not be the most revealing interview subject. How about Keena Turner and Michael Walter?" Thanks, Dave. Your job at the State Department should be coming through any day now.

The fourth round continued to be a 49ers bonanza with the back-to-back selections of offensive tackle Steve Wallace (101st) and defensive tackle Kevin Fagan (102nd). Wallace, who blocked for Heisman Trophy winner Bo Jackson at Auburn, replaced Bubba Paris when the "large one" went down with an injury in '87, and Wallace started every game in '88, including Super Bowl XXIII. Fagan starred on the '83 national championship team at Miami (Fla.) but missed the entire '86 pro season with a knee injury sustained in the Hurricanes' Sugar Bowl victory over Tennessee. He recovered and played in seven games in '87, then started 17 games, including the Super Bowl, the following season.

With seven Super Bowl starters chosen in just three rounds of the '86 draft, the 49ers could have packed up and gone home. But they stayed on the job and managed to pick up a couple more players before the day was done. Starting cornerback Don Griffin from Middle Tennessee State was the 22nd player taken in the sixth round—162nd overall. Like his '87 and '88 holdout compatriot Tim McKyer (they have the same agent), Griffin became an immediate starter in the Niners' defensive secondary and was named NFC Defensive Rookie of the Year. Rounding out a fruitful draft, the 49ers picked up pint-size University of Oregon running back Tony Cherry in the ninth round. The 5-foot-7, 180-pound speedster was the 240th overall selection and saw limited action with the team in '86 and '87.

For a change of pace, in 1987 the 49ers actually had two first-round draft choices and three of the first 37 selections. The team capitalized by strengthening the offense. North Carolina offensive tackle Harris Barton was the team's first choice (22nd overall), and just three picks later, the Niners picked Clemson running back Terrence Flagler. With their second-round pick, courtesy of the Philadelphia Eagles, the club selected guard Jeff Bregel from Southern Cal.

Barton started nine of his 12 games in the strike-shortened '87 season and made the NFL's All-Rookie team, then started 15 of 16 games in '88 as well as Super Bowl XXIII. Flagler, who was Atlantic Coast Conference Player of the Year in '86, has displayed vast talent when healthy, but has also had the misfortune of playing behind one of the NFL's best running backs—Roger Craig. Bregel, an Academic All-American and consensus All-American in '86, played little his rookie season because of a knee injury but has been a solid performer on special teams and is challenging for a regular position on one of the best offensive lines in pro football.

The '87 draft also yielded Stanford quarterback John Paye, in the tenth round—the 275th selection overall. Paye, who played three years of varsity basketball with the Cardinal, has had an injury-plagued professional career after a starring role in college. Of course, it probably doesn't help to be playing behind the greatest quarterback in NFL history, Joe Montana, and one of the league's best back-ups, Steve Young, but such is life on a Super Bowl championship team.

Five players from the class of '88 made the team, and all had significant roles in the 49ers' championship season. Once again the Niners found themselves without a first-round choice when they traded their number one —25th overall—to the Raiders for the 33rd pick, plus a fourth-round choice and wide receiver Dokie Williams. They used the second-round selection to take defensive end Danny Stubbs, another Miami Hurricane. Stubbs, a strong pass rusher, played in all 16 games his rookie season and started once. He also delighted his college fans with a sack in Super Bowl XXIII at Miami's Joe Robbie Stadium.

The 39th pick in the '88 draft also belonged to the 49ers. Walsh used the selection to take the oldest player in the draft (26 years old), who also had the most work experience. Defensive tackle Pierce Holt from NCAA Division II Angelo State entered college at age 22 after working on a farm, at a car dealership, on a construction crew and as an inspector for a mortgage company.

The 6-foot-4, 280-pound Holt went to work instead of college after high school to support his wife, Deana, and daughter Ashley. He took up football in college while also earning degrees in physical education and history and is nine hours short of a master's degree in education, in case anyone was thinking the Marlin, Texas, native was an academic underachiever because of his late start. Holt played in nine games his rookie season as well as both playoff games and Super Bowl XXIII. "I've had a pretty interesting life so far," he said in his Texas drawl.

The third round of the '88 draft yielded Boston College linebacker Bill Romanowski with the 80th overall pick. The versatile athlete started half the regular-season games his rookie season and made a key interception of a Boomer Esiason pass in the Super Bowl that led to a San Francisco field goal. After growing up in Connecticut and going to college in Boston, Romanowski was a little uncertain about the draft and apprehensive about where he'd be playing. "It's a little scary that you can end up in just about any city in the country," he said. "I'm from the East, and San Francisco is about as far away from home as I ever thought I'd get. But California is my new home, and I love it out here." A Super Bowl ring probably helped him get over any homesickness he may have felt.

In the fourth round, the 49ers took punter Barry Helton from Colorado. Drafting a punter is a rarity for the Niners, who selected only one other during Walsh's tenure with the team (Jim Miller in 1980). San Francisco also took Texas A&M cornerback Chet Brooks in the 11th round. The Dallas native not only made the team, which was against the odds for the 305th overall selection, but he played well in ten games before finishing the year on injured reserve after a blow to his left knee.

Tony Razzano thinks the '88 draft will turn out to be one of the team's best, but '89 worries him a little. "I don't think '89 was a particularly strong draft," he said. "At least not in the sense of an impact player. We got some talented kids. (Linebacker) Keith DeLong should do well, and (tight end) Wesley Walls is going to get a chance to make this team. (Wide receiver) Mike Barber, too. It's a good group, I think, but we won't know if it's a great one until they get us to another Super Bowl."

Of course, the 49ers did make it to a fourth Super Bowl in 1989, although it probably had more to do with the success of the veterans than the minimal impact of DeLong and Walls. But such is a statement on the team's depth. Immediate help was not needed from the '89 draft.

There is much more to the draft than the average football fan sees. For most, the extent of the commitment to the event begins with the pre-draft scouting reports and form charts that attempt to predict the exact order in which the players will be selected. On draft day, many will tune in to see the selections being made, thanks in large part to modern technology and the die-hard nature of the game's followers. And finally, the day after the draft, all the day's activities will be conveniently reported in the daily newspapers for closer scrutiny. Unfortunately, a lot of the most interesting facets, such as the maneuvering and jockeying for position, rarely get disseminated to the public.

For example, in 1979, Dallas, Seattle and San Francisco—all thinking they knew something the others did not—made a three-way trade in the third round. The Cowboys and Seahawks wanted to move up, and the 49ers seemed ambivalent after taking James Owens in the second round. San Francisco was drafting in the first position because it finished the 1978 season with the league's worst record, Seattle was picking 21st, and Dallas was drafting in the 27th position by virtue of its loss to the Steelers in Super Bowl XIII.

To start things off, Dallas sent its third-round pick— the 82nd overall—plus defensive lineman Bill Gregory to Seattle for the Seahawks' third-round pick—the 76th overall. The Cowboys used the choice to select tight end Doug Cosbie from Santa Clara. Seattle then traded the pick it got from the Cowboys, plus linebacker Bob Jury, to San Francisco for the Niners' third-round pick—the 56th overall. The Seahawks chose University of Washington linebacker Michael Jackson. The 49ers used the 82nd pick, which originally belonged to Dallas, to take a lightly regarded quarterback from Notre Dame named Joe Montana.

Everybody got that?

For those of you scoring at home, Dallas gave up Bill Gregory and got Doug Cosbie. Seattle lost Bob Jury and added Gregory and Michael Jackson. San Francisco received Bob Jury and Joe Montana. You decide who got the best of the deal.

In 1985, the 49ers pulled off another one. Coming off the Super Bowl victory over the Dolphins, San Francisco was stuck drafting in the 28th position. Walsh decided it was worth trading up to get an impact player the 49ers had their eyes on from a small college in Mississippi. The Niners sent their first-, second- and third-round choices to New England for the Patriots' first- and third-round selections. The Pats took center Trevor Matich, defensive end Ben Thomas and defensive back Audrey McMillan with the 49ers' picks, and San Francisco used New England's first-round choice—the 16th overall—to select Jerry Rice.

The only real downside to the draft day maneuvering the 49ers have executed so deftly is that it often embarrasses the other teams. And without the cooperation of another willing trader, you have to play the hand you are dealt. Walsh's reputation worked against him in trying to complete a similar transaction during the 1989 college draft.

In his new capacity as executive vice president, Walsh wanted to get new head coach George Seifert off on the right foot. But as in 1985, the Niners were coming off a Super Bowl victory and drafting in the 28th position. As the first round unfolded, Walsh noticed two potential superstars, Florida State defensive back

Louis Oliver and Michigan State wide receiver Andre Rison, slipping from their projected draft positions. He immediately hit the phones to try and make a deal to trade up for either player.

But Rison went to Indianapolis with the 22nd pick, and Oliver was taken by Miami at No. 25 after a deal was struck with Chicago. Later, Walsh insisted he had offered the Bears greater value than the Dolphins had, but they declined. After all, who wants to help San Francisco win another Super Bowl?

One man who would like to help the 49ers win another Super Bowl is Eddie DeBartolo. As you might expect, the record of his organization in the college draft is a source of great pride. "Our entire effort in the area of scouting and drafting has been superb," the owner said. "Starting with our scouts, to (general manager) John McVay and obviously Bill Walsh, who has been magnificent in judging talent, it's been a well-coordinated operation. They've worked hard, they've spent a lot of hours on the road, and all our people have been phenomenal. The big success of our franchise has been the ability to find talent in the middle to late rounds. Dwight Clark obviously comes to mind, but also in the third, fourth and fifth rounds especially, we've gotten the likes of Michael Carter, Jeff Fuller and Don Griffin. That is really the mark of an extremely capable group of men doing a very good job."

According to quarterback Steve Young, the 49ers' strong showing in the draft is more than just judging talent.

"There's a definite reason why this team does so well, and it's really very simple," he said. "You get a guy that is a great player, bring him to the 49ers and show him the work ethic that we demand, the standards we set, and he becomes a better player. It's a lot like the Lakers and Celtics. A guy could be drafted by the Clippers and he wouldn't be half the player. Because of the high standards and the examples set by guys like Joe (Montana) and Roger (Craig) and Ronnie (Lott), and our coach and owner especially, we feel we're achieving our full potential.

"Just watch Roger Craig sometime during practice. When he carries the ball, he doesn't stop after the coaches blow the whistle. He sprints downfield 40 to 50 yards on every run. Even in the 100-degree heat. A young guy can't help but see that and be motivated. They pick great athletes, and then they bring them in and make them great players."

Like many players, Lott, the 49ers' All-Pro safety, was watching the '89 draft with more than passing interest. As it was reported that San Francisco was trying to make a deal to acquire Louis Oliver, a hard-hitting safety often compared to Lott, he was asked how he felt about his team considering a player at his position. He responded in All-Pro form. "Success is not measured in terms of your own ego," the future Hall of Famer said. "Success is measured in terms of working together as one. That's the only way you can reach the top. If you become selfish, you'll never reach the top."

With team leaders like Ronnie Lott, Steve Young, Joe Montana and Roger Craig, it is no wonder the 49ers have reached the top three times in the 1980s.

Chapter 7

FILM AT ELEVEN
Three Moments That Shook the City

'I could never describe in words what it was like. At the time, it happened so fast, it's hard to put into words. On the other hand, I look back and everything happens in slow motion. My friends always kid me that the play could have been' 'The Drop.' "

— *Dwight Clark on "The Catch"*

*M*ention "The Catch," "The Goal-Line Stand" or "The Drive" to a San Franciscan, and chances are a smile will cross his lips and a warm, satisfied look will appear on his face. He'll lean back in his chair, gaze skyward and get a faraway look in his eyes that would make you swear he was recalling his first love.

It is that kind of emotion that is attached to three of the franchise's most thrilling moments, forever etched in the minds of Bay Area sports fans.

132   The San Francisco 49ers

"The Catch"
NFC Championship Game
Candlestick Park
January 10, 1982

In years to come, at least 200,000 people will say they were at Candlestick Park on that blustery 10th of January in 1982 when the 49ers and Cowboys played for the NFC championship; nearly 140,000 of them will be lying. It was the kind of event that prompts such embellishment. It had the kind of excitement that, after the story is told for years, causes the line between fact and fiction to become blurred.

By most accounts, the Niners were one of the least likely teams to be playing that day, having come off a dismal 6–10 season in 1980. But despite the poor record, the offense had established itself as one of the most dangerous in the league, and the defense was strengthened by the addition of six regulars through the 1981 draft and the acquisitions of veterans Jack "Hacksaw" Reynolds and Fred Dean.

Dean recalled the emotions of the season and the game: "Going to the 49ers was like a breath of fresh air for me, a new start. They were underestimated in '81, and we took a lot of teams by surprise. But by the Dallas game, people knew we were for real. That game was important for the franchise. And the catch? Well, the catch was the most important play of the season. Getting to the Super Bowl is every player's dream. It was the catch that put us there."

The most memorable afternoon of Dwight Clark's brilliant football career began like any other game day for the 49ers' all-time leading receiver. He had a good feeling about the game from the start. "I remember feeling very confident. We matured a lot that season, and by the NFC championship, we felt we could play

with anyone. The turning point was when we beat Pittsburgh in Pittsburgh."

Confidence? Maturity? Turning point? Was this the
same San Francisco 49ers who had underwhelmed their
fans with a combined record of 10–38 in the three previous seasons? Could they really be playing "America's
Team" for the right to go to Super Bowl XVI? Surely it
would take a superhuman feat of athletic ability to win
on this day.

It did. And the greatest passing combination in
49ers history provided the drama.

One of the other starting wide receivers that day,
Mike Shumann, added this unique perspective to the
game: "I started the championship game and made the
first catch, but for some reason the last catch overshadowed mine."

No kidding, Mike?

"I always ask people, 'Do you remember who made
the first catch? Me.' Hey, if I had dropped that pass, it
could have changed the whole history of the San Francisco 49ers," he added.

The game began at 2:01 P.M. Pacific Standard Time
in clear, cool weather. Dallas' opening possession
proved not to be a very good indication of the excitement the afternoon would bring. Three plays yielded
minus-9 yards. The first touchdown of the day was
scored by 49ers quarterback-turned-wide-receiver
Freddie Solomon on an 8-yard pass from Joe Montana
with 4:19 gone in the first quarter. Dallas answered
four minutes later with a 44-yard Raphael Septien field
goal after a nine-play drive stalled.

On the third play of the Niners' ensuing drive, fullback Bill Ring—who normally was sure-handed—was
hit at the line of scrimmage and surrendered the football to Dallas linebacker Mike Hegman. Less than one
minute after the Septien field goal, the Cowboys were
in ideal position on the San Francisco 29-yard line.

Quarterback Danny White needed just two plays to put his team into the end zone, hitting Tony Hill for a 26-yard touchdown that put the Cowboys up 10–7.

"No, I can't say I was really worried at that point," 49ers linebacker Dan Bunz said. "Both teams were playing well, and I knew it would be a good game."

The San Francisco offense continued sputtering, and ugly reminders of the '78 and '79 seasons were appearing. The running game netted only 6 yards in the first quarter, and the entire offense gained only 5 yards in the quarter after the opening drive. Dwight Clark hadn't caught a pass, and Montana seemed out of sync. On the San Francisco sideline, Bill Walsh pursed his lips and wore his familiar furrowed brow. He gripped his play card even tighter and tugged on his headset cord while he wondered whether his improved offense would begin hitting on all cylinders.

Clark's drought was broken on the second quarter's initial drive. On second-and-eight from the Niners' 35, Montana bootlegged right and found Clark on a deep post pattern, delivering a strike for a 38-yard gain to the Dallas 27. Joe was sacked on the next play for a loss of 5, then hit Clark again on the left side for 10 yards. But the drive ended abruptly when Dallas cornerback Everson Walls picked off a pass intended for Mike Wilson on the Cowboys' 2. The collective sigh of 60,000 fans was such that one might swear it could be heard for miles down the Bayshore Freeway from the 'Stick.

"That was a little depressing," Keena Turner said. "I thought we would score for sure on that drive. But Walls made a good play. I just strapped my helmet on and went back out there."

"It's definitely depressing," Bunz added. "I hate it when we hold them on defense and the offense turns it over. Especially that close to scoring. But the good part is we got the ball back and Joe and Dwight punched it in."

Starting a drive at the Dallas 47, Montana needed only four plays to put six more points on the board. Earl Cooper went up the middle for 11. Then Solomon caught a 12-yard pass, and Lenvil Elliott ran for 4. The fourth play in the series was vintage Montana and perhaps a hint of things to come.

Chased out of the pocket by a heavy Dallas rush, Montana scrambled to his left, avoided the blitzing Walls, then stepped up and fired a strike to Clark, who was alone in the middle of the end zone. The sure-handed receiver cradled the ball in his arms and drew it to his chest as he slid to his knees and rolled over on the painted section of the Candlestick turf. Montana, buried under three Cowboys, never saw the touchdown. But the hometown crowd let him know immediately his pass was successful.

"Dwight was so wide open I just knew it was a touchdown," Montana recalled. "Then the crowd noise confirmed it. I kinda like when that happens."

In true championship-game form, Dallas scored again on its next possession when Tony Dorsett went in on a 5-yard sweep to cap an 80-yard drive and make it 17–14. The touchdown would not have been possible without a controversial interference penalty against rookie Ronnie Lott, who intercepted a White pass but was flagged for making early contact with wide receiver Drew Pearson.

"My concentration was on the ball all the way," he would say later. And Walsh later made a veiled reference to the play when he said, "We overcame a lot of adversity and questionable calls."

The teams traded punts to open the second half, then traded turnovers when first Montana, then White, threw a pass that was intercepted. It was becoming apparent that this game might be decided in the final minute, even after the 49ers took a 21–17 lead on a 2-yard run by Johnny Davis. "It was an incredible game," said Turner, who was fighting off chicken pox and feeling a little woozy. "Going back and forth like that with the score, it must have been fun to watch."

It was. Another Septien field goal capped a 64-yard Dallas drive to cut the lead to one point to begin the fourth quarter. Then a San Francisco fumble at midfield set up another Dallas score, a 21-yard TD pass to tight end Doug Cosbie that gave the Cowboys a 27–21 lead.

"They took the lead, and a big hush came over the crowd, and it was as if the coffin had closed on our season," tight end Charle Young said. "We were somewhat dejected on the sideline because the defense had allowed them to score a touchdown, but we rose to the occasion. Nothing could stop us." Not the Dallas Cowboys anyway. Not in the end.

After intercepting a Montana pass, Dallas got conservative trying to preserve the lead. The Cowboys' nine-play possession stalled just across midfield, and White delivered a high, end-over-end punt that was fair-caught by Solomon on the 49ers' 11-yard line. With 4:54 to go to the Super Bowl, the stage was set, the lights were on, the cameras rolling. One of the greatest sequences in the franchise's history was about to begin.

Joe Montana took his place at the head of the 49ers' huddle standing near his end zone. Like mighty Casey, he quickly had one strike against him, missing on a screen pass to Lenvil Elliott. Three of the next four plays also involved Elliott, a former Cincinnati Bengal who was activated for the playoffs. A 6-yard run up the middle preceded a 6-yard pass to Solomon in the left flat. Another run by Elliott, this time around right end, gained 11. A 7-yard run to the left was followed by an incomplete pass; then Dallas was offside on the next play, and the 5-yard step-off gave the 49ers a first down at their 46-yard line. Montana hit Cooper over the middle for 5 to move into Dallas territory, and play halted for the two-minute warning. Finally, with the clock stopped everyone had a chance to take a deep breath.

Walsh and Montana powwowed on the 49ers' sideline as the sun fell behind the press box and the fans shifted restlessly in their seats. A Super Bowl berth was as unfamiliar to this crowd as a World Series is to Chicago, and tension filled the chilling air.

Was this kid from Notre Dame, this third-round draft choice with the skinny legs, the one to lead the 49er Faithful into the sport's greatest game?

It didn't take Joe long to move the team into position. On second-and-five from the Dallas 49, Solomon gained 14 around the left side on a reverse, and Montana passed for 10 to Clark. On first-and-ten, Montana hit Solomon over the middle for 12 more yards to the Cowboys' 13 and called the 49ers' first timeout with 1:15 to play.

Known to thrive well under pressure, known to keep his head while others lost theirs, Montana returned to the field and, after an incomplete pass, handed off to Elliott for a sweep that netted 7 yards. Walsh and Montana met on the sideline for the final time and discussed the next two plays—both passes designed for Freddie Solomon. The first was the same play he had scored on in the first quarter.

"Look for Freddie," Bill said to his star quarterback. "Hold it, hold it, hold it or throw it high for Dwight so that if he can't get it, it'll be thrown away." Joe called both plays in the huddle, and Dallas dug in with its goal-line defense. The world will never know what the second play was; the first was all the 49ers needed.

"You could feel the momentum growing that whole drive," offensive tackle Keith Fahnhorst recalled. "Every guy in the huddle was thinking, 'I hope the play is called over me. I hope I'm the one who has to make the catch, or the run, or the block.' There was that kind of confidence. With other teams in similar situations, it's like, 'Oh shit, I hope we don't run to my side.' "

The play is still in the 49ers' playbook, although it's difficult to imagine that it will ever be used at a more dramatic time. It's called "Sprint Right Motion," and the play was designed for Dwight to line up wide to the right and Freddie to line up in the slot on the right side. Clark was to run an inside hook, and Solomon was to take three steps and then go out along the sideline. If the pass was delayed, the instructions were for them to go as deep as possible and slide along the back line of the end zone looking for the ball. The only problem was that Dallas got a great rush on Montana and chased him out of the pocket before he could find an open receiver.

Fahnhorst's memory is flawless. "I remember that play because (Ed) "Too Tall" Jones was over me, and he didn't come rushing upfield to contain Joe like he usually does. He kind of looped around the linebackers. I thought it was strange that he did that and was wondering where he was going. I chased after him, but Earl Cooper cut down his guy and got me at the same time. I always wondered what would have happened if Too Tall had kept coming like usual and cut Joe off."

All teams practice emergency procedures for when the quarterback is forced to scramble, but with the Super Bowl riding on the outcome, it would have been understandable for a mistake to occur. The playoff-green 49ers, however, delivered a masterpiece of improvisation.

Solomon slipped and struggled to regain his feet while Clark was being double-covered by Walls and Michael Downs in the end zone. Joe sprinted out to the right, but with no receiver open he was getting dangerously close to the sideline. He scanned the end zone looking for a red jersey, but all he could see was linebacker D.D. Lewis and Jones bearing down on him. With nowhere to go, Montana backpedaled a couple of steps, then suddenly caught a glimpse of Clark running along the back line. A split second before Lewis and Jones made him a hood ornament, Joe got off a floating pass from his back foot and was buried under 520 pounds of Dallas Cowboys.

Clark remembers the next few seconds as though they were a dream. He jumped as high as he could, with his 6-foot-4 frame fully extended, and stretched his arms above his head reaching for the ball. Later, many would say the pass was a fluke, that it was a throw-away. But Joe disagrees. "I didn't think I had overthrown it," he said, "I was surprised to see on the replays that Dwight had to jump that high."

"I remember being so high," Dwight said in slight understatement. "I thought I had jumped too soon. I thought I'd miss it. It hit my hands, and I juggled it, but I caught it on the way down."

His gloved hands squeezed the ball, and he gently came back to earth with the franchise's future firmly in his grip. Momentarily he cherished the prize, then slammed it to the turf in triumph. Sixty thousand mouths roared, 120,000 hands thundered their approval, and in millions of homes and bars across the country 49ers' fans rejoiced.

As it turns out, the stadium contained an extra spectator on the play, All-Pro center Randy Cross, who watched from a most embarrassing vantage point: the playing field. "I was doing what I wasn't supposed to be doing," he said, breaking into a wide grin. "I was watching Joe scramble. I was watching my guy, Larry Bethea, chasing Joe. I saw the whole thing. It was really pretty."

Oh sure, there was the matter of the PAT and the kickoff and Dallas' valiant attempt with 51 seconds still to go to get within field-goal range. But as far as the San Francisco 49ers were concerned, the game was in the history books and they had a date with the Cincinnati Bengals in Super Bowl XVI.

In the 49ers' locker room, Bill Walsh was concise as usual. "We tried to methodically cut them apart," he said. "We were able to do that because we have a resourceful quarterback."

The players were euphoric. "This victory today made my career," defensive end Jim Stuckey exclaimed.

"We proved today we can make things happen," Fred Dean said. "We came from behind; that's what it takes to make it to the Super Bowl. We knew we could stop them on their final drive, and we did. It feels great. We deserved it!"

To this day, teammates vividly recall The Catch and the man who made it happen. Ronnie Lott: "If anybody on the team deserved to catch the winning touchdown pass, it was Dwight Clark."

Randy Cross: "The one thing that stuck out in my mind, and still does to this day, is how high Dwight jumped to get that ball. Everson Walls in his wildest dreams never thought Dwight could get that ball or he would have gone for it. I think he just figured it was being thrown away. I think he knew Dwight could get up. But whether he knew Dwight could get up that high . . ."

Joe Montana: "All quarterbacks have a vision of the ball as you release it, whether it's going to be high or low or where it's going to be on the receiver. I knew it was going to be a little high, but I thought it would be one of those where it would be a little above his head and he'd just reach up and grab it. I got knocked down, and the crowd went crazy. I found out later it was not only because of the touchdown, but because he had to go up and get the ball. I didn't see it until we got into the locker room and watched it on the TV replay. It was one heck of a catch."

Many players had a lot to celebrate that day: Hacksaw Reynolds, who had come north from the Rams to bring a veteran's stability to an otherwise very young defensive unit; Fred Dean, who was acquired in mid-season from the Chargers; Dwaine Board, who was cut by the Steelers in 1979 and was denied playing in the Super Bowl that season.

Bobby Leopold spoke for many of his teammates when he said, "Nothing compares to this win. This is the highest point of my career." The rookies expressed similar sentiments, from Ronnie Lott to Eric Wright, from Carlton Williamson to Lynn Thomas, who exclaimed, "From 6–10 to the Super Bowl! Nothing could be finer than to be a 49er!"

Years later, Clark's best friend, Montana, summed up the great receiver's attributes: "When you're scrambling around out there looking for someone to throw the ball to, he'd come and find you. He wanted the ball. That's the way you've got to be. You've got to want to be in the situation. You can't be afraid of it—and he wasn't. He wasn't afraid to go anywhere to get the ball."

Befitting the accomplishment, the last word on the subject belongs to the man who joined an elite group of 49ers when his uniform number, 87, was retired in 1988 on "Dwight Clark Day" at Candlestick Park.

"That one play didn't make me financially wealthy or anything. I didn't all of a sudden get a ton of commercials. But not a single person who knows anything about football doesn't know about 'The Catch.' "

"The Goal Line Stand"
Super Bowl XVI
Pontiac Silverdome
January 24, 1982

The city of San Francisco had not been exactly well-known for its pro sports champions. Despite five professional franchises and a few major colleges spread throughout the area, the City by the Bay had not actually been home to an honest-to-goodness champion since Sir Francis Drake sailed proudly past the Marin Headlands and first gazed upon what is now the city's waterfront.

Oh sure, first cousin Oakland was doing well enough with the A's and Warriors to win four world titles in as many years in the '70s; and little brother Palo Alto claimed two Rose Bowl champions with Stanford in 1971 and '72. But poor old San Francisco had to satisfy itself with being famous by association, a Frank Stallone kind of thing.

Then Eddie DeBartolo entered the picture. "This would be a pretty good place for a championship football team," he seemingly said. So he and his father peeled off $16 million from their shopping center wad and set out to bring the city what it wanted—what it deserved—a champion it could call its own.

In many ways, the 1981 49ers would be the team DeBartolo would most admire. No NFL team ever went from the basement to the penthouse more quickly. Not that it was a walk in the country to get there; Eddie had his critics. He was always "too" something. Too young, too spoiled, too rich, too loud. Too good would be a few years off. He had to pay his dues.

In truth, the teams he fielded those first couple of years were weak, but no one suffered more than Eddie. He was booed, he was jeered, and he was spit on by a "fan" in his team's home ballpark. Imagine the humiliation. A $16 million cover charge just to join the party and your guests spit on you.

But Super Bowl Sunday in 1982 would be the day all the itches would be scratched.

With a backdrop of anticipation that only a history without a championship can provide, Walsh brought his team to the frozen confines of the Pontiac Silverdome fresh from victory over Dallas—"America's Team"—in the NFC championship game. His players could not have been blamed for a loss of concentration amid the media circus, but they somehow managed to maintain their focus.

"It was definitely a new experience for us," Keena Turner said, laughing as he recalled the scene. "I had never seen so many reporters in one place at the same time. I couldn't believe some of the questions: 'What kind of T-shirt did I wear under my pads? How did I pick my number?' Crazy stuff."

Crazy stuff indeed. But not one 49er regretted being in that situation when the alternative was watching the thing on television from the La-Z-Boy in the den.

Super Bowl XVI is still the highest rated sports event in television history, and the more than 110 million Americans who tuned in were treated to a classic confrontation between two surprisingly well-matched, first-time participants.

The uneasiness of world championship football was evident from the outset, as both teams turned the ball over on their opening possessions—the Niners on a fumble and the Bengals on an interception. But the two conference champions soon settled into their game plans, and the 49ers dominated the first half with a pair of touchdowns and field goals to take a 20–0 lead.

"We felt satisfied that we'd done what we wanted to do in that first half," Fred Dean said. "But no way did we think it was over. Hacksaw (Reynolds) was the only one with Super Bowl experience." Then a smile broke across his lips, and he quickly added, "But it's not easy to talk to Hack during games."

The 20-point deficit the Ohioans found themselves saddled with at halftime was reduced to 13 on a 5-yard run by veteran quarterback Ken Anderson that capped the opening drive of the second half. There's nothing quite like an 83-yard, nine-play drive to reaffirm a team's stature as a worthy champion, and Cincinnati's hopes were bolstered. For their part, the 49ers seemed a bit bewildered by their opponent's newfound spirit and tried vainly to rekindle the offensive fire that had blazed so brightly in the first half. But Joe Montana was sacked by Ross Browner, and then a pass to Freddie Solomon was broken up by All-Pro cornerback Louis Breeden. Suddenly, the Niners felt their grip on the Lombardi Trophy begin to slip.

"Cincinnati came out fired up in that second half," Turner said. "We definitely lost our momentum at that point."

The 49ers' second possession of the second half was not an improvement as they went three and out again, and Jim Miller's punt was returned to midfield, giving Anderson an excellent opportunity to trim the margin further. The confidence that had been apparent along the 49er sideline just minutes before, though not completely gone, was weakened by the Bengals' surge. And without a doubt, the most concerned spectator among the 81,270 in attendance was one Edward J. DeBartolo Jr.

"I don't want to say I was nervous or anything," he recalled. "But I wasn't exactly thinking of victory speeches either."

The team that had gone from 2–14 to 13–3 in just two seasons was starting to feel the growing pains of the transition from doormat to contender, its character was once again being tested.

From midfield, Anderson moved his team quickly toward the end zone, trying to capitalize on the three rookies in the 49ers' secondary. Cornerback Eric Wright was victimized twice on the drive, although a 15-yard holding penalty voided one of the plays. The real damage was done on a 49-yard toss to wide receiver Cris Collinsworth on a third-and-23 play that gave Cincinnati a first down at the 49ers' 14-yard line. Stunned but not yet beaten, the Niners' defense stiffened and stopped the Bengals on the next two plays, but yielded a 10-yard pass to Dan Ross. On fourth-and-one from the

Craig soars with Rice (80) and Rathman (44) pitching in. (Photo by Jeff Bayer)

Sure-handed Clark (87) is the 49ers' all-time leader in receiving yards. (Photo by Jeff Bayer)

*Notre Dame star Montana was a steal in the third round of the 1979 college draft.
(Photo by San Francisco 49ers)*

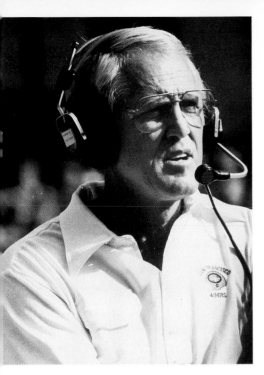

Walsh was dubbed "the Professor" for designing the offense and providing the leadership that led to three NFL championships. (Photo by San Francisco 49ers)

"I didn't think I had a chance at all," said Clark after being drafted in the tenth round in 1979. He stayed for nine seasons, two Super Bowls, and two Pro Bowls and had his jersey retired in 1988. (Photo by San Francisco 49ers)

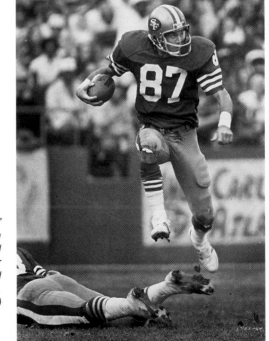

Walsh and DeBartolo didn't always see eye to eye. (Photo by Jeff Bayer)

Montana was the perfect choice to run Walsh's innovative offense. (Photo by Jeff Bayer)

Reynolds (64) brought veteran stability to a young defense in 1981 that featured Lott (42). (Photo by Bill Fox)

Bunz stopped Alexander on the 1-yard line to preserve the win in Super Bowl XVI. (Photo by Heinz Kluetmeir/ Sports Illustrated)

Dean was one of the NFL's fiercest pass rushers. (Photo by Bill Fox)

Craig brought his rugged high-knee-action style of running to the team in 1983. (Photo by Jeff Bayer)

Francis shows his All-Pro form on this touchdown catch. (Photo by Jeff Bayer)

"Playing for Mr. D. is great," say several 49ers who hold the popular owner in very high esteem. (Photo by Jeff Bayer)

Tyler (26) scored in the NFL championship game vs. Chicago, January 5, 1985. (Photo by Jeff Bayer)

Carter won a silver medal in the 1984 Olympics, then anchored a defense that was often overshadowed by Walsh's elaborate offense. (Photo by Jeff Bayer)

*Montana and Clark celebrated a 15–1 season in 1985 with the NFL champion-
ship, routing Chicago 23–0. (Photo by Bill Fox)*

*Montana scrambled for a 6-yard touchdown in Super Bowl XIX against the Dol-
phins. (Photo by Jeff Bayer)*

Ellison (50) and Carter (95) buried Dickerson in 1985. (Photo by Bill Fox)

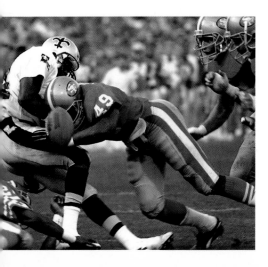

Fuller (49) terrorized opposing running backs with his hard-hitting style. (Photo by Jeff Bayer)

It was smooth sailing for Rice on this touchdown run in his rookie season. (Photo by Bill Fox)

Montana finds Craig while McIntyre (62) has his hands (and face) full with Millard (75). (Photo by Bill Fox)

Clark leaves Candlestick Park for the last time after the loss to the Vikings in the 1987 playoffs, but Rice had already begun to pick up the slack. (Photo by Bill Fox)

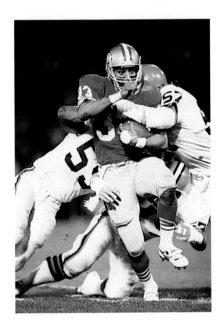

Craig often got wrapped up in his work. (Photo by Dave Stock)

Just ten weeks after major back surgery in 1986, Montana threw 60 passes for 441 yards against the Redskins. (Photo by Jeff Bayer)

*Rice opened the 1987 NFL cham-
pionship game against the Giants
with a bomb from Montana . . .*

*. . . but dropped the ball in open
field while Montana celebrated
prematurely. (Photos by Jeff Bayer)*

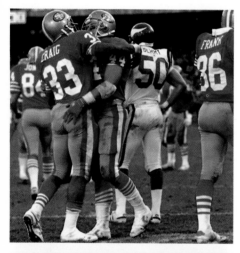

*Walsh's offense really clicked
when Rathman (44) and Craig
made an all-cornhusker backfield.
(Photo by Jeff Bayer)*

*Young (8) was acquired in 1987 to
back up Montana, and is
expected to inherit the team.
(Photo by Dave Stock)*

Rice has become the NFL's most lethal weapon. (Photo by Bill Fox)

The 49ers beat the Vikings in 1988 with an incredible 49-yard run by Steve Young. (Photo by Bill Fox)

The 49ers are ready for the '90s with Walter (99), Carter (95), Haley (94) . . .

. . . and Fuller. (Photos by Dave Stock)

Rice displays total concentration on this catch in Super Bowl XXIII despite early compromising contact from Billups. (Photo by Jeff Bayer)

The championship drive for Super Bowl XXIII was a group effort by Barton (79), McIntyre (62), Rice (80), Cross (51), Sapolu (61), Montana (16), and Paris (77). (Photo by Jeff Bayer)

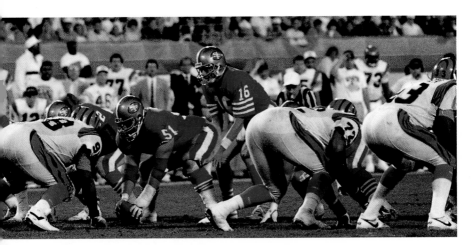

Cross (51) retired in 1989 after 13 seasons and 3 Pro Bowls. (Photo by Jeff Bayer)

Montana hit Taylor (right) with the winning touchdown in Super Bowl XXIII. (Photo by Jeff Bayer)

Walsh is all smiles in the post-Super Bowl XXIII press conference . . .

. . . then retired four days later as DeBartolo promoted Seifert. (Photos by Jeff Bayer)

"Without Joe we're not the team of the decade," said Razzano. (Photo by Bill Fox)

Many were calling Montana the greatest quarterback of all time after the 55–10 rout of Denver in Super Bowl XXIV. (Photo by Jeff Bayer)

Veterans Jim Burt and Matt Millen gave stability to the defense, and the organization demonstrated its willingness to add depth at key positions. (Photo by Jeff Bayer)

Guy McIntyre was the only offensive lineman to make the Pro Bowl in 1989. (Photo by Jeff Bayer)

George Seifert was in total command in his first season as head coach. (Photo by Jeff Bayer)

Ronnie Lott played with the exuberance of a rookie as he took another giant step toward Canton and the Hall of Fame. (Photo by Jeff Bayer)

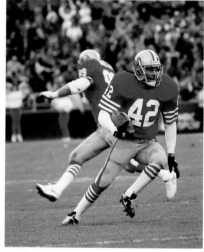

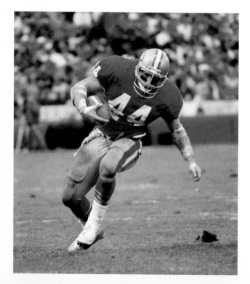

Tom Rathman's offensive production included 73 receptions during the regular season. (Photo by Jeff Bayer)

Chet Brooks did an outstanding job taking over for the injured Jeff Fuller. (Photo by Jeff Bayer)

Montana shows he's not just a finesse quarterback. (Photo by Jeff Bayer)

Rice broke the team record for career touchdowns receiving with 66. (The previous record of 59 was held by Gene Washington.) (Photo by Jeff Bayer)

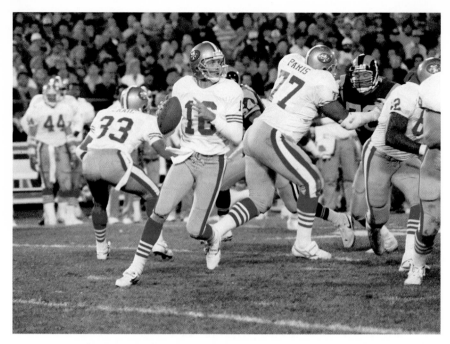

Montana gets ample protection as he passes for a club record 30-42/ 458 yards and 3 touchdowns. (Photo by Jeff Bayer)

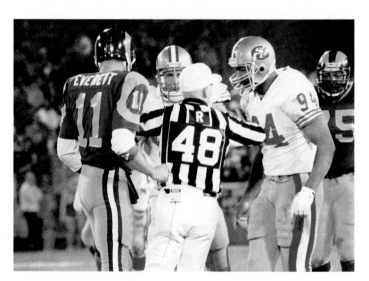

Emotions ran high as Charles Haley was ejected from the game in the third quarter. (Photo by Jeff Bayer)

The 49ers signal victory after the winning touchdown.
(Photo by Jeff Bayer)

Team owner Eddie DeBartolo celebrates one of the most
dramatic victories in franchise history. (Photo by Jeff Bayer)

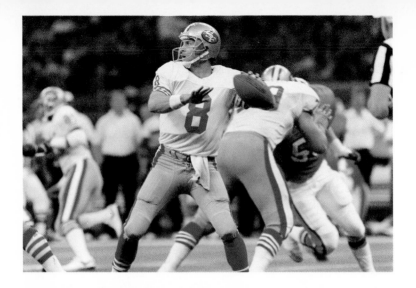

Once again, Steve Young's versatility gave the 49ers an extra dimension at quarterback. (Photo by Jeff Bayer)

*Offensive line coach Bobb
McKittrick's intricate blocking
schemes provided for . . .*

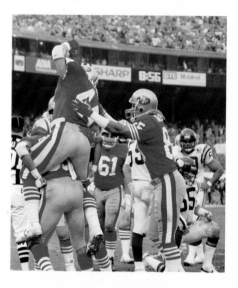

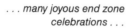
*. . . many joyous end zone
celebrations . . .*

*. . . as the running game reached
a peak during the playoffs.
(Photos by Jeff Bayer)*

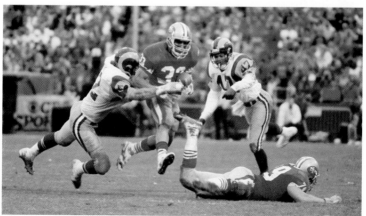

Coach Seifert was given a surprise 50th birthday party . . . followed by a Super Win . . . that ended with a chant of "Threepeat"! (Photos by Jeff Bayer)

5, fullback Pete Johnson hit the line for 2 yards, and suddenly the AFC champs were knocking on the door for the second time in the half.

The 49ers' destiny as the best professional football team of the 1980s began for certain with the nose of the ball on their 3-yard line and the Bengals in possession with four cracks at the end zone. A defense that was a blend of veteran ingenuity and youthful exuberance came of age that day in a valiant goal-line stand.

The gang of 11 braced for the Bengals' best assault —and responded with the most famous defensive series in club history.

First-and-goal from the San Francisco 3.

Anderson, brimming with newfound confidence, sent Johnson up the middle in one of the trademark plunges that made him college football's all-time touchdown leader at Ohio State. Dean made the initial contact, but the huge fullback drove forward for a gain of 2 before the defense could collapse on him.

The 49ers huddled in their end zone.

"Everybody was pretty hyped up in that huddle," Dean says. "My feeling was, either we could stop them here and be the champs, or we could lose it and think about it for the rest of our lives."

Forrest Gregg, the Bengals' head coach and a former Green Bay Packers offensive lineman, sought the counsel of his assistants. Though a veteran of two Super Bowls as a player, Gregg was making his first appearance in the NFL championship game as a coach. He had been receiving wide criticism for his coaching style since being hired in 1979 and was looking for a victory to serve notice of his arrival among the league's top coaches. But nothing comes easy in the last few yards of a touchdown drive in championship football, and the Hall of Famer from the Packers' glory years didn't want to make a mistake.

Not here. Not now.

Gregg settled on a plan. On second down from the 1, he made a bold decision to go for six points no matter the cost. After all, the worst that could happen would be that the 49ers would get the ball back in terrible field position. The best that could happen, what Gregg was counting on, would be a Bengals touchdown that would put them back into the game and perhaps shift the momentum in their favor. Championship teams, he reasoned, had to make the best of opportunities. And in the Super Bowl, history showed, opportunities were few and far between.

He would send Johnson, his human bulldozer, one more time into the line, hoping to ride his ample shoulders into the end zone. Then, if unsuccessful, the Bengals would try to catch the 49ers off guard with a swing pass to a running back. If both attempts failed—God forbid—they could always go back to Johnson on fourth-and-goal.

Second-and-goal at the San Francisco 1.

Forty-Niners defensive tackle John Harty, in his rookie season, was a-wonder at his good fortune. The second-round draft choice out of Iowa had been a solid contributor all season and now was digging in on all fours in a goal-line defense in the Super Bowl. Sandwiched between veterans Dwaine Board and Archie Reese, Harty glared across the line at Bengals left guard Dave Lapham, searching for a clue as to the Cincinnati intentions. At the snap of the ball, Lapham sprang forward and collided with the former Hawkeye, sending shock waves all the way down to his size 13 Nikes. Harty grunted at the impact and struggled to maintain his ground, feeling his knees stiffen in response to the blow his body was absorbing. Then with movement that had become instinctive after nine years of organized football, he shed Lapham's block and momentarily saw wide open AstroTurf all the way to the opposite goal line.

But just as quickly as it had opened, the hole began

to close, the plug being an oncoming freight train with number 46 across its chest.

Harty lowered his shoulder, took the blow that Johnson laid upon him and won the battle as he stopped the beefy fullback in his tracks. Then in quick succession the other Niners defenders piled on to make sure Johnson didn't get free.

Third-and-goal at the San Francisco 1.

Gregg clenched his jaw in typical stoic form and watched intently as his team broke its huddle and approached the line of scrimmage. Waiting for the Bengals with renewed confidence was a 49ers defense that had twice responded to the call of greatness and was surging with adrenaline.

If a thousand football fans were asked to name their favorite team's greatest defensive play, chances are most would pick a spectacular interception for a touchdown or maybe a fumble recovery for a touchdown. But in the case of the 49ers, the play that stands out above all others did not score a touchdown; it prevented one.

Linebacker Dan Bunz scraped his cleats along the carpeted end zone and eyed running back Charles Alexander as he took his place in the Bengals' backfield. In the goal-line coverage the 49ers had called, Bunz's responsibility was to go one-on-one with the former LSU tailback, nicknamed "Alexander the Great," wherever he went on the field. But as outside linebacker on the left side, Bunz was also the 49ers' only contain man at the line of scrimmage if Cincinnati decided to run wide.

It had been a rough season for Bunz, a rugged former Long Beach State star. A first-round draft choice in 1978, Dan had lost his starting job when the 49ers acquired veterans Reynolds and Dean. Nagging injuries had also played a part in Bunz's season, as well as playing on a team loaded with linebacking talent. In addition to Reynolds and Dean, who was interchanged between defensive end and linebacker for the Super Bowl, the Niners also had Bobby Leopold, Keena Turner, Milt McColl, Craig Puki and Willie Harper.

The only tackle Dan Bunz would make in Super Bowl XVI was destined to become the most memorable single defensive play in 49ers history, and one of the NFL's finest as well.

With the snap of the ball, the play was set in motion. Bunz was frozen momentarily with the rest of the 49ers as Anderson faked a handoff into the middle. But when Dan saw Alexander break out of the backfield around right end in the familiar motion of a pass pattern, his instincts took over. He shuffled laterally to his left along the goal line, trailing the movement of his target and all the while glancing back at Anderson to try to read the play. Once Alexander got clear of the pack at the line of scrimmage, he cut sharply to his right and sprinted for the sideline. Bunz dug his cleats into the plastic rug and shot after the fleet-footed running back, fearing for just a moment that he might be beaten.

"It's that brief feeling of panic a linebacker gets when the man he's covering breaks his pattern off," Bunz said. "After all, he knows where he's going and all you can do is follow."

Under pressure, Anderson wheeled and fired a pass to his running back in the right flat and was delighted to see it completed. But his joy turned to sadness when a blur of white shot across the field and Bunz dropped Alexander squarely in his tracks just inches from the goal line.

"Danny's thing on the sideline was just a great defensive play," Randy Cross recalled. "And a momentous blunder by Alexander for cutting off his pattern before he got into the end zone."

Fourth-and-goal at the San Francisco 1.

On the Cincinnati sideline, Gregg let out a groan

and slowly shook his head. On three plays his team had managed just 2 yards, and the momentum had unquestionably shifted to his opponent. Hardly anyone in the stadium was surprised when Pete Johnson got the ball on fourth down and was smothered by the 49ers' defense in his vain attempt to plow through the line. A lasting memory of the series was Archie Reese rolling onto his back on top of the pileup and flailing his arms in celebration.

Cross exalted on the 49ers' sideline: "We were ecstatic. Jumping for joy and screaming and yelling until we realized, 'Oh shit, now that means we get the ball on the one-foot line.' But we start those drills from the first day of training camp."

Said wide receiver Mike Shumann: "We were going nuts along the sideline. From that point on, we realized we could win the thing."

Baseball is supposed to be the game of inches. But in Super Bowl XVI, the 49ers won the war of inches with an incredible goal-line stand. Though the Bengals scored a touchdown just minutes later in the fourth quarter to make it 20–14, the Niners responded with two Ray Wersching field goals to put the game out of reach. A meaningless Cincinnati touchdown with 20 seconds to play made the final 26–21 and put the finishing touches on a very satisfying season for a young 49ers team.

"The Drive"
Super Bowl XXIII
Joe Robbie Stadium
January 22, 1989

For nearly a quarter of a century, football fans had been waiting every January for the scenario to unfold: Football's best quarterback taking football's best team the length of the field for the winning touchdown in the waning moments of an NFL championship game. In Super Bowl XXIII at Miami's Joe Robbie Stadium against the Cincinnati Bengals, Joe Montana and the San Francisco 49ers finally delivered.

Considering the way both teams played in the first half of the game, it's amazing anyone stayed around for the conclusion. The 49ers' opening possession was marred by a sack and a fumbled snap that fortunately was recovered by Montana. Cincinnati played just as poorly, managing just one complete pass in a seven-play series. San Francisco drew first blood, however, when a 41-yard Mike Cofer field goal sailed between the uprights after a promising drive stalled.

The second quarter brought more frustration to the 49er Faithful as their team, which had been widely favored, couldn't score despite moving the ball at will. First, Cofer's chip-shot field-goal attempt went wide to the left after Montana engineered a beautiful drive from the 49ers' 30-yard line to the Bengals' 2. Then, normally reliable Roger Craig coughed up the ball when he was hit after a 13-yard run on the 49ers' next possession, and Cincinnati recovered in Niners territory. But true to this game's emerging form, the Bengals' drive ended when quarterback Boomer Esiason was sacked, taking his team out of field-goal range. And when two penalties on the next San Francisco series eliminated any possibility of a score, football fans from coast to coast must have scrambled to check their program guides to make sure this really was the Super Bowl.

The Bengals broke their scoring drought after Barry Helton's punt netted only 32 yards, giving Cincinnati a first down at the San Francisco 44-yard line. Six plays later, Jim Breech split the uprights with a 34-yard field goal. At halftime, the 49ers were stunned to be in a 3–3 tie despite managing more than twice as many first downs and total net yards as their opponents.

"Needless to say, we made some adjustments at half-time," Bill Walsh said after the game.

Breech capped the opening drive of the third quarter with a 43-yard field goal, putting the Bengals in front for the first time. The 49ers' problems continued on offense as a sack and an incomplete pass on third-and-nine led to a punt, but a clutch interception by rookie linebacker Bill Romanowski gave the Niners an excellent scoring opportunity at the Bengals' 23-yard line. Four plays later, Cofer drilled his second field goal of the game, a 32-yarder, to tie the score 6–6.

The tie lasted exactly 16 seconds.

On the ensuing kickoff, Bengals kick returner Stanford Jennings took the ball on his 7-yard line and sped up the middle of the field for a spectacular 93-yard touchdown. Later, Walsh would say: "That was a great job by their kick returner. He did a brilliant job breaking it, and they did a good job blocking for it. We knew we had our backs against the wall at that point."

The touchdown was like a wake-up call for the San Francisco offense. From his 15, Montana hit Jerry Rice for 31 yards, then went to Craig on a perfect timing pattern down the right sideline for 40. On the third play of the drive, the Niners got a little lucky. From the Cincinnati 14, Montana tried to hit Rice in the end zone on a post pattern, but cornerback Lewis Billups read the play perfectly and stepped in front of the receiver for what appeared to be a certain interception. Incredibly, the ball hit his hands and bounced off his chest before falling incomplete.

"We got lucky on that one," Joe admitted. "J.R. (Jerry Rice) slipped a bit on his pattern, but I had Roger Craig open also. When I threw it, I took a little too much off the throw. It definitely should have been intercepted, and I breathed a little bit easier after the drop."

The miscue would come back to haunt the Bengals

on the very next play. Non-plussed by the near-interception, Montana stepped up and hit Rice on the right edge of the Cincinnati goal line, and the acrobatic receiver dived in for a spectacular touchdown. Cofer's extra point tied the game for the third and final time at 13–13.

Cofer missed his second field-goal of the game, this one from 49 yards out, with just under nine minutes to play. Then Breech put the Bengals up 16–13 with a 40-yarder after Esiason led his team on a 46-yard, 11-play drive that used up nearly 5½ minutes. As the ball sailed over the crossbar, Steve Young turned to Montana on the 49er sideline. "Well," the backup quarterback said, "It's set up perfectly for us."

When a holding penalty was assessed against the 49ers on the ensuing kickoff, the ball was spotted on the San Francisco 8-yard line and the clock showed 3:10 left in the game. For the second time in just over seven years, the curtain was about to go up on a sensational Joe Montana-led scoring drive in a championship game.

Later, when Walsh was asked if he was surprised to be in a comeback situation after being heavily favored, he said: "By that time I wasn't. But if somebody had said before the game we would get as many yards as we did but not score a lot of touchdowns, I wouldn't have thought that likely. If somebody had said, 'You're going to get over 400 yards and score two touchdowns,' I would have been surprised because we don't have those kinds of games very often."

Randy Cross agreed and added, "I was surprised in that I thought we should have been ahead by three touchdowns."

So, what was the plan? "The key was to get into field-goal position, then go for the touchdown," Walsh explained. "But we had to get to a point on the field so that if time ran down we could kick before we went for the touchdown with time running out. The key to the drive would be the execution of the entire team—not just Joe. One breakdown anywhere could cost us the game."

Cross disagreed slightly and offered the players' perspective: "We were not thinking field goal. We were going to score a touchdown even if we had to throw Joe through the air 10 yards to do it."

Along the 49ers' sideline, emotions ran high. All-Pro linebacker Charles Haley: "I was confident that the offense would score, but a lot of things run through your mind during that time. I knew if we got the ball to Jerry we would make things happen, and Joe is a veteran who has been in this type of situation before."

Ronnie Lott: "It was just like 1981 against the Cowboys. Don Griffin came up to me and said, 'You've got to believe we're going to win this one.' The same thing happened in 1981. Archie Reese came up to me and said the same thing."

Bill Romanowski: "We all had a feeling our offense was going to pull it out. Joe Montana has done it before."

The 49ers' offense huddled on its goal line. No rah-rah speeches were made, no talk about destiny. Just a confident, business-as-usual approach. "Joe was real calm," fullback Tom Rathman said. "Basically, that's the way he has to be, just trying to get things organized. Because of Joe, everyone was calm. I think that's why we were so successful."

Cross agreed. "It was typical Joe Montana—cool and calm," he said. "He's not a 'rah-rah' kind of guy. He just keeps hitting those passes. He tells you what to do. He tells you what play he wants or how to change the blocking schemes to make a play work. You just do it because he is going to come through."

Montana passed over the middle to Craig for 8 yards to begin the drive, then hit tight end John Frank on a curl for 7 and a first down. Rice was open in the right flat for another 7 yards, and Craig got a yard on a run to the right. Then Craig got 4 yards on a run over right tackle for a first down, and Montana called his first timeout with 1:54 to play. Joe was in complete control, throwing easy, sure passes and mixing his receivers and plays in trademark fashion.

On first-and-ten from his 35, Montana hit Rice on the left sideline for a gain of 17, then came back to Craig for 13 and another first down. But something was wrong. Joe looked panicked and tried to signal Walsh for a timeout. Walsh turned him down and on the next play, Joe threw an incomplete pass, way over the head of Rice on the left side.

"I was hyperventilating," Montana would later say. "I felt like I was yelling as loud as I could, but no one could hear me over the crowd noise. I threw the ball away on purpose because I didn't know what would happen after it left my hand. I didn't want to risk a turnover at that point of the drive."

Along the Cincinnati sideline, the unfolding events were all too hauntingly familiar for head coach Sam Wyche. The previous season, Montana and Rice had combined to come back and beat the Bengals on their home field with a last-second touchdown pass. "Deja Vu," Wyche mumbled, as he paced the sideline.

With 1:22 to go, the Niners faced another setback when a pass to Craig over the middle was nullifed because of an ineligible receiver downfield. Randy Cross was the culprit, but Walsh took the blame. "He (Cross) was supposed to pull down the line of scrimmage and fake a screen pass," the coach said later. "Roger was to start out as though he was going out on a screen and then break back up the middle. It had been a good play for us in the past in games like this, and they were in the right defense for us to utilize it. I wasn't happy with myself even as I called the play because it was too low a percentage play for that situation. Randy was knocked downfield inadvertently, and Roger was hit. We completed a short pass out of it, but it was too risky a play for that situation."

The second-biggest play of the drive occurred after the 10-yard step-off moved the ball back to the Cincinnati 45. Montana passed to Rice over the middle, and the fleet-footed receiver split two defenders and raced downfield before being stopped after a 27-yard gain. An 8-yard pass over the middle to Craig moved the ball to the Bengals' 10-yard line, and with 39 seconds left in the game, Montana called his second timeout.

The execution had been perfect. Montana had moved the team 82 yards in ten plays using three different players, and the only mishaps had been an intentionally incomplete pass and a 10-yard penalty against Cross.

Niners' broadcasters Lon Simmons and Joe Starkey watched the drive with the appreciation of true fans of the game. "It's such a sight to watch this," said Starkey. "Whether it happens now or not. To watch Joe Montana do this for so many years. To watch this absolute surgeon on the football field, one of the all-time greats do his thing again. It's almost like poetry."

For the record, the play Walsh called during the timeout was "20 Halfback Curl, X Up." It was designed to go to Craig, but just as in '81 it turned out to require improvisation. Rice was the decoy. He had been double-covered most of the game, so Walsh lined him up wide right and sent him in motion to the left to get the defense shifting. A moment before the snap, Walsh and his staff noticed Craig had lined up incorrectly in the backfield, but their frantic shouts could not be heard above the din. In hindsight, the mistake may have helped wide receiver John Taylor get wide open across the middle.

With Taylor split wide left and Rice in motion to the left, Craig lined up over left tackle, in effect flooding that side with bodies. At the snap, Rice and Craig went to the left side of the end zone and drew most of the defense's attention. Taylor, on a post pattern broke inside when the defenders moved up to check Rice and Craig. All of a sudden, Taylor was open as he headed toward the back of the end zone. Without hesitation, Montana stepped up and fired a strike that Taylor snuggled into his arms with 34 seconds remaining for the game-winning touchdown. Final score: San Francisco 20, Cincinnati 16.

All in all, 25 Super Bowl records were tied or broken, and the finish was the most exciting in history.

The biggest story of the week preceding the game was Jerry Rice's tender ankle, injured in practice on the first day. All week there had been speculation he would not be 100 percent for the game, but the superstar was fittingly named MVP after a Super Bowl record 215 yards receiving. Ronnie Lott: "I've said all along that Jerry Rice is the best wide receiver ever to play this game. Yes, ever. I've never seen a guy that has those kinds of tools work as hard as he does. When you have guys like that on your team, it tends to rub off."

For his part, Rice would say: "I'd rather give Joe the MVP any day because he held the leadership. He took total control and typified the leadership we needed."

Although Walsh did not necessarily agree that Joe deserved the MVP over Jerry, he did credit Montana for another clutch scoring drive to win a championship.

Said the professor: "People have dropped back and thrown a 50-yard pass and won a game, or dropped back and thrown a long pass to pull a game out. But to orchestrate a drive that would be a series of plays from your own 7- or 8-yard line using the clock, utilizing the timeouts, using good judgment on who to throw to and then, of course, making the big pass when he had to, . . . (that) would indicate to me that he has been the very best in football for some time."

Chapter 8

SIDELINES
The Players Speak

"He always thought he was a piece of crap. He always thought he had no talent—and we would always agree with him."
—*Keith Fahnhorst on former teammate Paul Hofer*

*T*hrough the decade, one could easily make the case that the most interesting events involving the 49ers occurred away from the field, away from the fans and the television cameras. Never mind "The Catch." Never mind "The Goal-line Stand" and "The Drive", and those three championship rings.

Ask former Niners offensive tackle Keith Fahnhorst about one of his favorite memories of the 1980s and he will describe a scene in the locker room during an exhibition game in 1982, the year the team spent its second-round draft choice on tackle Bubba Paris of Michigan.

"Our former starting tackle, Dan Audick, came back in the locker room real upset one time in a preseason game," Fahnhorst said. "The day they drafted Bubba, they gave him Audick's job. I remember Audick beat the hell out of a locker in Seattle before the game, but the coaches didn't say anything to him because they knew his intentions were not to hit the locker but to hit the coaches. Finally, he cut it out. But about halfway through the first half, Dan got hurt and had to go to the locker room. Then Bubba tore up his knee, and he had to go to the locker room. So there's Bubba, sitting on the training table, his knee wrecked, and he's left alone in the training room with Audick, the guy who lost his starting job to him. From what I heard, Audick looked at him like he was going to kill him. On the flight back, John Ayers, who was afraid to fly, was paranoid that Audick was going to open the door of the plane and jump out."

Although every player has his favorite story, practically every 49ers player and coach agrees that team's most unusual character of the decade was linebacker Jack "Hacksaw" Reynolds. Waived by the Los Angeles Rams after the 1980 season and picked up by the Niners, Reynolds quickly established himself as a defensive leader on the field and a certifiable, well, character, off it.

He brought a stack of freshly sharpened pencils to each team meeting, but almost never let anybody borrow one. Unlike his teammates, who would suit up at the stadium, Hacksaw dressed in his hotel room and wore his full gear at the team breakfast table. He kept notes and files on almost every offensive player in the league. And he had earned his nickname in college when he sawed in half, by hand, a '53 Chevrolet to work out his aggressions after his Tennessee team was blown out by Mississippi 38–0. It took him eight hours and 14 blades.

The eccentricities don't stop there, and neither do the recollections from some of his former teammates.

From All-Pro free safety Ronnie Lott: "I remember when he first got here he used to live out of his locker. Here was a man who had been in the league for a long time, and we all knew he could afford an apartment. He didn't even get an apartment for the first two or three weeks. Everything was in his locker. His film projector, his clothes—that was just Hacksaw."

From former running back Bill Ring: "I couldn't believe the first time I saw him come downstairs in the hotel at 9 a.m. for a 1 p.m. game and he had his eye-black on, his uniform, the whole nine yards. The first thing he would do when he got to the hotel was rip the sheet and hang it on the wall so he could watch film."

Of Hacksaw's famous pencil collection, Ring said: "He let me borrow one once. I felt privileged."

From former wide receiver Mike Shumann: "I stayed away from Hacksaw before games. His coffee kicked in earlier than everybody else's. He was just too intense for me. But he was among the core of leaders who really helped us through that 1981 season."

From Fahnhorst: "There weren't many people like Hacksaw. He lived and died football. I don't know if you'd call it dedication or obsession. I rode up with him to training camp his first year. Now, I love to talk about football, but nothing like that guy. He didn't talk about anything else."

Because the 49ers' roster has included so many players with so many unique personalities—Paris, center-guard Randy Cross, and tight-end Russ Francis among them—each deserves his own little category, his own little niche. His own little award:

Secret Disguise Award: To former coach Bill Walsh, who dressed up as a bellhop and fooled most of his players when they arrived at the team hotel before Super Bowl XVI in Pontiac, Michigan.

"I was the first one to get off the bus, and I see this guy coming up to me," former wide receiver Mike Shumann recalled. "I started thinking, 'Great, here's somebody who's already trying to make some money off of us.' So when he reached for my bag, I literally armed him away from me. I didn't know it was Bill until later on when I was riding down the elevator with John

Ayers and he said, 'What do you think of Bill dressing up as a bellhop?' I said I didn't know that was Bill, and Ayers said, 'No wonder you're not playing Sunday.' I saw Bill later, but he wasn't upset. He just thought it was great that he fooled somebody."

Shumann wasn't the only player fooled. Said former running back Bill Ring, "I was carrying a light bag and he said, 'I'll take that for you.' I said, 'No thanks,' but he kept insisting, and I got irritated. When I finally looked up at his face, I started dying." Fahnhorst added, "I just walked right by him. I didn't know it was him until somebody told me later.

Reverend Roy Award: To offensive tackle Bubba Paris. Although a great number of professional athletes are deeply religious and often express their faith during interviews, none has taken it to the extent of Paris, who in his early years actually "witnessed"—that is, shared his religion with—players across the line during games.

"It started in Seattle against Jeff Bryant," Paris recalled. "It got to the point where he was talking to me and battling me at the same time. I said, 'Jeff, have you been saved?' He thought about it, and I knocked him down."

Predictably, not all opponents took to Preacher Paris. "Dexter Manley kicked me," he said. "He didn't like anybody witnessing him. He would act crazy, beating me up, but because of it he didn't have time to sack Joe (Montana).

"Howie Long was a crybaby. He used to cry all the time, and for some reason he had something against me. He didn't think I deserved the accolades. He yanked my helmet off and threw it to the ground. He told me he read I was a Christian and he was going to convert me. Convert me to what, I don't know."

Keith Fahnhorst recalls that Paris often would pray before games. "Before we'd go out, you'd hear Bubba saying, 'Help me, Jesus. Help me, help me.' That always disturbed me. I always hoped Jesus was doing something more important with his time than watching Bubba play a football game."

Breakfast of Champions Award: To defensive lineman Pierce Holt, who enjoyed a fine rookie season in 1988, but after the season almost lost his life to a bowl of Grape Nuts. Honest.

Holt ran into the problem when a spoonful of the cereal became lodged in his throat because, Holt later reasoned, "It must have not soaked up the milk." Holt began choking, panicked and for some reason felt the urge to get some fresh air and headed toward the backdoor of his Los Gatos home. But as he reached for the handle on the sliding glass door, he staggered and fell through the glass, cutting his forehead and left arm.

Credit Holt's wife, Deana, with the Red Cross award. She performed the Heimlich maneuver to force the Grape Nuts from Holt's throat and then drove her husband to the hospital where he received 100 stiches to close the wounds. A toe injury that wiped out half his rookie season seemed almost trivial compared to that. Holt's post-Grape Nuts perspective: "It really wasn't that bad."

The makers of Post cereals will be happy to know that Holt plans no lawsuit and, in fact, still eats the cereal regularly.

National Enquirer Award: To running back Roger Craig, who was victimized by one of the infamous Fleet Street tabloids when the 49ers visited London for an exhibition game against Miami in 1988.

The screaming banner headline in Sunday Sport read: "ROGER'S 49 WAYS TO PLEASE HIS MISSUS." No explanation necessary. (It should be pointed out that Sunday Sport is the same publication that carried a story, "Adolf Hitler was a woman.")

In the Craig "exclusive," the story the "sex-mad

49ers start" had a rollicking good time during the team flight to London from San Francisco. Of course, Craig denied the story and the Sunday Sport "reporter" was conspicuous in his absence from the game.

Craig: "This is bad for my reputation. Good for my ego, but bad for my reputation."

Obsessed Athlete Award: To tackle Harris Barton, a tireless worker and admitted insomniac. He explains:

"I guess I take the job home too much," he said. "I'll be watching television, and suddenly I'll jump up and start working on a 'reach block' I missed or a pass set, right there in the living room. But that's nothing. There have been times in college when I've done it out on the balcony at my dorm room at 3 in the morning."

Lee Gliarmas, a kicker who was a teammate of Barton's at North Carolina, said, "Harris was legendary. We would be on the road and there were coaches who would wait for Harris to come out on the balcony and work on his techniques. The man is the biggest insomniac in the world. He would go out there and stare at the moon for a few minutes; then he'd start working on his blocks. I remember one time we were walking down the middle of Franklin Street in Chapel Hill and, out of nowhere, he'd go into a pass set."

Golden Tonsils Award: To retired guard and center Randy Cross, who during his career was regularly surrounded by reporters after games and practices because of his quick wit and insightful comments.

One example came during Cross' final training camp in 1988, after he realized he was the oldest player on the team: "To me, Merlin Olsen was the greatest defensive player I've ever played against. To these young guys here, he's some old, gray-haired announcer who talks too much on TV."

Selected other comments: "Everyone sees the light at the other end of the tunnel, but not everyone recognizes that it's a train." And this: "It bothers you when you're called a finesse player. We're not interior decorators. Finesse is something you see in the ballet." And this, on his father, Dennis, a retired actor: "He's died more times than Lee van Cleef and all of the other bad guys put together. The only time he didn't get killed was on 'Get Smart,' when Agent 99 knocked him out."

George Hamilton Tanning Award: To tight end Russ Francis, in a runaway vote. As with Reynolds, nobody was ever quite sure which drumbeat Francis marched to. He was a little flaky, a sky diver, a pilot, a surfer and a solid tanner. Once asked during a brief retirement what it would take for him to return to the game, Francis said, "Move the training camp to Hawaii and exclude me from practices and team meetings."

Francis excelled at bronzing his body during hot summer days in training camp at Sierra College in Rocklin, a community just east of Sacramento in Placer County. The reason he was able to tan during camp is because he rarely had his uniform on . . . because he rarely practiced. For all of his success on the field, Francis never was a strong practice player. He always seemed to be rehabilitating from some injury in the swimming pool. Consequently, teammates nicknamed him "Flipper."

"Russ was different from most of the guys on the team," Fahnhorst said. "A lot of guys resented his attitude, but it never really bothered me because I knew Russ would be there when it came time, when they were shooting live bullets. I remember games when his elbow would pop out of joint and he'd turn to me and have me pop it back in between plays."

Lott echoed those remarks. "He would have been a joker if we were winning or losing. Russ had a great time while he played the game. But on Sunday he was always there. It took everyone a while to understand what Russ's intentions were. He was the one guy whom everyone could look forward to coming up with something a little different."

Best Practical Joke Award: To former defensive end Dwaine Board, who wasn't as frequent a prankster as some of his teammates but undoubtedly pulled off the practical joke of the decade. It came at the expense of defensive end-linebacker Charles Haley, who earned a reputation as a prankster at James Madison University, where he used to "persuade" freshman players to shave their heads.

Haley's sometimes-irritating clowning began to wear thin with veterans early in his rookie season in 1986, so Board decided to get even and brought Michael Carter, Ronnie Lott and a police officer into the gag. Board, Carter and Lott began spreading stories that the police department in Redwood City, where the team's training facilities were then located, was loaded with "redneck cops." They told Haley that the officers were known to pull guys over, drag them into back alleys, beat them up and leave them for any passing vultures.

One night, the four players were in a car, and Carter intentionally ran a red light and was pulled over. Haley panicked; the others only pretended to. After pretending to run a check on everybody's driver's license, the officer returned to Carter's car, asked Haley to step out and informed him that there was a warrant out for his arrest for drunken driving and a hit-and-run accident. In mid-protest, Haley was handcuffed and taken away, while the other three players rolled over with laughter."

Haley eventually was set free and told the truth. Funny. He couldn't find the humor in the joke.

Reassessed Priorities Award: To guard Jeff Bregel, who enjoyed All-America status, even Academic All-American status at Southern Cal, but had a rocky beginning in his first two years with the 49ers.

Bregel missed most of his rookie season in 1987 with a knee injury, which worsened when he took a shower and the water hit his post-surgical stitches, giving him a staph infection. And he spent most of his second year as a seldom-used reserve on the offensive line and on goal-line defense (which, incidentally, he actually likes).

But Bregel's worst setback came in May 1988 when he was arrested and charged with drunken driving and resisting arrest. By the time he arrived at training camp '89, Bregel was a prospective starter again, but it came as no surprise that football suddenly didn't seem as important.

"You get a different outlook on life when you talk to people from your hometown who haven't had the opportunity you've had. I think now I get happiness and a better quality of life just from doing things the right way. The last incident with the police taught me a lot. I can't keep living on the edge all the time. I have to sit down once in a while and enjoy everything around me."

Locker Room Intimidator Award: To free safety Ronnie Lott, whose pregame disposition has rivaled Reynolds'. Translation: Don't bug him. Former defensive coordinator George Seifert found this out the hard way.

"He has this 'don't fuck with me' look," Seifert said. "I did once early in our relationship, and I haven't since. It was one of those deals where players get a mindset before a ballgame and you can see them when they're sitting at their locker when they're in a trance, preparing themselves for a ballgame. That's about the time I walked up and made some comment like, 'Don't forget to watch for this guy on this pattern. His response was something like, 'What the fuck are you doing? Leave me alone.' "

Bronco Billy Award: To kicker Steve DeLine, a 1987 draft pick who became part of a long line of players who failed to beat out veteran Ray Wersching for the 49ers' place-kicking chores. After being released,

DeLine returned to his family's ranch in Rand, Colo., to resume practice—to practice bronco riding, to practice team roping, to practice not getting maimed by some wild four-legged creature.

Typical of a cowboy—the real kind, not the phonies with stars on their helmets—DeLine also can negotiate the difficult tobacco chew-spit combination with the best of them. He used to spit after nearly every sentence until, he said, "My mom bet me and my brother $50 that we couldn't quit. We did."

Wild Man Award: To linebacker Riki Ellison, who since as a rookie from Southern Cal in 1983 has found himself in some abnormal situations. On the Fourth of July in 1984, Ellison and teammate Tom Holmoe took a boat out into the Foster City lagoon and brought a bag of firecrackers with them.

Holmoe recalled, "(Ellison) threw a match into the bag of fireworks. He didn't mean to. It was an accident. So I jumped off the boat. He put out the flame with his hands. Otherwise, we would have blown up."

Among other Riki-isms: He often overturns golf carts, obviously mistaking that narrow paved path for a grand prix course. He wrapped his old pickup truck around a telephone pole one summer on the way up to camp, then got out of the car and cut away the mangled mudflap with a pocket knife so he could continue driving. (Of course, he offered a wonderful explanation: "The telephone pole must have jumped into the street. These things always seem to happen to me." And, the horn of his Mercedes Benz plays "Fight On," the USC fight song.

Now, given all of that, consider this: Ellison is a staunch Republican and spends his off-seasons working for Lockheed on strategic defense research and often debates teammates on the importance of the Strategic Defense Initiative (SDI).

Unwanted Room Mate Award: To defensive end

Kevin Fagan, whose incredibly loud snoring dissuades teammates from wanting to room with him during training camp.

Fagan shrugs. "Gee, you know some people think you do it on purpose or something," he says. "It never bothered Vinny Testaverde when I was rooming with him at Miami. He just wadded up some toilet paper and stuck it in his ears. Someday when I get married, I might have an operation because, let's face it, I really do snore super loud. In fact, sometimes I snore so loud, I wake myself up."

Sudden Royalty Award: To former wide receiver Mike Shumann, who was traded to St. Louis after playing on the 49ers' first championship team. "It was incredible. I was like a God to (the Cardinals). That ring probably gave me three more years in the league. All of a sudden, I was the Hacksaw of the Cardinals."

Writing on the Wall Award: To former running back Bobby Ferrell, who, according to teammates, would often stroll around the locker room, singing, "Bobby Ferrell, Bobby Ferrell, he works real hard, but he never gets to play."

Houdini Award: To Sam Wyche, the former 49ers quarterbacks coach who is now the head man for the Cincinnati Bengals. Wyche loved to perform magic and often would do tricks during team meetings.

"He would do it in meetings, and Bill (Walsh) would walk in and give everybody a look like, 'What the fuck is going on?' " said former wide-receiver Mike Shumann. "Sam would be pulling a rabbit out of a hat instead of going over 22-Z-in."

Enterprising Businessman Award: To reserve linebacker and special-teams player Sam Kennedy, who as a rookie in 1988 had an original thought: charge for interviews.

The way Kennedy figured it, sportswriters make money to write about athletes, so why shouldn't athletes make money to provide sportswriters with quotes. Without debating the subject, we will just tell you that his price was 25 cents. When the Niners visited Tokyo for an exhibition game in August 1989, Kennedy raised his rate to 100 yen (about 70 cents).

Kennedy's most depressing interview session followed a pre-Super Bowl workout. He counted his earnings, and the change came to a total of $1.55. "Somebody slipped me a nickel," he said. "Do you believe that?"

Worst Timing Award: To defensive lineman Pete Kugler, who after making 10 tackles in the 49ers' 1983 NFC title game loss to Washington signed with the Philadelphia Stars of the now-defunct USFL. The following year, when Kugler reported to the Stars' camp, it was the same night the 49ers walloped Miami in the Super Bowl.

"It was one of the toughest nights of my life," he said, "The grass is always greener on the other side until you get to the other side. Then it's brown. I hear guys complaining, I just shake my head."

Hard Luck Award: To linebacker Todd Shell, who was nicknamed "Crystal" by his teammates because he seemed to have as many injuries as tackles in his career. He finally had to call it quits after suffering a spinal-cord injury during training camp in 1988.

Shell should at least be well-prepared for a career in sports medicine, having memorized every bone in his body. After emerging from the training room one day in full uniform—shorts and an electronic muscle stimulator on his knee—Shell explained, "The thigh would have never healed without the surgery. I had myositis ossificans. See, the muscle fascia and rectus femoris calcified."

Huh?

"It's another way of saying I had calcium deposits. I knew a lot of this stuff before. Microbiology was my major in college, and I had to take a few anatomy classes. But as far as the myositis ossificans, that was a term I learned. You know, you pick these things up as you go along."

Negotiating Rhetoric Award: To owner Edward DeBartolo Jr., whose patience with holdout cornerbacks Tim McKyer and Don Griffin had run out by the second exhibition game of the 1988 season.

"If those guys don't show up by 6 P.M. Wednesday, it's over," he said. "That's my deadline. If they don't show up by Wednesday night, everything we've offered those guys starts going down. Those guys can sit out the year. I don't care. I need nothing and I ask nothing."

In the same conversation with a reporter, DeBartolo threatened to tie the players up in court "for 40 years." When a reporter made the mistake of asking the 49ers owner if he was serious, he glared at the reporter and shot back, "Is death serious?"

Postcript: Neither McKyer nor Griffin met DeBartolo's deadline, but both soon signed contracts, and the two sides lived happily ever after.

Happy Feet Award: To Steve Young, the 49ers' quarterback of the future. When he was asked to fly to the Bay Area for a workout with the Niners in May 1987, shortly after being acquired from Tampa Bay, Young was in such a hurry that he forgot his football cleats. But Niners equipment manager Bronco Hinek told Young not to worry about it and gave him a pair of Joe Montana's cleats, figuring Joe was not expected in that afternoon. But about a half-hour later . . .

"Hi, Joe," Coach Bill Walsh said. "I'd like you to meet Steve Young. Steve, this is Joe." As Young shook hands with Montana, he stood against a wall to conceal the red No. 16 on the back of each shoe.

"Frankly, I didn't know how he'd react," Young recalled. "Maybe he would think I was walking right in and trying to take over. I mean, this guy is a legend. We all went into a room and talked and watched some football film, until Joe had to go. As he left, he smiled at me and said, 'Steve, a pleasure meeting you. And, oh, by the way, nice shoes you're wearing.'"

Comeback Quote Award: Outgoing 49ers coach Bill Walsh said upon his exit, "I don't want to put too much of an onus on George Seifert but I think the 49ers have as good a chance as anyone to repeat as world champions."

When Seifert heard this, he responded, "Not to put the onus on *him* or anything, but I'm sure he'll have the highest Nielsen ratings of all broadcasters."

Chapter 9

FIELDS OF GLORY
Super Bowls XVI
and XIX

"I guess we were all young and dumb. It got to be like a college atmosphere. It had been so long since we won that everyone was going nuts."
—Keith Fahnhorst on the 1981 season

When he played at Southern Cal, Ronnie Lott became accustomed to winning. Conference titles and Rose Bowl berths were commonplace for the Trojans; losses were not. It was an atmosphere that he had hoped would stay with him throughout his career.

Imagine Lott's surprise when he arrived for his first day of professional football training camp in July 1981, a few months after the San Francisco 49ers made him the eighth overall selection in the 1981 college draft.

"There were a lot of rookies on that team," Lott recalled. "We had a lot of people who didn't have great attitudes. There wasn't any sense of pride during that training camp. It wasn't training camp like we have now, where guys say, 'Boy, we're going to the Super Bowl.' Back then it was, 'Like, hey, man, I hope we make the team.'

"It was really weird, because at Southern Cal, you set

a standard. You learn how to compete, on the practice field as well as the playing field. I was surrounded by a lot of guys who didn't have that attitude."

Things changed quickly, however, in Lott's rookie campaign. By the time the 1981 season ended, the defeatist attitude of the 49ers' players had dissipated, as had Lott's concern that he would be stuck playing with a perennial loser. The 49ers stunned the NFL—its participants as well as its followers—with their first league championship by defeating the Cincinnati Bengals 26–21 in Super Bowl XVI at the Silverdome in Pontiac, Mich.

That initial title had followed eight straight non-playoff seasons, including two under Bill Walsh, who had not yet attained genius status as an NFL head coach. The Niners had finished 8–24 in his first two seasons, including 2–14 in 1979. But with the 13–3 regular-season record in '81, the 49ers became the first team since the Chicago Bears (1945–46–47) to go from the league's worst record to the best in three seasons. Predictably, the suddenness of the franchise's turnaround in 1981 aroused skepticism whether San Francisco deserved mention as one of the NFL's elite teams, but those doubts were smothered three years later. The Niners won a league-record 18 games, including play-offs, dominating the opposition from start to finish, and slammed the door closed on their 1984 season by slamming the Miami Dolphins 38–16 in Super Bowl XIX at Stanford Stadium.

Now there was no doubt—just as there were no available seats at Candlestick Park. In the first five seasons of the decade, three teams shared the league championships. Two were owned by the Raiders of Oakland and later Los Angeles; one belonged to the Washington Redskins; and two Super Bowl trophies were in the possession of a team that not long before had, in Lott's estimation, a defeatist attitude: the San Francisco 49ers.

Joe Montana mentioned that the 49ers' third championship, in the 1988 season, seemed the sweetest because "at 6–5, everybody was counting us out." But in 1981, it was more a case of not being counted at all. From the time the Niners lost their season opener at Detroit, Bay Area football fans (those remaining few, anyway) expected another year that would end with the final regular-season game.

Although there seemed to be a more professional, at least positive, atmosphere from the time Walsh was hired in 1979, some players couldn't break old habits.

"We had much more fun as a team when we were losing," retired center Randy Cross said. "Of course, a good reason we were losing is we were having so much fun. It was the old Raiders' mentality of going out and getting shit-faced a couple of nights a week with the boys. It was great in the '60s and '70s, but it just didn't make it anymore."

Walsh could not be faulted for many of the 49ers' early problems. The problem was not his system; it was the parts he had to work with. The organization, in the words of owner Edward DeBartolo Jr., "needed a franchise cleaning," and this was no more evident than on the player roster. Previous General Manager Joe Thomas, DeBartolo said, "did a tremendous amount of damage."

That is why for the first two years of the Walsh era, in particular, it seemed as though a revolving door had been placed in the locker room. Every game, every practice, was more like an open-to-the-public tryout. Very few players could afford the risk of signing a long-term lease at their apartments for fear they might be working at a convenience store or the family's ranch in Texas the following week. Tackle Keith Fahnhorst, who had been with the team since 1974, has a clear recollection of the 1981 season, because that year included one of the low points of his career.

"I was just hoping we'd have a winning season," he said. "But Joe was just starting out as a starter, then we lost the opener in Detroit and I figured, 'Here we go again.' Also, I was in the middle of a contract dispute, and I asked to be traded a few weeks into the season. Thank God, John McVay (who was in the front office) didn't go through with it. All I remember is there was a lot of frustration."

Even when the 49ers were a respectable 3–2 through the first five weeks of the season, with victories over Chicago, New Orleans and Washington, Fahnhorst wasn't convinced the team was headed upward. "We didn't have the confidence we were going to win all the time. The atmosphere was more like, 'What's going to go wrong today to make us lose?' But after the '81 season, we always figured someone would do something, someone would make it possible for us to win."

Two victories during the regular season convinced many that even if the 49ers weren't destined for a decade of excellence, they would at least be a force in the 1981 playoffs. The first came in the sixth week, when San Francisco ripped the Dallas Cowboys 45–14—and this was back when a win over Dallas meant something. Montana, in his first full season as starter, threw for 279 yards and two touchdowns, including a 78-yarder to Dwight Clark that was his longest of the season. The Niners had beaten the Cowboys only once in the previous nine meetings, and the last time the teams had met, in 1980, the 49ers were the main course in a Texas barbecue—59–14.

Three weeks after the win over Dallas, the 49ers, at 6–2 off to their fastest start in five years, visited the Pittsburgh Steelers, winners of four of the previous seven Super Bowls. Although some doubted the Steelers would make a fifth trip to the championship game, they were 5–3 and still considered a league power. But the 49ers won 17–14, their sixth straight win in a streak that would reach seven. Overall, San Francisco lost just once in the final 13 weeks of the season en route to its best record ever and its first NFC West Division title since 1972.

"I remember feeling more and more confident that year, thinking something's got to happen. The winning has got to stop," Clark recalled. "I don't remember being overconfident. The confidence was growing, but all along we were wondering how good we were. Every time we would win, the newspapers would say, 'Well, the 49ers got lucky again.' To me, the turning point of the whole season, the game when everybody started to say the 49ers were good, was when we beat Pittsburgh. They had guys like Terry Bradshaw and John Stallworth. Most of the guys on our team watched them since we were kids. When we got into the locker room after that game and even Bill Walsh was jumping up and down like we were, you knew we were a good team."

"We got to the point that year where we were walking around and thinking, 'Hey, we're not supposed to lose.'" Lott said. "I remember that year we had beaten some team, I think it was Houston, and I came into the locker room and everybody was upset because we had played terribly. Nobody was jumping up and down or anything."

Strangely, this attitude permeated the defense as much as the offense. After being tattooed for 416 and 415 points in Walsh's first two years, the 49ers yielded only 250 points in 1981, second-best in the league to the Philadelphia Eagles (who had reached the Super Bowl the previous year). Whereas Cross noted of previous years, "We had to score 45 every week because everyone else was scoring 42," the offense had now discovered that scoring a few touchdowns was often enough for a victory.

The mixture of players on defense that caused this

was as curious as it was effective. Three rookies started in the secondary—Lott and Eric Wright at the cornerback positions and Carlton Williamson at strong safety. They joined free safety Dwight Hicks, who had been cut by two teams in the NFL and one in the Canadian Football League but led the 49ers with nine interceptions that season.

Leading the assault on quarterbacks was sack specialist Fred Dean, who had been acquired a week before the Dallas game. Dean led the team with 12 sacks that season, was named to the All-Pro team, played in the Pro Bowl and was honored as Defensive Player of the Year by United Press International and as Outstanding Defensive Lineman by the NFL Players Association.

It was Dean who, in the words of former tight end Charle Young, served as "the last piece to the puzzle. Fred solidified the defense, the defense solidified the team, and we won every game the rest of the year except for one. Fred was such an awesome force, he had to be reckoned with."

The glue that held the team togther was inside linebacker Jack "Hacksaw" Reynolds, who had been released by the Los Angeles Rams after the 1980 season and signed with San Francisco as a free agent. Reynolds' contribution did not show much on the statistics sheet, but his mere presence in the locker room and work ethic in games, practices and team meetings seemed to rub off on other Niners.

"He created a lot of good habits for this organization," Lott said. "He taught a lot of people how to win. He taught some coaches how to win. He did a lot more for this organization than people know."

"Guys like Jack Reynolds," said former running back Bill Ring, "showed us the way. We went to our first two Super Bowls because people like Charle Young and Keith Fahnhorst and Hacksaw were there."

There was a dash of everything in the first championship team. The 1981 49ers included five rookies, 10 free agents and five players who were acquired by trade. "We sure didn't expect miracles, like winning the championship," Clark said.

And why should they have? Cross described the previous seasons as "real bad. It was like not being professional at what you did. It was like, 'Gee, wouldn't it be nice to play for a real good football team sometime in your career? Wouldn't you rather be with the Raiders or the Rams?' Nobody would take you seriously."

It's understandable that Walsh was optimistic but cautious going into the 1981 season. He was quoted before that year as saying, "We have been able to add slowly potentially better athletes to our squad, especially with this year's draft, and that's working to make us potentially better overall."

Two of those potentially better athletes were the only survivors of Walsh's first draft in 1979. They were the same two players who fueled the offense of the '80s: Joe Montana and Dwight Clark.

In his first complete season as the No. 1 man on the depth chart since he left Notre Dame, Montana led the National Football Conference with an 88.2 efficiency rating—a statistic based on percentage of completions, percentage of touchdowns, percentage of interceptions and average yards per attempt. That standard proved to be no fluke. Going into the 1989 season, Montana ranked as the NFL's all-time passing leader with a career rating of 92.0, throwing for more than 27,000 yards with almost twice as many touchdowns (190) as interceptions (99).

Even one of Montana's worst games in 1981—the one against Pittsburgh—was inspiring to his teammates. Unbeknownst to the Steelers, the fans or the media until after the game, Montana played that afternoon with extremely sore ribs and wore a flak jacket. The pain was so bad that Montana, despite throwing a 5-

yard touchdown pass to Charle Young, was not used as
the holder on the extra-point attempt after the 49ers'
second TD because he couldn't catch his breath.

Montana's most active receiver in his first three seasons as starter also happened to be his best friend—
Clark. A lightly regarded 10th-round draft pick two
years earlier, Clark had little confidence in his future as
a football player. But his size (6-foot-4, 215 pounds),
strength and leaping ability made him a prototype possession receiver for Walsh's offense. He had 85 catches
in the '81 regular season, though none was as big as the
one he would make in the NFC title game against
Dallas.

Indeed, going into San Francisco's first post-season
appearance since 1972 (when they had lost their second
playoff game to Dallas in as many years), it was apparent that Walsh had pieced together an efficient
machine from an odd collection of parts. There were
victories over Washington, Dallas and Pittsburgh, and
two over the 49ers' NFC West Division rivals, the Los
Angeles Rams.

But the biggest win for Walsh—and, in a sense, even
bigger than the Super Bowl—was a 21–3 victory over
the Cincinnati Bengals in the 14th week. In terms of
revenge, this game meant more to him than the title
because it was his first return to Cincinnati since he had
been snubbed for the head-coaching job by Paul
Brown.

"It was the key game for me," Walsh said. "We had
clinched our division, and they were going for theirs
and had tremendous momentum. We sort of shut them
up a little bit. I made some off-handed remark about
resting some of our players, and then Howard Cosell
was really critical of me for being able to rest some of
our players for this big game, and he said the Bengals
should have all the competition they can get: 'Just
because the 49ers had clinched their division doesn't

mean they shouldn't make it tough on the Bengals.' It was never in my mind not to play our best guys and go for that game because it was a big game to me."

The victory fell in the middle of a five-game winning streak that the 49ers carried into the playoffs. San Francisco then opened with a convincing 38–24 win over the New York Giants, to land in the conference championship game against Dallas. The Cowboys had whipped Tampa Bay 38–0 in the first round and had won eight to their previous 11 playoff games, including a Super Bowl title four years earlier.

For three hours and 13 minutes, the 49ers and Cowboys put on the type of show you would expect between one of the league's new forces and a perennial power. Montana threw a touchdown pass to Freddie Solomon four minutes into the game; Danny White threw a scoring strike to Tony Hill eight minutes later; then Montana found Clark for a score; then Tony Dorsett ran 5 yards to the end zone for Dallas. Back and forth.

"They wanted revenge for losing to us in the regular season, and they were the last team in our way," Young said. "It was the ultimate. The Super Bowl was almost anti-climactic. It was like two prize fighters getting hit and coming back. Then they took the lead late in the game and a big hush fell over the crowd, as if that was the final nail in the coffin and our season was ending."

Indeed, with 4:54 left, the 49ers found themselves on their 11-yard line, trailing 27–21. But Montana, as would become his trademark, seemed as relaxed in those final few minutes as if this was a pickup game, with the losers buying a round of beer. In the next four minutes, he moved the Niners 89 yards to the end zone, capping the winning drive with the now-famous 6-yard touchdown pass to Clark.

On the decisive play, The Catch, Montana rolled right, eluded the Cowboys' pass rush and threw the ball high into the end zone for Clark, who was guarded by

Everson Walls. "I really thought he overthrew him," said Ring, echoing the feelings of most who were in attendance or watching on television. But Clark leaped, made the catch and came down with the ball with 51 seconds left, giving the Niners a 28–27 victory and forever changing the course of team history.

"It was hard to believe I have been in the position and had the opportunity to do something as great as, that for the city and the team," Clark said. "You don't get too many of those opportunities in your life. I was so tired after the game that I went home and to bed. I partied the next night, though."

Clark and his teammates had two weeks to sleep off their hangovers before meeting the Bengals in Super Bowl XVI at Pontiac, Mich. (ironically, the same city in which the 49ers had opened the season). But for most San Francisco players, the two-week buildup merely made them more nervous.

"I had to pinch myself," Ring said, "It was unreal. The adrenaline going through my body at the time was like nothing I had ever been associated with."

That was nothing compared to what Young experienced when he walked out of the locker room, through the tunnel and onto the field at the Silverdome. Young, like Montana on the winning drive in Super Bowl XXIII seven years later, hyperventilated.

"I walked onto the field and it was like all the waiting was over. You walk onto the field and you realize that is the only game; you realize a hundred million people are going to be watching you. As I jogged around the field, I began to hyperventilate. My body was being transformed. There was so much electricity going through my body, so I had to relax. So I went to the center of the field and lay down and crossed my legs and wondered what it would feel like if we won. I sensed victory, I tasted victory, I saw victory. I went back to the locker room and I wrote, 'World Champions' on the chalkboard."

The Bengals almost won the title by default. Many of the 49ers' players and coaches—including Montana and Walsh—did not arrive at the stadium until about 30 minutes before the scheduled kickoff, partly because inclement weather had created traffic jams and partly because the team buses were held up so then-Vice President George Bush's motorcade could get through.

"It was like, 'Hey, we have to get Bush here so they blew us off," Shumann recalled. "What about the players? There was a point where you could cut the tension with a knife. Then Bill stood up and said, "Don't worry. Chico just threw a touchdown pass to Cosmo,' and we all let out a nervous laugh."

Chico Norton and Greg Cosmo were the 49ers' equipment managers. They had arrived at the stadium early—to hang jerseys, not go over the game plan.

The bus ride did little to calm the atmosphere around the 49ers, and it showed in the game: Amos Lawrence fumbled the opening kickoff at the 49ers' 26-yard line. The reaction on the Niners' sideline was predictable. "Oh God, that wasn't a good way to start the game," Ring said.

But the Bengals bungled the scoring opportunity, a common occurrence on this day. After Cincinnati moved to the Niners' 5-yard line, running back Charles Alexander was stopped for no gain, quarterback Ken Anderson was sacked by Jim Stuckey for a 6-yard loss, and Anderson's attempt for wide receiver Isaac Curtis at the 5 was intercepted by Dwight Hicks.

Walsh wasted no time in making full use of the 49ers' playbook. On first down, Montana threw a screen pass to Ricky Patton. A few plays later, the 49ers ran a flea-flicker, when Patton took a handoff and reversed it to Freddie Solomon, who lateraled back to Montana, who completed a 14-yard pass to Young to the Cincinnati 33. Montana eventually capped the 11-play drive with a 1-yard dive into the end zone for a 7–0 lead.

The Bengals, whose arrival in the championship game also followed seasons of mediocrity, were a mess throughout the first half. They were in scoring position early in the second quarter, but wide receiver Cris Collinsworth, after making a catch, was stripped of the ball by Eric Wright at the Niners' 8. That set up another improbable Montana scoring drive, this one measuring 92 yards and ending when the quarterback tossed an 11-yard touchdown strike to Earl Cooper.

Before the half was over, the Bengals added another fumble, and the 49ers added two field goals: San Francisco 20, Cincinnati 0.

At halftime, Walsh warned the team about becoming complacent and told the players that 20 points would not be enough to win the game. Some players didn't realize it at the time, but their coach was right on target with his comments.

Cincinnati scored on its first possession of the second half when Anderson ran 5 yards for a touchdown. It didn't even help that the 49ers' defense mistakenly had 13 men on the field at the time. It appeared the Bengals would close to 20–14 later in the third quarter when they found themselves first and goal at the 3-yard line. Then came the Goal Line Stand which will be remembered along with The Catch, and The Drive as one of the most memorable segments in team history.

Bengals fullback Pete Johnson was held to a 2-yard gain by Dean on first down and was stopped short of the goal line again on second down, this time by John Harty. Anderson then completed a swing pass to Alexander, but the running back was dragged down at the 1 by Dan Bunz. On fourth down, Johnson ran into a wall up the middle, and the 49ers erupted into a celebration.

"We were going nuts on the sideline," Shumann

said. From that point on, we realized we could win this thing."

"We knew it was do or die," Lott said. "We also knew they were going to give the ball to Pete Johnson. Everybody on our team knew we could stop him. That's why Danny Bunz' play was so significant, so great, because it was the one play when they thought they could score on us."

The momentum may have shifted back to the 49ers, but the Bengals kept it interesting. Anderson threw a 4-yard touchdown pass to tight end Dan Ross, but the Niners responded with two field goals by Ray Wersching (giving him four, tying a Super Bowl record). Cincinnati closed to 26–21 on another short Anderson scoring pass to Ross, but by then only 20 seconds remained.

Dwight Clark, who made The Catch to get San Francisco to the Super Bowl, made a different kind of catch to secure the Niners' first title when he cradled an onside kick in the final seconds. At 7:41 P.M. Eastern time, the 49ers became world champions. Heads were spinning in the locker room and back in the Bay Area. Walsh, who was voted Coach of the Year by seven different sanctioning bodies, was not immune to this euphoria.

"You don't realize it at the time, but when you have that kind of success and that kind of attention, you're affected by it, regardless of how often you remind yourself that you're very mortal," he said. "You begin to act a little differently around the edges of your contact with people. You start to become too self-assured, and if you're suddenly very quotable you can overstate things in more of a dramatic way, even a reckless way."

The 49ers were brought back to earth with a thud: They finished only 3–6 in the strike-shortened 1982 season, a year so filled with frustration and rumors of drug use by his players that Walsh seriously considered resigning. But he decided to stay on as coach, and in 1984 the Niners put together one of the most dominating seasons in the history of sports.

As in 1981, the 49ers opened the '84 campaign against the Detroit Lions. Unlike in 1981, they won, although only 30–27. They won their first six before losing to Pittsburgh 20–17. So much for the season's only losing streak. The next nine weeks produced nine victories, including lopsided results against the Los Angeles Rams (33–0), Cleveland (41–7), New Orleans (35–3) and Minnesota (51–7).

"Talk about confidence," Clark said. "It was like, no matter what the other team does, no matter what the refs do, we can win, we can overcome it. That season there was no doubt we would go all the way. You always hear things from coaches like every player plays a part on the team. But that was the only year I recall when everyone was really involved, down to the 10 guys on injured reserve. Every guy contributed something."

This team was much different from the 1981 version. For one, it included a potent running attack with Wendell Tyler, acquired from the Rams, and Roger Craig, acquired through the draft, giving the team a more balanced offense. Other additions included tight end Russ Francis, tackle Bubba Paris, linebacker Riki Ellison, nose tackle Manu Tuiasosopo and defensive end Gary "Big Hands" Johnson.

There also was an intangible connected to the '84 season: motivation. The Niners had been knocked out of the playoffs the previous year by Washington, 24–21, in a game that included a questionable interference penalty on the 49ers' defense. "I remember the emotion in the locker room after we lost to Washington," George Seifert recalled. "Players were really in the tank. But that loss vaulted us into next season."

Said Tyler, "We all believed that if we could get close

again the next season we could win. We felt we got robbed, but we knew we were the better team."

From the opening week in Pontiac, Mich., to the Super Bowl at Stanford Stadium, there was no doubt who rated as the NFL's best in 1984. After blowing through their regular-season schedule with a record 15 wins, the 49ers shredded the New York Giants and Chicago Bears in the playoffs by a composite score of 44–10.

Walsh, perhaps rubbing it in slightly in the Chicago game, even lined up guard Guy McIntyre as a blocking back on a touchdown run. It became known as the "Angus" play, because McIntyre sometimes ate at Black Angus restaurants. He was so nervous when he brought the play in from the sideline, "I stepped on Joe's foot. I thought I put him out of the game. I ran onto the field to tell him the play because I didn't want to forget it. I stepped on it so hard, he pushed me back. He was hobbling around for a while."

Eighteen opponents couldn't stop Montana that season, and neither could McIntyre. Neither could Miami two weeks later. You could have counted XIX ways the 49ers' offense pummeled the Miami defense in Super Bowl XIX. Among them, there was the score (38–16), the 49ers' record yardage total (537), their running game (211 yards to Miami's 25), their advantage in time of possession (37:11 to 22:49), Roger Craig's three touchdowns. But the biggest factor was Montana, who threw for a Super Bowl record 331 yards and three touchdowns and earned his second MVP award.

Montana's performance was remarkable when you consider that the quarterback getting most of the media attention that week was the Dolphins' Dan Marino. Nobody viewed Montana as a schlemiel. But Marino seemed to be on another plateau . . . by himself. In only his second season out of the University of Pittsburgh, he eclipsed NFL records by throwing for 5,084 yards and 48 touchdowns. His wide receivers, Mark Clayton and Mark Duper had combined for 144 receptions. The Dolphins' offense averaged four touchdowns per game.

But Seifert, the secondary coach on the 1981 team and by then the defensive coordinator, designed a scheme to shut down the seemingly unstoppable Marino. The Niners harassed him with a strong rush up the middle, putting pressure on center Dwight Stephenson. There was little reason to be concerned if Marino got outside, because his immobility as a quarterback had been well-illustrated.

As a result, the 49ers sacked Marino four times, and the secondary intercepted two passes and broke up eight others. Showing San Francisco's strength on defense that season, all four members of the secondary —Lott, Wright, Hicks and Williamson—earned spots in the Pro Bowl.

Conversely, the Dolphins' defense, directed by Chuck Studley, was stepped on all afternoon. Montana threw touchdown passes in the first half to Carl Monroe and Craig, and Montana and Craig each ran for one TD to give San Francisco a 28–16 lead at intermission. About the only down point for the 49ers was a fumble late in the half by, of all players, McIntyre, who couldn't handle a squib kickoff by Miami's Uwe von Schamann. The pratfall set up a Dolphins' field goal.

"That was my fiasco," McIntyre said, "I went down to get the ball, and by the time I got up, somebody hit me and the ball came out. I was feeling real down. I remember I wanted to go into the locker room and hide."

There was no need for that because the Dolphins never got any closer. In the third quarter, San Francisco added window dressing to the win with a Wersching field goal and a 16-yard touchdown pass from Montana to Craig, making it one of the most lopsided Super Bowls. It was a microcosm of the season.

"We kept building momentum and confidence, but the pressure kept building that year, too," Fahnhorst said. "When you're the favorites, it's even tougher because everyone is gunning for you. But we had the type of people who could handle it."

"The thing I couldn't believe about that year," Craig said, "was we scored so many points." Including play-offs, the 49ers totaled 557 points, an average of more than 29 per game. The balance between the passing and the running attacks, which did not exist in 1981, kept defenses off balance.

But the difference between the first championship team and the second was not evident just on the score-board.

"The '84 team had a much different makeup from the '81 team," Ring said. "A lot of the rookies had now been in the league for three or four years. We were veterans. We were more dominant because great players like Lott and Wright and Keena Turner and Montana and Clark got better with age."

Chapter 10

MONEY MAKES THE TEAM GO ROUND
Owner, Edward J. DeBartolo Jr.

"The longer I play for him, the more I realize I'm a part of his family. And when I go out onto the field, I want him to be proud of me."
—Riki Ellison, linebacker

Bathed in champagne, 5-foot-8, 160-pound Eddie DeBartolo was being bear-hugged by 6-foot-3, 225-pound tight end John Frank. The shirt-sleeved, 42-year-old businessman was lifted off the ground by the player and carried across the locker room. The trip was cut short, however, when DeBartolo slammed into defensive end Larry Roberts' locker stall, banging his head. Frank roared in celebration.

Veteran cornerback Eric Wright sprayed the helpless DeBartolo with champagne and later dumped a Gatorade bucket filled with cold water and ice on him. Laughing through it all, Wright yelled: "You'd better be a happy man now."

No, this was not a Stephen J. Cannell script for an episode of "The A Team." This was the victorious

189

locker room of the San Francisco 49ers immediately
after Super Bowl XXIII. DeBartolo is the owner of the
team, and believe it or not, he was thoroughly enjoying
every minute of the cavorting with his players. Bruises,
soaked shirt and all.

Not all NFL owners are treated this way. Why, some
players don't even like their owners. Others view the
man who signs their paychecks as the enemy, or the
patriarch, the grand old man of the team. Can you
imagine dear, sweet Art Rooney, the Pittsburgh Steelers' owner from 1933 until his death in 1988, being
bear-hugged and slammed into a locker by one of his
players? Or doused with ice water? How about Wellington Mara, the New York Giants' owner whose family
bought the team in 1925? Lamar Hunt? Or Jack Kent
Cooke?

Eddie DeBartolo is at home with that kind of behav-
ior. He is also at home in the winning locker room. "I
don't mind being regarded as a player's owner because
I really think I am," he said. "I really care about my
players. It bothers me very deeply when something bad
happens to them. Their families mean a lot to me, and I
think we'll always have this rapport, this closeness, this
bond between us."

If Eddie DeBartolo sounds like your kind of guy—
he probably is. The billionaire Ohio real estate devel-
oper and sports impresario extraordinaire is pretty
much loved and admired by virtually everyone who has
played football for him. "I really enjoyed playing for
him," former All-Pro defensive end Fred Dean said. "I
always felt good in his environment. To me, he was just
a great owner."

A great owner. When was the last time you heard
that from a player? With the 49ers, you hear it quite
often. "Eddie is very committed to winning," Joe Montana said. "You have to put forth money to produce a
great team. Eddie did that. He found the best person-

nel for this organization, spent money to get them here and spent money to keep them here. The results speak for themselves."

DeBartolo has had three Super Bowl wins, more than any other current NFL owner. And whether it is the elegant and extravagant parties he throws for his team in such places as London and Tokyo, or the state-of-the-art sports training complex he built in Santa Clara that includes a leather floor in his office, Mr. D. makes sure everything associated with him and the San Francisco 49ers is first-rate. Including their prized Super Bowl XXIII rings.

"Eddie spent a lot of extra money on our Super Bowl rings to thank us for winning," Montana said. "That's the kind of gesture that makes players say, 'I worked my butt off to win this championship for a good man, and in return, he's shown us his gratitude.' That's respect, and that creates a winning atmosphere."

A winning atmosphere was about the last thing DeBartolo acquired when he purchased the 49ers in 1977. "I just remember sitting in the company jet on the way back to Youngstown and thinking, 'That's it then; we're going to do it.' And all of a sudden we were in the football business," he recalled. From that rather inauspicious beginning sprang the pro football reign of Edward J. DeBartolo Jr.

It's safe to say that the previous owners—the Morabito sisters, Jean and Josephine, and minority partner Franklin Mieuli, the Golden State Warriors owner and a Bay Area sports impresario in his own right—probably didn't realize the impact the young Notre Dame alumnus would have on the 49ers, the NFL and the city of San Francisco when they agreed to sell him 90 percent of the franchise in 1977 for $16 million.

"Looking back on it now, they were a hell of a bargain," DeBartolo said about the team, which a national sports magazine estimated is now the NFL's most valuable, worth more than $120 million. "But in 1977 the price tag was, well, it was a lot of money—still is," he added. But don't get the idea the president of the De-Bartolo Corporation, the nation's largest owner and operator of shopping malls, is a penny-pinching, cost-cutting taskmaster.

To the contrary, Eddie DeBartolo—at 42 the youngest NFL owner—pays the highest salaries in the league, treats his players like family and is having by all accounts, the time of his life. And he's never happier than when he's watching his favorite football team win a Super Bowl. In fact, even when Eddie and Bill Walsh had their much-publicized falling out, which led to Walsh losing the title of club president in 1988, the local newspapers called it a "49ers Family Feud." DeBartolo's presence was both needed and felt soon after his arrival.

"I used to be a lot worse than I am now," he said of his reputation for becoming "physically involved" in some games from his perch in the owner's skybox, where he, his family and a regular group of close friends have been sharing 49ers football weekends for the past 13 years. The accounts have ranged from how he broke a glass refrigerator door after a loss to the Raiders in 1988, to how he ripped a locker room phone off the wall and marched around in a rage with phone in hand, the severed cord trailing like a tail.

Most successful businessmen, it should be pointed out, don't accept losing well, whether it's a sale/leaseback or a football game in a "nice guys finish last" world. But more than anything else, Eddie DeBartolo is happy when his team wins football games—something it has done with regularity since Bill Walsh and Joe Montana signed on in 1979.

With all the success Eddie has achieved during the 1980s, it is sometimes hard to recall all the negative rumors and controversy his purchase of the team set in motion. He was, after all, just 30 years old when he acquired the 49ers, and a lot was said about his ability—or lack thereof—to run an NFL franchise. It was suggested that he was a spoiled rich kid whose father had bought him the team to give him something to do. It is a notion he has been trying to live down since the ink dried on the purchase agreement. And even now, as he basks in the glory of his achievements, his discomfort is evident when the suggestion is made by his critics that the only credit he deserves for his success in football is for having the foresight to choose wealthy parents.

"I don't know how much credit anybody needs," he said in the mature, self-effacing tone that has become his style. "I really enjoy what I'm doing out there, now more than ever. How much credit? I think you're only as good as the people you surround yourself with, and I've hired some very good people."

Funny how the brash, overbearing, spoiled little rich kid (by some accounts) who came to San Francisco in 1977 has been replaced by the poised, sensitive adult. And it only took three Super Bowl victories to accomplish the transformation.

In all fairness, Eddie has been blessed—or cursed, depending on your point of view—with his birthright in one of this country's wealthiest families. His good fortune is not without a downside, however, for it carries an enormous amount of expectation and responsibility. And in many ways, his motivation is to prove himself worthy of the adulation that is a part of a winning pro football franchise and to define himself outside the DeBartolo legacy. To prove he is no longer just a rich man's son, but rather, his own man.

Money was not, and is not, the paramount concern. He certainly has more than enough to maintain his comfortable lifestyle. Establishing himself as a respected, successful businessman in his own right is the driving force behind his efforts. In 1989, Eddie

DeBartolo has finally, unquestionably, emerged from the giant shadow cast by one of America's most successful businessmen: Edward J. DeBartolo Sr.

Of course, it does not hurt a guy to have a little bit of money in the bank before he decides to buy a pro football team. In that regard, it is important to understand how deep the DeBartolo family pockets are in order to put into context the magnitude of their achievements.

More than 40 million people shop each week at DeBartolo Corporation malls in more than 70 locations nationwide, and at least 80 new projects are being planned for completion before the turn of the century. With more than 15,000 employees, eight hotels, 13 office buildings and 75 million square feet of total leasable area, the 45-year-old privately held DeBartolo Corporation is one of America's largest and most successful family-run businesses.

Begun in 1944 in Youngstown, Ohio, by Edward Sr., the multi-billion dollar corporation is generally regarded as enormously profitable, although financial figures are never officially released. With large cash reserves, the company often finances multi-million-dollar projects internally for a year or two until institutional lenders—banks, insurance companies or pension funds—can be brought in to provide permanent financing. And with strong ties to international capital markets, the financial subsidiary DeBartolo Capital Corp. once arranged a $100 million Eurobond financing deal at extremely favorable rates to obtain mortgage money for its retail properties.

By most accounts, Edward Sr. is still very much in control of the operation. He is often described as a soft-spoken, unassuming man, a characterization that seems far removed from his public persona of a shrewd businessman and tough negotiator with a short fuse. Dubbed the "lord of discipline" because of his commitment to a rigorous daily routine that includes eating six

times a day and sleeping just four hours a night, the elder DeBartolo outworks people half his age (he's 79).
His 14-hour days begin at 5:30 A.M. when he arrives at
his office. He works seven days a week and has not had
one vacation in 40 years. Eddie often joins his father in
the pre-dawn hours at the company's work sites to
drink coffee out of styrofoam cups and discuss business. A close family friend says he's seen the elder Mr.
DeBartolo—an extremely shy and formal man—
without a necktie only twice, and one of those times he
was in a swimming pool.

It has been said that the future belongs to those who
correctly anticipate it, a concept in which the DeBartolos have clearly excelled. Edward Sr. accumulated his
fortune by being one of the first to build regional shopping malls just before the initial wave of suburban
development. The first, a 48,000-square-foot plaza that
opened in 1948, was seen as radical in design mostly for
its size, and was followed three years later by the 17-
store Boardman Plaza in Youngstown, the company's
first "major" center. Local real-estate experts proclaimed the development's life expectancy to be about
six months in the untested market, but today the half-
mile-long center thrives as a vital retail hub offering 50
stores to service the heart of an expanding community.

During the ensuing ten years, the corporation concentrated on the development of similar centers
throughout the Midwest, and by 1965 DeBartolo had
earned the reputation of "Plaza King" with more than
100 projects to his credit. The next year, Summit Mall
in Akron became the only fully enclosed regional center
in the state, heralding the beginning of a new retail era
for the firm as well as the country: the era of the covered, climate-controlled shopping center.

Accurately anticipating the trend of migration away
from downtown areas to the suburbs, DeBartolo
formulated an ambitious schedule for regional mall

development in the heart of new growth areas in Florida and the Midwest. This aggressive plan of expansion raised the company to the zenith of the shopping center industry in the 1970s, a position it has maintained for nearly 20 years. The flagship project for the dynamic company was Cleveland's Randall Park Mall, a 2.2-million-square-foot center that at its opening in 1976 was the world's largest shopping mall. With five anchor tenants and more than 200 retail shops, it became the premier shopping destination for the region.

By the 1980s, in-depth market research by the DeBartolo Corporation indicated that the population of Florida would triple by the end of the decade and that the entire Southeast would provide enormous potential for the firm. To exploit the emerging market, the primary development thrust of the company centered in the Sunshine State and included more than 20 centers and 25 million square feet of total leasable area. To service the needs of the changing demographics of the American public, the company incorporated several new features in its developments, including food courts to give patrons a convenient respite from the rigors of power shopping.

In addition to creating enormous wealth for the family, the DeBartolo Corporation has made millionaires of a number of top executives. Loyal employees are rewarded with percentage ownerships in its regional malls, and Edward Sr. once told Shopping Center World that every company-developed mall has returned at least $200,000 per percentage point of ownership. The price for such largesse is absolute loyalty and dedication to the integrity of the company, something three top executives failed to heed when they accepted a plumbing contractor's offer of a European vacation in exchange for some subcontracting work on a company project. They were immediately terminated.

The huge success of the company in real estate development naturally prompted diversification, first into professional sports ownership in the 1970s, then with equity investment in large retail firms via the stock market in the 1980s. Edward Sr.'s interest in professional sports began in the 1950s with an unsuccessful attempt to purchase the Cleveland Browns before they were sold to current owner Art Modell. He settled for the ownership of two racetracks in Cleveland, which turned out to be sensational investments: On one site, the DeBartolos built the highly successful Randall Park Mall, and the other is Thistledown, one of four DeBartolo-owned racetracks.

The family's first foray into major sports ownership was completed with the purchase of the Pittsburgh Penguins of the National Hockey League. For many years a struggling franchise, the Penguins seem poised to challenge the NHL's leaders in the 1990s after qualifying for the playoffs in 1989 for the first time since 1982.

In 1977, with a real estate empire expanding almost daily because of the inflation-assisted economy, the DeBartolo family made its second purchase of a major sports franchise with the acquisition of the San Francisco 49ers. At the time, the NFL team had been floundering, posting losing seasons three out of the previous four years with three different head coaches and losing money at the ticket window as well. The Morabito family—Jean and Josephine—was the principal owner, with Mieuli controlling a minority stake. The sale was further complicated by various estates, trusts and partnership agreements that had to be dealt with before the deal could be completed.

"It took an awful lot of negotiation," said Eddie, who was spearheading the discussions for his family, though he was barely 30 years old and less than 10 years out of Notre Dame University. "After many days of talks, always very above board and very pleasant—and, of course, we were flying back and forth from Youngstown—we finalized the deal. I can remember sitting on the plane and thinking what a phenomenal city San Francisco was and what a great opportunity this was going to be for us."

The decision was made for Eddie to assume ownership of the team, not, as was widely reported, so he would have something to do, but rather to keep the operation separate from the corporation's real estate holdings. The young entrepreneur had his own thoughts about the transaction. "I knew what was happening with sports, and with cable TV and everything else it was very exciting. I thought they (NFL franchises) were going to go up in value, but I never thought a team would be worth $100 million. I just didn't think—even if the team didn't perform up to par on the field—that there was any way you could lose your investment."

Eddie's detractors almost always insist that the purchase was made by the father for the son. And although it is easy to see that a 30-year-old without family money and influence probably could not have afforded an NFL team alone, it is hard to imagine that Edward Sr. would spend $16 million on a mere diversion for his son. It is, however, a notion that the young DeBartolo has tried to play down. Even today, as he's risen to the unofficial leadership of the group of insurgent NFL owners who challenged the establishment on the election of Jim Finks to succeed Pete Rozelle as commissioner, one senses the brashness of a young man attempting to stake his claim as a sports mogul in his own right.

Eddie graduated from Notre Dame in 1968 and joined the DeBartolo Corporation in an executive training program designed to give him experience in each of the firm's departments and, naturally, wind up with his ascension to the top position. He was appointed vice president in 1971, became executive vice president five years later and in 1979 was elevated to his current post of president and chief administrative officer, which carries responsibility for the company's 15,000 professionals worldwide.

Opinions vary as to the weight of his title. Some say the father still makes all the decisions; others insist they carry equal authority. "I don't think Ed Jr. is that much involved in the shopping center phase of the business," said Murray Shor, publisher of Shopping Center Digest. "Ed Sr. is still very much in control of the entire operation, and (senior vice president) Bill Moses is the number two man as far as shopping centers are concerned."

Paul Martha, a DeBartolo vice president in Pittsburgh who formerly was an assistant to Eddie with the 49ers, said most of the company decisions are made jointly by father and son. "But obviously the predominant figure as far as real estate and shopping centers are concerned is Mr. DeBartolo Sr.," he said. "Eddie concentrates on the sports and entertainment side of things." Which seems only natural considering the history of the company. But with the rapidly escalating value of professional sports franchises and the success Eddie has achieved in managing that segment of the business, it would not be hard to imagine a time when the two achieve near parity. This could certainly be true in terms of public exposure, although the real estate operations will most likely continue to be the dominant asset base of the corporation.

Whether Edward J. DeBartolo Jr. is as good a businessman as his namesake is not relevant to the matter of the San Francisco 49ers. What is, however, is that the diminutive Mr. D. has guided a team that was the poster child for mediocrity in the 1970s to the NFL's best record and an unprecedented three world championships in the 1980s. And even more important

—if you ask him—he is held in the highest esteem by those who really matter: his players and employees. No small feat considering the skill required to navigate the minefield of professional football.

"It was just great playing for Mr. DeBartolo," Fred Dean said. The All-Pro defensive end from Louisiana Tech came to the 49ers in a 1981 mid-season trade with the San Diego Chargers, who accepted a second-round draft choice for one of the NFL's legendary pass rushers. Coming to a team that had gone 2–14, 2–14 and 6–10 in the three previous seasons and leaving a club that had narrowly lost in overtime to the Miami Dolphins in the AFC championship game the year before, Dean wouldn't have been blamed for being a little miffed at the trade. But he describes the feeling as a breath of fresh air, and a rich, rewarding breath it turned out to be as he earned pro sports' greatest prize —a Super Bowl ring—twice in a little more than three years, while his former team missed the NFL playoffs entirely.

From the beginning, the task of rebuilding the 49ers proved great and at times must have seemed like the challenge of rebuilding Western Europe after World War II. "We didn't have good teams, and it was a tough situation with Monte Clark," Eddie recalls. "God, I was booed. I got hit with things in the stadium. I was spit on. It was a very tough few years. And there were times when I thought, 'This is crazy; who needs this? Is this really worth it?' But then you stop and say, 'Well let's try and get things together. Let's try and regroup, get the troops together, put the wagons in a circle and we'll see what we can do.' And you know, that's about the time I met Bill Walsh."

On January 9, 1979, Bill Walsh became the 49ers' sixth head coach in five years and the 11th overall. After a wide-ranging career that included stops as an assistant in Oakland, Cincinnati and San Diego in the pros, Walsh was the head coach at Stanford University from 1977 to '78 when Eddie DeBartolo decided Walsh was the man he wanted to lead his team into the 1980s. "We needed an entirely new attitude, a new look, a franchise cleaning," Eddie said.

"Joe Thomas (former 49ers general manager) did a tremendous amount of damage. He was a very good man, a nice man, but he just didn't know people," DeBartolo said. "Joe lived with the football, he was only pigskin. But everything is not pigskin. People did not mean a whole lot to Joe Thomas. Their feelings, their likes, their dislikes. He alienated a lot of people, especially the fans. It was not the way I operated, but I was in Youngstown and he was in San Francisco. I knew something had to be done. I don't think I had fired three people in my entire life, and it wasn't easy going out there to fire Joe Thomas, but it was something I had to do."

Eddie had been following Walsh's career, especially at Stanford, and decided to hire him after their one-on-one meeting at San Francisco's Fairmont Hotel. At first, the job was only head coach, but as Eddie's confidence in Bill grew and his performance improved, he was given more and more responsibility, becoming team president in 1981. "I just knew it," Eddie says about their first meeting. "And I think he knew it, too. I think we both knew after five or six minutes that it would be a good relationship."

The DeBartolos place enormous emphasis on the family. Edward Sr.—for all his criticism in the business arena—is a devoted husband and father who keeps the walls of his office filled with pictures of his children and grandchildren. When his only daughter, Marie Denise, went away to college, he wrote her every day. (She has grown up to be a vital part of the family enterprise, serving as, among other things, governor of the Pittsburgh Penguins.) Sadly, he lost his wife of many years in August 1987, and as a loving tribute to his mother, Eddie Jr. dedicated the 49ers' new, state-of-the-art headquarters and training center to her memory. One year after her passing, the Marie P. DeBartolo Sports Centre in Santa Clara became the official residence of the San Francisco 49ers.

"The new facility is just great," Joe Montana said. "It's another example of the stuff nobody writes about, but it makes a tremendous difference to the players. Eddie does things for the team to let us know he's behind us. For years we practiced in a facility where, if you were showering and somebody upstairs flushed a toilet, you got scalded. You'd have to yell "Warning!' before you flushed, so everybody could get out of the water. And our locker room was the size of a living room. That's just not what you picture for a winning professional team."

Eddie had a little different picture in mind.

Located approximately 40 miles south of Candlestick Park on an 11-acre site near the Great America amusement park, the complex exemplifies the DeBartolo touch of quality and is a standing reminder of Eddie's dedication to the organization and his high standards for the operation of the franchise. With the emphasis on an environment designed for maximum performance of all personnel, the facility blends the opulence of executive offices suitable for world champions with a ruggedly functional workout and training facility to best serve the physical nature of the sport. Two natural grass practice fields with underground drainage and watering systems allow for workouts in all Northern California weather conditions, and a third field has an artificial surface (Omniturf) that features an innovative fiber-and-sand design to minimize the possibility of player injury. The two-story, 52,000-square-foot building includes upstairs offices for coaches, administration, video operations, business operations, public relations, pro and college scouting and marketing/ promotions staff.

The ground floor contains a spacious dressing room area with 60 permanent lockers and space for additional lockers when the roster swells during minicamps. There's also a players lounge, a well-equipped weight room, a 30-by-40-foot hydro-therapy indoor swimming pool and, in an adjacent building, two racquetball courts and a full-size basketball court complete with glass backboards.

The new team headquarters is only the latest example of Eddie's dedication to running a first-class operation with a tradition of rewarding excellence. A hardworking, generous man who enjoys all aspects of his life from business to family, Mr. D. has a commitment to the 49ers that includes spending a good deal of his life in the DeBartolo Corp. jet flying between Ohio and California. He estimates that he makes more than 40 trips a year to San Francisco for games and related matters, not including the traveling he does as president of the multi-billion-dollar real estate empire.

Like his father, Eddie places great value on loyalty and dedication to duty. Unlike his father, Edward Jr. appears to enjoy the public spotlight and is very accessible, whether it's a player asking for advice on a business deal, a sportswriter's request for an interview or a request for an appearance from one of the charitable groups he regularly supports. Eddie takes a genuine interest in the lives of his players and their families and has a reputation for always being the first to send flowers in the event of a tragedy or a happy occasion. The same is true for the office staff, who receive regular bonuses and praise for good work and are especially rewarded during championship seasons, further demonstrating his belief that successful businesses are products of superior effort at all levels of the organization.

Several players have benefited from Eddie's patronage in their off-the-field endeavors even after their playing careers with the 49ers were concluded. Former standout linebacker Dan Bunz, a 10-year veteran after being drafted out of Long Beach State in 1978, sought Mr. D's advice on a restaurant venture he was considering as a post-football career path. "Mr. DeBartolo was a great help," Bunz recalls. "I told him what I was thinking of doing, and he told me to send him the plans. He said he'd run them by his real estate experts and give me his opinion on the viability of the restaurant. I was real inexperienced, and he didn't want me to get taken advantage of. He saved me a lot in terms of both money and grief in starting up."

Now, three years after his retirement from professional football, Dan Bunz is, among other things, the owner/proprietor of "Bunz and Company," a highly successful restaurant and sports bar in Roseville, California. It's not far from the 49ers' summer training camp at Sierra College in Rocklin—a Sacramento suburb—where Bunz has also been coaching linebackers during the school year.

Players and coaches alike speak highly of DeBartolo, who has been everything from big brother to banker.

Linebacker Keena Turner: "I haven't played for anybody else, but in talking to players from other teams who have come to San Francisco, this is the ideal situation. The thing about Mr. D. is he pays you well, but he does so many other things that he doesn't have to do, and those are the things that touch me. In a lot of places they don't. I've never wanted to play anywhere else." Linebacker Bill Romanowski: "The bottom line for Mr. D. is, he wants to win. He's spoiled in a good way. He wants to win and he'll pay the price for winning, and that's what it's all about."

Tony Razzano, 49ers director of scouting since 1979: "There's none better as far as I'm concerned. He's proven himself. He's like Bill Walsh. He's generous, charming, dedicated, real well-grounded. He knows all aspects of this business."

The DeBartolos' generous nature has also benefited several charitable organizations, including those involved with heart and cancer research, as well as the Italian Scholarship League and St. Jude's Children's Research Hospital, which was the beneficiary of a Christmas project in which the corporation's malls sold shopping bags featuring the artwork of singer Tony Bennett.

The family also has supported several political campaigns of both national and local scope, including failed bids by Democratic candidate John Glen—the Ohio senator's run for the presidency in 1984—and San Francisco mayoral candidate John Molinari. "There isn't any question that they have political influence, but it's behind the scenes and isn't very obvious to the casual observer," said Ann Przelomski, managing editor of the Youngstown Vindicator in the DeBartolo's hometown.

Former San Francisco Mayor Dianne Feinstein has also been a beneficiary of DeBartolo financial support. Eddie hosted her fund-raiser in 1988 to kick off her California gubernatorial campaign. His legendary concern for employees was even in evidence at that event as he worked the room. "It was a glittering evening, a big success for him," said Leigh Steinberg, a prominent Bay Area player agent. "But the first question he asked me when I chatted with him evinced his interest in how one of his players was doing off the field. I think his concept is, the team is a family. There's a real warmth and camaraderie."

Lest the impression be given that Eddie DeBartolo is some sort of cream puff who busies himself with peripheral aspects of his team's affairs, he has proved over the years that he can be a very tough negotiator, especially in issues vital to the 49ers' presentation to the public. In 1985, calling the stadium a pigsty, he

threatened to move the team out of Candlestick Park—
its home since moving from Kezar Stadium in Golden
Gate Park in 1971—unless the city agreed to spend
more than $30 million on renovations and construction
of revenue-generating luxury boxes. His argument was
so compelling, and he was taken so seriously, that he
was given everything he wanted and now exalts in his
achievement.

"It's a great football stadium," he said. "I know (Giants owner) Bob Lurie's having his problems, but the
city and the Recreation and Parks Department have
worked very well with us. The boxes are satisfactory—
we may add a few more, and some more seats as well—
but the lavatories and concession stands have been
improved and are continuing to be improved, and the
parking conditions are much better, too. It serves our
purposes and our needs extremely well."

So successful, in fact, were his efforts in securing stadium improvements that the following year the DeBartolos used the same tactic to obtain $11 million in reno-
vations to Pittsburgh Civic Arena for their Penguins
hockey team.

Perhaps the best measure of the man was exempli-
fied by his handling of the situation surrounding the
1987 players' strike. With labor relations between
league owners and the NFL Players Association reaching an impasse, the union members walked out just two
games into the regular season. The owners were left
with two unappealing choices: Cancel the regularly
scheduled games while the parties negotiated a
settlement—which would cost them millions in lost gate
receipts; or field replacement teams from open tryouts
of non-professionals willing to cross the picket lines.
Reluctantly opting for the latter, all 28 teams set their
coaching staffs to work at evaluating the recruiting talent from all corners of the country, though no one

really thought the season would be completed with replacement players.

The 49ers had begun the 1987 season with a loss to
Pittsburgh and a victory over Cincinnati. The stoppage
sent Walsh and his staff combing scouting reports and
personnel files for able bodies to fill the 45 roster spots
and be in uniform and ready to play football in just two
weeks. While the task was formidable, the 49ers were
more than up to the challenge. Walsh fielded a team
that won all three of its strike games—although they
weren't pretty—and when the regulars returned, they
found themselves with a 4-1 record and the lead in the
NFC's Western Division.

In fact, the replacement games proved to be of such
poor quality that the TV ratings dropped significantly
—70 percent in some markets—and prompted numerous jokes about the backgrounds of certain players. In
one of his television monologues, David Letterman
quipped, "The replacement quarterback for the Jets
will not be able to play in this Sunday's NFL game—he
couldn't get the time off work."

No other single event in the 13-year history of
Eddie's ownership was more bitter in terms of dividing
his team than the 1987 strike.

The NFLPA tried desperately to close ranks on the
owners and present a united front during the walkout,
but many players grew weary of the diatribe and lack of
progress. A group of 11 49ers led by Montana, Roger
Craig and Dwight Clark came back to camp after only
two weeks, but Walsh encouraged them to stay out one
more week in hopes of settling the dispute. It was
widely reported, however, by local newspapers that the
group of 11 had been promised special bonuses for
their loyalty. The issue of the bonuses would be a
source of great controversy for the owner and place
him in the national spotlight for yet another time.

Although Eddie initially denied the offer had been

made, when the strike ended the following week and the rest of the players returned, it was learned that he had decided to reward the whole team with year-end bonuses. In effect, DeBartolo offered to match the league bonuses given to players whose teams qualify for the playoffs: $6,000 per player for wild-card teams and $10,000 for division champions. The move, which was meant to be a unifying gesture between management and labor, unfortunately would be considered an offer of incentive payments to win games, something specifically prohibited by NFL rules. Once the secret bonus plan was revealed to the rest of the league, the other owners acted swiftly to condemn Eddie and demand the league take action to punish him.

At first, every attempt was made to keep the payments confidential. But a copy of the letter Eddie sent to his players outlining the bonus plan was obtained by a local newspaper. While it was apparent that the owner was motivated by genuine concern for his players, it was an incriminating document to say the least.

October 22, 1987

Dear (Player),

To promote the most positive possible atmosphere in our organization, and to provide further incentive towards the success all of us look to achieve, I now commit the San Francisco Forty Niners to a double share for the first Playoff game. (This would be Wild Card or Divisional.) At this writing, $6,000.00 for a Wild Card; $10,000.00 for a Divisional. This will be accomplished by adding a clause to your contract for the 1987 season.

Best of luck for the remainder of the year.

Edward J. DeBartolo Jr.

While the debate over the bonuses swirled through the league, Eddie at first insisted he had sought league permission to make the payments, then later said he had misunderstood the rule. It was later determined that a front-office employee had incorrectly informed the owner that the bonuses were legal. "It was a miscommunication between our people and the league office," DeBartolo said. "As owner, I assume full responsibility for the error. But if I had known that it was unequivocably against league policy, I never would have done it."

In spite of his denials, however, to most people close to the team it seemed entirely within character for Eddie to support his players in this manner. "I don't think I did anything wrong," he said. "My team was divided on account of the strike, and I thought this was to pull all of them together. Let them work toward a common goal by giving them a bonus. It had nothing to do with getting home-field advantage in the playoffs or anything like that. It was just a way to avoid trouble on our team."

If the bonus plan was meant to avoid trouble on the team, it certainly caused trouble with the league. NFL Commissioner Pete Rozelle ruled the bonuses a violation but allowed the players to keep them and levied a $50,000 fine—the maximum amount allowable under league bylaws—against Eddie instead. But in a gesture befitting the popularity of the owner, the players voted unanimously to pay his fine themselves.

"It's more than just money with Eddie," linebacker Riki Ellison said about the incident. "Everybody says he's a player's owner because he pays us more money than the other teams do, but that's not why he's so popular. It's because he's so genuine. Players respect a man who treats them like men, not property. The bonuses were helpful—we all lost a lot of money during the strike—but it was really because he stuck his neck out for us. We paid the fine because we respect what he tried to do for the players. That's Eddie, and that's why I respect him so much."

With the cat out of the bag—so to speak—Eddie came clean on the whole affair and confided to a local sportswriter: "I've never been opposed to taking care of my players and coaches (monetarily). There's always ways around the rules. You know me—I like to win. I'm not a little angel sitting here in Youngstown, Ohio. I like to reward success. I appreciate good performances from my players and coaches."

The 49ers finished the 1987 regular season with the NFL's best record (13–2) and entered the playoffs with a full head of steam. But a stunning 36–24 loss to the Minnesota Vikings in front of a disbelieving Candlestick Park crowd was their third straight first-round playoff loss since winning Super Bowl XIX, and Eddie DeBartolo was not a happy man. Although the 49ers had an overall record of 33–16–1—including the three playoff losses—for a .670 winning percentage from 1985 through the 1987 season, and many teams would have been thrilled with that record, Eddie had set such high standards for success that nothing short of another Super Bowl appearance would suffice.

Maybe it was the agony of the strike and the controversy of the bonuses, or maybe it was the third straight playoff loss, or maybe it really was the need to "streamline" the operation of the club; but whatever the reason, less than 90 days after the loss to the Vikings, Eddie removed Walsh as club president and assumed the title himself. Although both men confirmed the move was to take away from Walsh the pressure of performing two jobs, a reliable account of the incident may have been provided by a front-office source who said: "I think what happened is that Eddie offered Bill a new two-year contract, which amounted to only a one-year extension of his existing contract. And although it was for more money, Walsh was insulted he didn't get a multi-year offer. At that point, Bill told Eddie, 'If that's all the confidence you have in me, you be president.'"

To those who know Bill Walsh, it seemed out of character for him to give up the presidency of the 49ers voluntarily and accept such a minimal contract improvement. More likely, the change was a precursor of Walsh's departure in 1989, first to the front office, then to the NBC broadcast booth. "This has been building for some time," said a source close to the team. "After a loss, you have no idea how hard Eddie comes down on Bill. It's very, very hard."

The playoff loss to the Vikings took a heavy toll on the Team of the Decade. Joe Montana found himself in the middle of a painful quarterback controversy after Walsh pulled him in the third quarter of the game in favor of Steve Young. And the off-season trade rumors made Montana feel unwanted even after the sensational regular season he had completed. Walsh was so devastated by the loss that he disappeared for nearly 30 days while rumors circulated about a feud with Eddie.

"We didn't talk much for up to two months after the game," Walsh said. "But he went his way and I went mine trying to just recoup. We knew the other person was there and we were functioning normally. But that game was a real shocker, less so to me than it was to Eddie. Being a coach for so many years and knowing the dynamics of the game, I understand a frustrating loss whereas Eddie just did not. It was difficult because we had played so well during a very distracting season, and Eddie really has a thing about winning. That was a very difficult time for me."

Although it seemed to some that Eddie was playing the heavy, Walsh was quick to defuse any suggestion of conflict between them. On the decision to relieve him of the title of team president, Walsh said: "I asked for this change. I had to decide between being an administrator and coach, or just a coach. I've been stretched too thin."

DeBartolo called Walsh the "best coach in the league," and said, "I want to make sure he has the ability to concentrate on that job." Eddie also was paying Walsh like the best coach in the league, with a $1.3-million-a-year salary.

Later, Walsh reflected on his relationship with the 1980s' most successful owner and credited DeBartolo with patience and support that most executives would not have exhibited under such circumstances. "He supported me in the toughest times—1979, 1980 and 1982," Walsh said. "Coaches are often given only two years to produce, and that's just unrealistic. We had an awful first year (2–14), although people who knew football knew we'd improve. Eddie was most supportive during that eight-game losing streak in 1980, then again in 1982 when I almost quit. Obviously he's been supportive throughout. He was frustrated after the Minnesota loss and about the team not making it past the first round of the playoffs for three straight years. We didn't take it out on each other, but we were both very frustrated. Then we broke through."

The breakthrough, of course, was the 1988 season and Super Bowl XXIII.

By far, the best of times for Eddie DeBartolo are his team's appearances in Super Bowls. Although he insists that as owner he never really relaxes enough to fully enjoy them, it is very clear that he is right at home in the environment of championship professional football. "It's pretty tough for me to entertain and be Mr. Congeniality when my team's out on the field," he said, and it is easy to believe him. "I can't just socialize or talk business on a Sunday afternoon, and I've never done it at the Super Bowl. I stay clear of everybody."

Super Bowl XXIII in Miami's Joe Robbie Stadium was typical of the spectrum of emotions Eddie travels when his team is on the field. "It was a real roller coaster ride for me. That final drive was just amazing," he said, recalling the 92-yard scoring drive Montana led the team on in the final three minutes. "It's the type of situation my franchise has thrived on throughout the '80s. And if I wasn't so emotionally involved in the game, maybe I would have just sat down and said, 'Boy, this really ought to be interesting. Let's just sit back and watch this surgeon go to work.' But that's not exactly what went through my mind at the time."

In spite of his statements to the contrary, Eddie DeBartolo is actually a very gracious and prophetic host. In the 1988 pre-season he took his team to London to play the Miami Dolphins in the annual American Bowl at Wembley Stadium. According to several players who made the trip, Eddie put on quite a spread, hosting some of the best parties they had seen. Former All-Pro center Randy Cross recalled the trip: "It was an incredible time. Eddie pulled out all the stops. I'm not saying that Joe Robbie is cheap or anything, but more than one Dolphin asked me if he could trade teams while we were there. Everyone wanted to be a 49er and go to Eddie's parties."

"But we lost the game," Eddie said in mock seriousness. "I know it was only a pre-season game, but I like to win them all. Seriously though, I thought it would be a great experience for the players, and it was. I think every single one of them enjoyed themselves, and that was important to me."

The London game must have been good for the team because it ended up winning 13 games that counted that season, including Super Bowl XXIII the following January. Curiously, the Niners repeated their belated thank you to DeBartolo in 1989. The owner took them to Tokyo in the preseason for an exhibition against the Los Angeles Rams. Once again, the 49ers lost the game. Once again, however, they also went on to win the Super Bowl.

In the wake of the retirement of NFL Commissioner Pete Rozelle after nearly 30 years of service, Eddie DeBartolo served notice to the rest of the league of his own arrival. During Rozelle's tenure, the commissioner saw the NFL come out from the shadows of the nation's pastime—Major League Baseball—to become the world's greatest sports enterprise. But, over the issue of Rozelle's replacement, two notable factions emerged among the league's owners. Loosely called the Old Guard and the New Guard, the two groups settled into opposing camps over the process for selecting a new commissioner.

In his surprise retirement announcement at the annual league meetings in March 1989, Rozelle agreed to stay on until a successor was chosen and was integrated into the operation of the NFL. Almost immediately a search committee was formed to choose the next commissioner. The result was a recommendation to the entire league that Jim Finks, president and general manager of the New Orleans Saints, be hired for the post.

Eddie DeBartolo, speaking for the New Guard, took exception to the way the search was handled and the fact that the league was presented with only one choice. "Jim Finks is a high-grade terrific guy," he said. "We just didn't like the selection process. It's one thing to vote a candidate. It's another thing to have a done deal."

Finks failed to get the votes needed for confirmation, and the six-man search committee, which initially was headed by owners Wellington Mara of the New York Giants and Lamar Hunt of the Kansas City Chiefs, was amended to include New Guard owners Pat Bowlen of Denver, Jerry Jones of Dallas and Ken Behring of Seattle. The selection process eventually resulted in the hiring of former NFL antitrust attorney Paul Tagliabue as Rozelle's successor.

The fact that Eddie took the lead on the issue of the new commissioner in direct opposition to the Old Guard of owners came as no surprise to anyone who had been following professional football. His opposition to the rubber-stamping of Finks was the strongest indication of his emergence as a powerful force in the NFL hierarchy after a 13-year struggle to create his own identity.

Once the spoiled little rich kid, Eddie has proven himself a capable and effective manager of a multi-million-dollar business. He has inhabited both the basement and the penthouse of the National Football League. He has lived through the boos and the cheers and has survived two labor strikes, five coaches and countless hundreds of thousands of miles of travel. And through it all, he gives the distinct impression that he wouldn't trade one minute of it for anything else on this earth.

Recently, he was asked to comment on an article in a national sports magazine regarding the current value of the 28 NFL franchises. The writer estimated the San Francisco 49ers were the league's most valuable at around $120 million. He answered without hesitation.

"I think the city of San Francisco has a certain magic, a mystique," he began. "Whether it's the culture or the restaurants or the landscape, I'm not sure. You can hear Chicago: great city; you can hear Boston: great city; you can hear New York: great city; you can hear Los Angeles: great city. But when you hear San Francisco, there's something about the name and what it stands for that is different than the others. It's special.

"I think the success of the franchise in the '80s has had a lot to do with the valuation. Winning organizations are always more valuable than others. And I certainly intend to keep the franchise as perennially competitive as I very possibly can as long as I am the owner. And you know, that probably has a lot to do with it."

Chapter 11

LIFE AFTER WALSH
The Fourth Championship

"After I took the job, somebody told me, 'If you win, it's going to be Bill Walsh's team, but if you lose, it's going to be your team.' I said, 'In that case, I hope to hell it's Bill Walsh's team.'"
—George Seifert

*F*rom high above the synthetic playing surface in the Superdome, Bill Walsh, the man who first gathered and programmed these players like they were chips for a state-of-the-art Silicon Valley computer, watched in amazement. The 49ers, once *his* 49ers, were well on their way to their fourth NFL championship of the 1980s, a 55–10 thrashing of the Denver Broncos in Super Bowl XXIV in New Orleans. Walsh had witnessed three other San Francisco title victories, but this was the first opportunity he had to view the team in a championship game without a set of headphones, without a script of plays, without Xs and Os flowing into and out of his mind. Without worry.

"I was sitting in Eddie DeBartolo's box, just marveling at the team's execution," Walsh recalls. "It was beautiful to watch and to just be able to sit back and

217

enjoy it as a spectator. I came to realize what a mechanism this team can be when it's in sync.

"I know what George was thinking, because when you're a coach, you're always wondering what could go wrong. But people like me who were watching could tell that wasn't going to happen. I think the score was 20–3 and Eddie turns to me and says, 'You think we can hold on?' I said, 'Eddie, we're going to score 50.' You could see the way things were developing. Just amazing. It's no wonder the team has been able to accomplish so much in recent years.' "

The ease with which the 49ers won their fourth set of Super Bowl rings in January was not a complete surprise, as oddsmakers had them favored by as much as two touchdowns. But six months earlier the championship wasn't necessarily a sure bet. Successfully defending a crown in any sport is difficult, and no NFL team had won consecutive Super Bowls since the Pittsburgh Steelers of 1978 and 1979. In fact, of the next eight Super Bowl winners, four missed the playoffs the following season and three lost in the first round. Only Washington, winner of Super Bowl XVII in January 1983, reached the championship game the following season. But the Redskins were blown out by the Roving City Raiders (then of Los Angeles) 38–9.

There was this little matter of the 49ers' organization adjusting to life without Walsh—who may not always have endeared himself to his players, but there is no doubt that he squeezed the most production possible out of each. Nobody, especially Seifert, knew how the team would react without Walsh's intimidating presence on the field. Nobody, especially owner Edward DeBartolo, Jr., knew for certain that Seifert and vice-president and general manager John McVay had the foresight and shrewdness to maintain the level of excellence in the front office and, by extension, the team's roster.

The latter area of uncertainty loomed larger,

because Walsh's departure from the organization to the broadcast booth was sudden and came less than two weeks before the start of training camp. No longer would he be orchestrating the trades; no longer would he be pulling the strings on draft day. And no longer was there the prospect of him sitting down the hall from Seifert, just in case the new head coach was perplexed as to how to attack a certain defense.

As Seifert remarked after learning of Walsh's resignation as executive vice-president of the team, "All hell broke loose a little sooner than I expected."

But hell soon turned into another football utopia. Oh, there were problems at the outset of 1989, as there are in any season: injuries, contract holdouts, even personality conflicts between Seifert and disgruntled cornerback Tim McKyer. There was the unexpected retirement of starting tight end John Frank, the midseason, career-ending injury to strong safety Jeff Fuller, the lineup shuffling on the offensive line (where familiarity and timing between players is essential) and the adjustment to three new assistant coaches and three others working in new positions.

The results were staggering. The Niners went 14–2 in the regular season, as Seifert won more games than any rookie coach in NFL history. The only losses came in week four to the Los Angeles Rams by one point (13–12)—the decisive field goal arriving with two seconds remaining—and in week 11 to the Green Bay Packers by four points (21–17). But the playoffs made San Francisco's regular-season showing appear trivial. The Niners dismantled post-season opponents Minnesota (41–13), Los Angeles (30–3) and Denver (55–10) by a composite score of 126–26. Overall, they won 17 of 19 games, including their final eight of the year and the last five by a combined score of 173–36.

Seifert didn't merely disprove the theory that Walsh's departure would signal the end of the team's reign; he smothered it. He *improved* the Niners, if that's possible. Offensive coordinator Mike Holmgren, elevated from quarterback coach, actually *improved* the play of quarterback Joe Montana by eliminating certain pass routes from the offense and helping the All-Pro cut down on his interceptions. And this all was done while Bill Walsh sat in various press boxes around the country. So much for the shortsighted predictions of such doomsayers as *San Francisco Chronicle* columnist Glenn Dickey, who shortly after Walsh's resignation began a story, "The departure of Bill Walsh means the end of the 49ers' dynasty."

Success came so quickly that Seifert never really had a chance to put things in perspective, and he prefers not to until after his coaching days are over. Why focus on the past, he says, when training camp is just six months into the future? Typically, his post-championship celebration was brief and low key. He spent a week in Mexico with his family, sunning and fishing for marlin, then returned to prepare for the draft in April.

For those who believe winning a league title lessened the weight on Seifert's shoulders, think again. Perhaps he has proven himself as a head coach and erased the memory of those two horrible seasons in his first top job at Cornell in 1975 and 1976. But Seifert says winning the Super Bowl in his first season—making him only the second coach to do so, after Baltimore's Don McCafferty in 1970—will only raise the expectation level. The weight has not been removed; it has only become larger.

"Now there are the questions of whether or not I'm a flash in the pan," he says. "People think a heck of a lot about the talent level of this club. There are real high expectations and reasons for me to feel anxiety."

Because of the Niners' talent level, the presence of a magical quarterback and the free spending by the owner, some had difficulty gauging after a 17-win season whether Seifert's direction was overrated or under-rated. It is a situation similar to that of Los Angeles Lakers head coach Pat Riley, who inherited a championship-caliber team and Earvin "Magic" Johnson, another magical player, at point guard, pro basketball's equivalent to a quarterback. But 49ers assistant coach Lynn Stiles may have put it best when he said, "You can't minimize what he did for this football team. Yes, he inherited a lot of talent. But he inherited a lot of problems, too."

The initial problem, or at least potential problem, was complacency. Many players were happy to see Walsh and his mind games leave and the down-to-earth Seifert promoted. But at least one veteran wondered as early as mini-camp in May, before the team even played a minute under Seifert, whether the change would be for the best. The player, speaking on the condition of anonymity, told the *San Jose Mercury News* he was "worried," explaining that Seifert "doesn't keep you on edge in meetings the way Bill Walsh did. And I think we need to be kept on edge. Things are definitely looser."

There also was a flurry of Walsh-bashing by some of the players during training camp, when Seifert would have preferred they spend more time digesting the playbook.

Montana remarked that Seifert's arrival was like "rolling down the window for a breath of fresh air."

Guard Bruce Collie referred to Walsh's "dark side" and called him "Darth Vadar."

Tackle Bubba Paris said, "It feels like I've got 200 pounds of genius off of my back."

Guard Guy McIntyre cracked, "Bill Walsh was the master of disguises. George Seifert is the master of being George Seifert."

Safety Ronnie Lott said, "The reason I was 'washed up' last year was because somebody with white hair thought I was too old."

It continued as the season progressed. Even at the Super Bowl, tackle Harris Barton said, "The guys have always felt we were here because of the talent level. The guys have always felt we were here because of Joe Montana. There would have been some rebelling against Bill. The change was good. Guys wanted to prove that it's not a one-man team."

Even linebacker Matt Millen, who didn't arrive until long after Walsh departed, felt he had gained the perspective to remark, "George has done a great job of letting the players play, and he's knocked off all of that stuff that surrounded Bill here. I do see a huge ego from Walsh. I don't see it when I look at Seifert."

My. Imagine the verbal bashing Walsh would have received had he not turned around a losing franchise, won three Super Bowls, revolutionized the game and possibly established himself as the greatest coach in NFL history. Walsh publicly shrugged off the remarks and attributed them to the players "bonding with a new coach." But team insiders say he was hurt and had hoped to leave the organization on better terms.

Seifert was merely hoping that his players could channel some of their emotion onto the football field and avoid the typical post-championship blues. Injuries and bounces were out of his control, but some potential key factors in the 49ers' success weren't. Most important, there was the question of attitude and motivation. Teams tend to return from championship seasons a little too satisfied to put themselves in a position to repeat. In effect, a group of overachievers becomes a group of underachievers. Although there were other factors, this no doubt contributed to the 49ers' two previous post-title seasons. After overachieving with a young and inexperienced team to win Super Bowl XVI, the Niners slipped to 3–6 in the strike-shortened 1982 season, missing the playoffs. After the dominating 1984 championship season, the Niners opened 1985 by losing four of their first seven games, finished 10–6 and were bumped from the playoffs in the first round by the New York Giants, 17–3.

Although hindsight tells us that the opposite probably was true, the switch from Walsh to Seifert seemed only to increase the possibility that the Niners would let down again in 1989. If innovation and foresight were Walsh's greatest assets as a head coach, motivation wasn't far behind. Personal pride was one reason players played hard for him, but fear was another. Walsh had a knack for getting the most out of players, sometimes "scaring" them into high gear by his mere presence. And Seifert? As a defensive coordinator, he sometimes screamed on the field or behind closed doors at his players, but it hardly was a habit of his, and, unlike Walsh, he didn't play mind games.

Almost predictably, a few players remarked during the early days of training camp that the atmosphere seemed more "relaxed" in practice. Alarms went off in Seifert's head. "The last thing I wanted to hear was that things were relaxed," he said. "But before I said anything to the players, I decided to evaluate things. I looked around and saw we were practicing hard. We weren't lackluster. That's all I'm concerned about. How they do on the football field and how they perform on game day. There's plenty of time for stress."

Seifert didn't feel it was necessary to "scare" the Niners into winning another title. He didn't change his personality a bit. "Everybody is their own guy," McPherson said. "There was an aura about Bill Walsh, but George didn't have to be Bill Walsh. He learned a lot from him, as we all did. George had ways to get the most out of players, different from Bill's ways. He really opened up the lines of communication, made himself a lot more available."

Says Seifert, "We have a lot of communication between players and coaches. We try to give them a feel for what's going on in our minds and allow them to think like coaches on the field."

Convinced he had done all he could for his players' psyches, Seifert quickly doused a few other potential problems:

1. He announced Joe Montana was his starting quarterback and did so without leaving open the possibility that Steve Young could beat him out for the job. This may sound obvious, given that Montana was coming off of another phenomenal season and Super Bowl, but it was a string of words Walsh never uttered the previous season.

2. Seifert also stopped hounding Paris about his immense girth. The offensive tackle, who has been known to top 350 pounds, was lampooned often by Walsh, and it created a season-long soap opera titled "The Bubba Watch." Seifert hardly turned Paris loose on the Bay Area's buffet lines, but he decided that an overweight but talented Paris could give the team two strong quarters before tiring. This decision was a major factor that led to the Niners' unique rotation on the offensive line.

3. With his expertise in defense, Seifert pretty much allowed offensive coordinator Mike Holmgren to run the offense from the start of the practice season. As the year progressed, Seifert felt more comfortable giving his input, making changes and calling plays. The two also decided to trim the 25-play pre-game script made famous by Walsh to 15 plays. Holmgren so impressed others with his play-calling abilities that he was wooed for two head-coaching jobs after the season by Phoenix and the New York Jets.

The pre-season wasn't a thoroughly enjoyable experience for Seifert. Starting linebacker Riki Ellison suffered a broken right forearm, four of the team's Plan B signees (linebacker Chris Washington, guard Terry Tausch, tight end Jamie Williams and wide receiver

Mike Sherrard) went on the injured list with various ailments, and there were a dozen players who missed
chunks of training camp because of contract problems,
including Michael Carter, Jeff Fuller, Charles Haley,
Kevin Fagan, Steve Wallace, Don Griffin, Tim McKyer,
Guy McIntyre and Larry Roberts.

Things settled down somewhat as the Niners
approached their season opener in Indianapolis, but
Seifert's stomach remained in knots.

"I'm always excited before a game, but there are two
in particular that have stood out in my career," he
recalls. "The first one was in my first year with the
49ers in 1980. We were getting ready to play an exhibition game against the Oakland Raiders. I remember the
rush of adrenalin I had before that game was incredible. It was like we were playing for the world championship. I had a similar rush going into Indianapolis. It got
so bad that my mouth was actually dry. You know, my
tongue sticking to the roof of my mouth. I didn't have
any trouble sleeping the night before, but that's typical.
That's my escape. I sleep well, but sometimes I have bad
dreams about the game the next day."

Some of Seifert's nightmares were realized in the
Hoosier Dome, but San Francisco escaped with a win.
The Niners seemed on their way to an easy win with a
23–10 lead in the fourth quarter, but a 1-yard sneak by
Colts quarterback Chris Chandler capped a nine-play
touchdown drive that made it 23–17. The Colts pressured Montana on the Niners' ensuing possession, but
on a third-and-long play from his own 42 and facing
the blitz, Montana found Jerry Rice on a crossing pattern and the wide receiver ran all the way for a 58-yard
touchdown play. Indy closed to within six points again,
30–24, when Albert Bentley recovered a blocked punt
in the end zone, but the play came with only 1:18 left
and the rally ended there.

It wasn't a dominating 49ers team that opened the

season, but, really, there were few games during the regular season where they tore opponents apart. "We were a good team, but we weren't as great as people thought," recalls free safety Ronnie Lott, one of only five players to participate in all four of the team's Super Bowls. "It wasn't until the playoffs that we really became a dominating force. Really, you look at some of our games, and we were playing teams that just didn't play that well. We could've blown some teams out in the first or second quarter."

Some teams are content with just getting a victory. When a team wins four Super Bowls in a decade, standards become a little higher. Post-games begin something like, "Yeah, we won, but . . ."

"I think that's why I still feel a lot of anxiety," Seifert says. "I'm coming off a season knowing that some of our wins could have been losses. When you're a head coach and you're specific and you pay attention to detail, you realize how much can go wrong, no matter how many people think how great you are."

Seifert mentions the Tampa Bay game in week two as a near-loss and, indeed, the 49ers' offense against the Buccaneers struggled early and often. Facing a team that hadn't posted a winning record the previous six seasons (and would go only 5–11 in 1989), San Francisco became engaged in a humdrum battle of field goals for most of the afternoon until Montana pulled out a 20–16 win with a 4-yard keeper with all of 40 seconds left in the game.

The 2–0 record looked nice in the morning paper, but Seifert and the coaching staff watched some rather ugly footage in film sessions in the ensuing days. The offensive line, which suffered in the pre-season from injuries and inadequacies and allowed the Colts three sacks in the opener, was a confused mess against Tampa Bay. Montana was dropped four times, pressured often and threw two interceptions, negating his

25-of-39 passing ratio and 266 yards. The real problems came on the ground. Roger Craig, who ran for a career-high 1,502 yards the previous year and opened 1990 with a 131-yard day, was held to 36 yards on 16 carries by the Bucs' defense. It was the first sign of what would be an up-and-down season for Craig. He ran for only 18 yards on eight carries in week three against Philadelphia and didn't have another 100-yard day until the 45–3 massacre of Atlanta in game 10.

After successful games, it is typical of Craig and most running backs to lay credit on the offensive line. It follows that the running game's problems for much of the season was the fault of the line. Guard Guy McIntyre and tackle Steve Wallace both missed valuable time in training camp with contract problems. Guard Terry Tausch, signed as a free agent, missed the first seven games of the season with an ankle injury. Bubba Paris often became winded due to his excess weight, and guard Bruce Collie was inconsistent. Perhaps the most solid performer from day one was Jesse Sapolu, who shifted from guard to center after the retirement of Randy Cross.

There also was the Jeff Bregel affair. A touted draft pick out of Southern Cal in 1987, Bregel suffered through an injury-plagued rookie season, playing in only five games, and failed to crack the starting lineup in 1988. Nonetheless, with Sapolu moving over to replace Cross, Bregel was expected to establish himself as a starting guard in '89. His reign was brief. Bregel, bothered occasionally by back spasms, started the first three weeks but was replaced in all three games by McIntyre due to poor play. When it became apparent after the Philadelphia game that offensive line coach Bobb McKittrick was pulling Bregel from the lineup, the player fumed, walked out of camp and was suspended by the team. Bregel eventually returned, but his playing days, at least for the season, were over, as he spent the rest of the year on injured reserve with a painful back and a bashed ego.

Such a compilation of problems to an offensive line usually spells trouble. In no other area of the team is each man required to be so familiar with the player standing next to him. Consequently, starters usually play the entire game and reserves are often relegated to special teams. But McKittrick and Seifert decided the only way to take advantage of the plusses of each of their linemen and negate the negatives was with a rotation system, foreign to the NFL. From mid-season, left tackle Paris played the first and third quarters and was relieved by Steve Wallace in the second and fourth. Right guard Collie played the first and third quarters and was replaced by Tausch. Left guard McIntyre, center Sapolu and right tackle Harris Barton played throughout.

The shuttle system made sense, McKittrick reasoned, because, "We don't have any players who we would consider to be the best. Otherwise, they would play the whole game. It was best for our situation."

Perhaps, but it wasn't best for the psyches of the players. Wallace, who lost his starting job to Paris, says the shuttle system "could be the start of a new trend in the league, but I don't want to be a part of that trend. I want to be a starter and I want to stay in there." Barton, who has the luxury of playing four quarters, nonetheless says, "It's tough for a tackle to go out there and play next to two different guards every game. It takes time to adjust because everyone does something different."

It's a little-known fact that minor adjustments were made to the shuttle system to conform to the players' financial interests. The substitutions come at the end of each quarter, even if the Niners are in the middle of a possession, unless they are close to the opponent's goal line. Collie explains: "We don't want to botch anybody's bonuses. We decided the most fair way to do this was right after each quarter because we all have playing-time incentives in our contracts."

If money is a constant concern for professional ath-letes, there is no greater joy than unplanned income: that of playoff revenue. For that, the Niners' linemen again could thank Joe Montana. After two close victo-ries, the Niners again tempted defeat against the Eagles. They trailed 18–10 through three quarters, and Montana had spent much of the afternoon in the hori-zontal position under part-human Philadelphia pass rushers. But then came the single best performance by any individual in a quarter in 1990.

In the final period, Montana threw four touchdown passes and completed 11 of 12 passes for 227 yards. There was a 7-yarder to John Taylor less than two minutes into the quarter, then a four-minute span late in the game that saw him throw scoring strikes to full-back Tom Rathman (8 yards), tight end Brent Jones (24 yards) and wide receiver Jerry Rice (33 yards). By the time the game had ended, Montana, despite being sacked eight times, threw for 428 yards, the third high-est total in club history.

In the locker room, Montana, typically, couldn't understand why people were making such a big deal about his dismantling of one of the league's most renowned defenses. "A quarterback relishes being in these situations," he said. Perhaps. But Sapolu, one of Montana's guard dogs, had the more appropriate remark when he said, "This guy laughs in the face of defeat."

Having won three straight road games in a year that would see them go unbeaten away from home, the Niners returned to Candlestick Park to play the NFC-West-rival Los Angeles Rams, who, with the develop-ment of quarterback Jim Everett and strong, recent drafts, were tabbed by some to dethrone San Francisco as division champions. The game was typical of the long-standing series: close. Atypically, neither Montana nor Everett was the game's star, rather kickers Mike Cofer of San Francisco and Mike Lansford of Los Angeles. Cofer kicked four field goals. Lansford had only two, but the biggest of the game—a 26-yarder with 2 seconds left to give the Rams a 13–12 win.

A 3–1 record with a one-point loss may not seem like much to be concerned about, but Seifert considers this to be a key time of the season. The three wins could have gone either way; the L.A. defense had held Montana without a touchdown; and another tough division opponent, New Orleans, was coming up in game five. "If we had lost two straight division games, there is no telling what would have happened the rest of the season," says Seifert. "I'm not saying we would have fallen apart. But the way the Rams were going, we might not have been able to get back to the top again."

Team Cardiac struck again in the Superdome. This time, the Niners found themselves down 17–3 in the third quarter. Once again, the running game was stagnant and the secondary had been dented for two touchdown passes by Bobby Hebert. But Montana, who hadn't thrown a touchdown pass in the six quarters since that magical fourth period in Philadelphia, resumed displaying the talents that lead passing-game guru Sid Gillman to call him "the Van Gogh of quarterbacks." He threw a 60-yard touchdown pass to Jerry Rice, then came back with a 21-yard scoring pass to John Taylor to tie the score 10 seconds into the final quarter. The Saints retook the lead on a Morten Andersen field goal, but less than three minutes later, Montana came back with another touchdown pass to Taylor to give San Francisco a 24–20 lead.

Victory was in doubt when the Saints were driving for the apparent winning score in the final minutes. But Eric Wright, whose knockdown of a Dan Marino pass for a potential touchdown in Super Bowl XIX remains one of the team's highlights of the decade, performed a similar feat to save this game. He swatted away Hebert's pass before it reached receiver Brett Perrimen's hands at the goal line, preserving the narrow win.

The season could have taken a turn for the worse in New Orleans, but not just on the scoreboard. Montana injured his elbow late in the game, and it forced him to miss the final series and the following week's contest at Dallas. So, enter Steve Young, whose duties in the first five weeks had been limited to signaling in plays. In a sense, perhaps no player felt worst about Walsh leaving than Young. Walsh may have let the quarterback debate fester longer than expected, but, from Young's point of view, at least it gave him a glimmer of hope that he could slip ahead of Montana on the depth chart.

Young started against the Cowboys and the Niners won easily, 31–14. Before the season was over, he started two other games for the injured Montana, against the New York Jets and against the Buffalo Bills —two other victories—and saw backup duty in nine games. But Young, despite having more playing time than the previous season, was no less frustrated. By the year 1989, Young, who arrived from Tampa Bay two years earlier, had expected to be the starting quarterback. Instead, Montana had one of his greatest seasons ever, was unstoppable in the playoffs and let it be known that he planned on fulfilling the three remaining years of his contract.

Young considered asking the team to trade him. Vice-president John McVay was concerned enough about Young's desires that he spoke to the Dallas Cowboys about acquiring Steve Walsh, but after much thought after the season, Young decided to stay. Seifert says he "wants to be a 49er." At least going into 1990, he wanted that a little more than a starting job, which he could have at any of half the teams in the NFL.

"I've put my investment in time here and it hasn't

worked out like I hoped," Young remarked Super Bowl week. "But if everyone turned back when things weren't looking good, you'd miss half the great opportunities in life. I'm willing to play this one out, as long as there's communication and I stay informed. I'm under the impression that if I keep working hard and preparing, I'll get the chance sometime. This time last year it was supposed to be real close between Joe and me, but he's played spectacularly and left me holding the bag."

The way Montana played down the stretch of the season, he might have left Johnny Unitas, Roger Staubach and Otto Graham holding the bag. His quarterback rating of 112.4 set a record. Few people actually know how to compute a quarterback rating, but trust us, 112.4 is good. During one stretch of the season, Montana threw 15 touchdown passes and had only one interception in six starts. The only loss in that stretch was a four-point defeat to Green Bay, the Niners falling 21–17 despite gaining 515 yards in offense to the Packers' 192.

We mentioned earlier that Montana improved as a quarterback in 1989. You can verify this through an examination of his totals in the three most important statistics for a quarterback: completion percentage (70.2), yards per attempted pass (9.12) and touchdowns-to-interceptions ratio (3.25 to 1). All were career bests.

Much of the credit goes to Holmgren, the new offensive coordinator, who only eight years earlier had been tutoring quarterbacks at San Francisco State. He broke down film of Montana's 10 interceptions in 1989 and of other miscues in recent seasons and found that a large majority of them occurred on two certain pass plays. Both were eliminated from the offense. "Joe's a gambling man sometimes," Holmgren says, "and I wanted him to cut down on some of those gambling tendencies."

Holmgren says his role in Montana's season has been vastly overstated, but there is little doubt about the impact he had on the team. At a luncheon prior to the season, Seifert stood before a group of fans, pointed to Holmgren, who was seated next to him, and said, "He's really the guy who is replacing Bill Walsh."

That wasn't far from the truth, as it is Holmgren who was left with the responsibilities of calling the offensive plays. It was the first time he had had that responsibility since 1981 and, going into the season, was barely confident enough to say, "I hope it's like riding a bicycle." The results speak for themselves, as the Niners tied for the league lead in points scored with 442, led all teams in total offense per game (391.8 yards) and were second in passing per game (268.9 yards).

Curiously, Holmgren has risen to prominence quickly, whereas Seifert and Walsh labored for years as assistants before being given their shots at an NFL head coaching job. Had he desired, he could have entered 1990 as head coach of the Cardinals or the Jets instead of offensive coordinator for the 49ers again. But family considerations (such as transferring his teen-age daughters to a new school), a hefty raise from owner Eddie DeBartolo, Jr. (close to a 50 percent raise from his $150,000 '89 salary) and perhaps the feeling that one more season as an assistant could only help round him as a head coach persuaded him to stay.

"I really want to be a head coach," he says. "The more I think about it, I realize that it was mostly a family decision, a personal decision, than a career one. I just didn't think the time was right to uproot my family. I think—I hope—I'll get another chance at a head coaching job. I suppose I'm betting on the come line a little bit because not everybody gets another chance."

Through 16 weeks of the regular season, Seifert, Holmgren and the rest of the coaching staff seemed to make few wrong moves. One example was expanding the role of fullback Tom Rathman, who finished second on the team with 73 receptions. After some fortunate wins early, the Niners blew out Atlanta 42–3 in game 10, stunned the Rams 30–27 after twice trailing by 17 points to clinch their seventh NFC West title of the decade and smoked the Chicago Bears in the year's finale 26–0 when there was nothing at stake.

As the playoffs approached, many wondered how the Niners managed to avoid a post-title letdown. How was it that these players still seemed hungry? How did they maintain that edge without Walsh? In truth, many players intimated that it was Walsh's very departure and their respect for Seifert as both a coach and a person that inspired them to a strong season. They wanted to show that things would not crumble under the new regime.

To quote Sapolu before the Super Bowl, "I think everybody knows that George isn't going to get the credit he deserves because everybody's saying that Bill handed him a team that was already tuned up, prime for a championship and ready to go. But I don't think that's true. All of the credit should go to George for motivating us and keeping us together."

Seifert showed he could get things done in a "kinder, gentler way," as linebacker Michael Walter put it. At halftime of the second Rams game, when the Niners trailed 17–10, Seifert asked his assistants not to scream at the players, even though they had played like their minds were somewhere else. "That game defined him as a dominant motivator without having to scream," Paris says. "He makes players motivate themselves."

The best example of Seifert holding the team together came seven weeks into the season, when strong safety Jeff Fuller, one of the team's defensive leaders, suffered two fractures near his vertebrae and damaged a nerve in his right shoulder during a head-on tackle against New England running back John Stephens. The injury ended Fuller's career and left him partially paralyzed in his right arm. It had already been such a strange atmosphere that week, as the game was held at Stanford Stadium because Candlestick Park was being repaired from the devastating Bay Area earthquake days earlier. A number of players dedicated their season to Fuller, including second-year safety Chet Brooks, who even tucked a towel with Fuller's number 49 on it into his pants.

"That was a very emotional time for everybody," Seifert recalls. "It was very upsetting, not just because of what happened to Jeff but because everybody realized that things like that can happen in this game. It was a tough thing to get through, but we managed to stay together."

Nobody seemed more inspired than Brooks, Fuller's replacement, in the playoffs. In the first-round game against Minnesota, he recorded a team-high eight solo tackles and had an interception with a 28-yard return that set up a touchdown. The Vikings had their day against the 49ers in the playoffs two years earlier, but that may be the last time in a while that they celebrate in Candlestick. They were shellacked by San Francisco 41–13, as Montana threw four touchdown passes in the first half.

Free safety Ronnie Lott, another of Fuller's closest friends, returned an interception 58 yards for a touchdown. "The only way I could make myself feel better about what happened to Jeff was to play the game the way it should be played, the way Jeff would have wanted it to be played," Lott says.

The entire team, to use a common sports cliche, seemed to play on another level against the Vikings. It left such an impression on Minnesota defensive coordinator Floyd Peters that he could manage only a one-adjective analysis afterward. "Awesome," he kept saying. "They were just awesome."

Philadelphia coach Buddy Ryan was well aware of the 49ers capabilities. All he had to do to remember was to check the film from week three. But before the Eagles' wild-card playoff game against the Los Angeles Rams, Ryan already was looking forward to a potential meeting with San Francisco. "We're probably the only team in the NFL who can beat their butts," Ryan boasted. "I think we can go out there and beat the 49ers, and I think they think so, too."

Poor Buddy never had the chance to find out. The Eagles lost 21–7 to the Rams, who went on to dump the New York Giants in the next round and earn a shot against the Niners in the NFC title game. Rams coach John Robinson felt throughout the 1989 season that his team finally was at the level of the 49ers. Jim Everett had come of age, the Rams had more overall team speed than San Francisco and they came close to sweeping both regular-season games from the defending champions.

Fortunately for Robinson, he didn't echo Ryan's blustering. Otherwise, he would have had a few words to eat. Everett was a confused mess facing the Niners' defense, throwing three interceptions (by Ronnie Lott, Tim McKyer and Keena Turner), and the Rams were held to nine first downs and 156 total yards. The result was another playoff mugging, this one by 30–3. Montana threw for two touchdowns and completed 26 of 30 passes, a team record 86.7 percent.

So arrived another Super Bowl berth, the team's fourth of the decade. Some wondered aloud, "Why bother playing it?" Even fans in Denver, whose Broncos carried the memories of three Super Bowl defeats with them to New Orleans, were pessimistic. One Denver radio station polled listeners and determined that most Bronco backers would prefer seeing the team lose early in the playoffs than have to subject themselves to watching it get stomped in another championship. (Denver had lost three previous Super Bowls to Dallas, the New York Giants and Washington by a combined score of 108–40.)

Few expected this to be different. In Las Vegas, where, rumor has it, people like to bet on this game, the Niners were installed as 11-to-13-point favorites. In Irving, Kentucky, a rooster tabbed San Francisco by 14—at least so said the rooster's owner, noting that the bird pecked 14 kernels of corn when "asked" to pick a point spread. On a slightly more scientific footing, a football software inventor in Tennessee, Dave Holt, played 5,707 games between the Niners and the Broncos on his computer, and the Niners won 4,434 of them (78 percent). His prediction: San Francisco 34, Denver 21.

Nobody was close—nobody except Walsh, at least, when he turned to DeBartolo and said, "We're going to score 50." Walsh wasn't quite as bold in his daily Super Bowl column written for the *San Francisco Chronicle*, when he projected the 49ers winning 35–17. But he also said the Niners would have 460 yards in offense (they had 461), and Montana would complete 24 of 32 passes for 320 yards (Montana ended up not playing the whole game, but he and Young combined for 24 of 32 passes and 317 yards).

San Francisco dismembered the Denver Broncos 55–10. Seifert never dreamed his team could win by such a landslide. CBS never dreamed that their megabuck event would turn into such a yawner. Montana and Holmgren never dreamed that the Denver defense would sit back and hardly blitz for four quarters, that the Broncos would make *NO* adjustments from their standard 3–4 alignment, the perfect defense for San Francisco's possession/passing game.

"They could've lined up in the single wing and we could've had nine men on the line, and we still wouldn't be able to stop them," said Denver defensive coordinator Wade Phillips.

Yes, it was that one-sided. Montana remarked, "It was so much fun, we couldn't wait to get back onto the field." By halftime, he had already thrown for 189 yards and three touchdowns and clinched his third Most Valuable Player award. He finished with five touchdowns in the game and in four Super Bowls has thrown 11 touchdowns and no interceptions on 83-of-122 passing.

Denver owner Pat Bowlen, one of the few to predict a Broncos victory (well, what else was he going to say?), was succinct when asked what the Broncos could do to improve: "Send an assassin after Montana," he quipped.

Says linebacker Matt Millen, "You can talk about Gordie Howe and Wayne Gretzky and Joe DiMaggio and Babe Ruth. You can talk about Wilt Chamberlain. You can talk about anybody in the National Football League. But I've never seen anybody who can dominate a game or a season like him. It was the greatest season I've ever seen anybody play."

Consequently, the 49ers joined the Pittsburgh Steelers as the only team to win four Super Bowls, became only the fifth team to repeat (Pittsburgh did it twice, Green Bay and Miami once) and laid claim to their own decade. If there was any disputing it before, their frightening march through the playoffs doused remaining skeptics. "The 49ers have created their own level of play," remarked Broncos safety Dennis Smith.

The bad news for the rest of the NFL is that there's no reason to believe San Francisco can't be the team of the '90s as well. Months after their fourth championship, San Francisco was the league's most aggressive team during the Plan B free-agency period, signing defensive backs Hanford Dixon, Dave Waymer and Greg Cox, nose tackle Fred Smerlas, defensive tackle John Shannon and center Wayne Radloff. Those moves, combined with the draft, allowed the team to fill voids left by the retirements of defensive lineman Pete Kugler and Jeff Stover and also to deal away three players: cornerback Tim McKyer (to Miami), running back Terrence Flagler (to Dallas) and defensive end Dan Stubbs (also to Dallas).

McKyer, one of the self-proclaimed "Cover Brothers" during the 1988 championship season, had contractual problems in training camp, suffered a groin injury early in the season, lost his starting job, fell out of favor with management, was suspended for three games for "insubordination" and never worked his way back into Seifert's good graces. Flagler had been seeking a trade due to lack of playing time behind Roger Craig, although management preferred not to part with him, and Stubbs never developed the work ethic that the coaching staff was hoping for.

The bottom line is that Seifert and McVay proved that they could handle their increased load of front office duties and that another voice was not needed to replace Walsh. McVay, who has been referred to as the most important invisible man in the organization, was out front enough in 1989 to be named the NFL's Executive of the Year by the *Sporting News*.

McVay often deflects praise to others and prefers being in the background. Part of that is because he had enough of the spotlight when he coached the New York Giants for two and a half seasons (1976–78) and too much time on football blooper films for the infamous "Miracle of the Meadowlands." McVay was on the sidelines when his team was trying to run out the final seconds of a victory against Philadelphia in '78, but quarterback Steve Pisarcik fumbled the ball before getting it to Larry Csonka on a handoff, and it was picked up by Philadelphia's Herman Edwards and returned for a touchdown and a 19–17 stunner. "Oh Lord. Isn't anybody ever going to forget that?" McVay often says when asked about the nightmare.

Blooper shows may prevent that from ever happening. But he has been involved in few front-office blunders, helping put the Niners in a position to "Three-Peat." That chant was heard in the locker room after the thumping they gave the Broncos.

No doubt, Montana headed into the 1990 Super Bowl thinking of another championship. His wife Jennifer, had arranged for a plaque to be hanging in his locker at the Superdome when he arrived for the game. It included a picture of his three children Alexandra, Elizabeth and Nathaniel, each wearing one of Joe's Super Bowl rings. Below the picture an engraved plate read, "OK, Daddy, the next ring is yours." But after securing ring number four, Montana had other plans.

"That's OK, Jennifer can have this one," he said. "I'll take the next one."

Chapter 12

EPILOGUE
Team of the Decade?

"I can't say this is the team of the 1980s. I leave
comparisons to others."
— *Bill Walsh, after Super Bowl XXIII*

We know what you're thinking . . . and
you're right: Sure, the 49ers are a nice little franchise
on San Francisco Bay with a couple of dozen great players, a handful of Hall of Fame candidates, a legendary
coach, superior organization, a blue ribbon owner and
the greatest quarterback in NFL history. But there are
28 teams in the National Football League and you've
only shown us one. How about the other 27 teams?
Aren't there other candidates for Team of the Decade?

We want to be fair. So . . .

In the category of "Best Professional Football Team
during the Decade of the 1980s," the nominees are:

The Cleveland Browns, Denver Broncos, Miami Dolphins, San Francisco 49ers and the Washington Redskins.

Football fans in Chicago, Cincinnati, Los Angeles,
New York and Oakland: Do not throw this book into
the fireplace until you hear the criteria.

To determine the Team of the Decade, we evaluated
the entire period through the 1989 season, taking into

account overall regular season record, number of winning seasons, division titles, wild card playoff berths, overall playoff records and strength of competition. In one or two cases, the results were a little surprising, but mostly it was what we expected.

Although the Bears, Bengals, Raiders, Rams and Giants had outstanding achievements during the '80s—six Super Bowl appearances and four wins among them —and are among the NFL's powers as we move into the next decade, they did not make the top five. Consider them semi finalists.

What follows is a most-of-the-time objective, some-of-the-time subjective, review of the decade in professional football.

The 28 NFL teams are divided into three groups:

1) The Field. All teams not considered serious candidates, plus cities the Raiders have not taken a deposit from. There are 13 teams in this group, ranked from 16th to 28th.

2) The Semi finalists. The ten who came the closest to making the top group. Teams that were, on balance, winning programs, but not quite as consistent throughout the entire period as the five finalists.

3) The Finalists. The five most qualified to be considered Team of the Decade

With the ground rules established, let's get started.

16–28) The Field

Believe it or not, every NFL team qualified for the playoffs at least once during the decade. The **St. Louis/Phoenix Cardinals, New Orleans Saints, Green Bay Packers** and **Kansas City Chiefs** made it by the slimmest of margins: each appeared only once, as a wild-card representative. And in the case of the Cardinals and Packers, their only experience in post-season play came in the strike season of 1982 when only 56 percent of the regular season games were played, and 16 teams—more than half the league—were allowed into the post-season.

The Cardinals, Saints, Packers and Chiefs combined for just nine winning seasons in the 1980s—the 49ers alone had eight—and won just one playoff game. (Green Bay defeated St. Louis 41–16 in the first round of the 1982 season's playoffs, then lost to Dallas in the second round.)

The **Atlanta Falcons, Baltimore/Indianapolis Colts, Detroit Lions** and **Tampa Bay Buccaneers** are also hereby eliminated from contention. With only eight winning seasons and four playoff appearances among them—excluding the '82 season—the only factor elevating these four a notch above the previous group is that they've each won a division championship—Atlanta in '80 (12–4 record); the Colts in '87 (9–6 in the strike-shortened season); the Lions in '83* (9–7); and the Bucs in '81 (9–7). While winning a division championship is certainly a worthy accomplishment, the fact that none of them won a playoff game is enough for us to wish them well and move on.

The next group in our move up the ladder is made up of the **Buffalo Bills, Houston Oilers** and **San Diego Chargers**. With the exception of Houston, these teams each won at least one division title and, including Houston, made at least one appearance in the playoffs as a wild card team. Also, each had at least three winning seasons during the decade. The three teams, all from the AFC, had a combined playoff record of just 5–9, however, and advanced to the conference championship game only twice, losing both times.

Buffalo and Houston became contenders late in the decade, thanks in large part to several years of high

* Detroit tied with Minnesota for the NFC Central Division title in 1980, but the Vikings went to the playoffs by virtue of a better conference record (8–4 to 9–5).

draft choices, and San Diego seemed only a couple of years away. But with 10-year regular season winning percentages of .454, .407 and .474, respectively, they are simply not legitimate contenders for Team of the '80s.

The **Philadelphia Eagles** emerged as one of the NFL's best teams as the decade came to a close. But since we are talking about the 1980s, the Eagles are also eliminated from consideration for Team of the Decade. Philadelphia made a total of four playoff appearances in the '80s—including a losing effort in Super Bowl XV —but had a regular-season winning percentage of .507 and only four winning seasons. Not bad really, but not good enough to make it out of the bottom group.

The **New York Jets** round out the first group. No one needs to remind us about the Jets' stunning victory in Super Bowl III over the heavily favored Baltimore Colts. But seriously, folks, how much mileage can they get out of one moment of glory more than 20 years ago?

In the '80s, the Jets were not even the best team in their city, with a winning percentage of only .487. Also, many of their wins came against teams in the pitifully weak AFC East Division. The Colts and Bills took turns playing doormat. Both assumed the role early in the decade while the Dolphins ruled the division, and later, when Miami slid to the bottom of the division and the Colts and Bills resumed prominence, the Jets managed to maintain their mediocre form. Five total playoff appearances and a 3–5 post-season record further weaken any possible claim to being Team of the Decade.

The Semi Finalists

These fine teams distinguished themselves in one

way or another during the decade but fell short of making it into the final group.

15) Pittsburgh Steelers

They won Super Bowl XIV against the Los Angeles Rams in Pasadena on January 20, 1980. But the best regular-season record they showed the rest of the decade was 10–6 in 1983, and they made the playoffs only three times.

Can a team with a starting quarterback named "Bubby" really be considered great? Team of the '70s? Unquestionably. Team of the '80s? We think not.

14) Minnesota Vikings

This is a tough one to figure. It seems as if the Vikings have been a power in the NFL forever. The all-time roster has included All-Pros Mick Tingelhoff, Carl Eller, Ron Yary, Paul Krause, Fran Tarkenton, Ed White, Chuck Foreman and former league MVP Alan Page. Not to mention media darling Ahmad Rashad and Bud Grant, the seventh winningest coach in NFL history. Oh yeah, do not forget four Super Bowl appearances. Maybe you did because all four appearances were losses.

In the '80s, the Vikings have had Pro Bowlers Doug Martin, Tommy Kramer, Joey Browner, Chris Doleman, Gary Zimmerman, Anthony Carter and Keith Millard.

But they also have been inconsistent. A .507 winning percentage and a 4–5 post-season record have been the signposts of mediocrity for a team that plays in the division that is the league's weakest overall. When Pete Rozelle issued his famous "parity" speech, he might have had Minnesota in mind. Regular season records of 9–7, 7–9, 5–4, 8–8, 3–13, 7–9, 9–7, 8–7, 11–5 and 10–6 read like the parity handbook. So unless we are talking about the "Parity" Team of the Decade, let's keep going.

13) New York Giants

The Giants have only seemed like a great football team in the 1980s. In reality, they have been just good for most of the decade. Want proof? How about regular season records of 4–12, 9–7, 4–5, 3–12–1, 9–7 and 10–6 before going 14–2 and winning Super Bowl XXI, and 6–9, 10–6 and 12–4 after. A .537 winning percentage. So why do the New Yorkers have such a fearsome reputation? Well, in a word: 1986.

That was the year the Giants breezed through the regular season with a 14–2 record, then steamrolled two of the NFC's best teams in the playoffs. A devastating 43–3 victory over the 49ers was followed by a 17–0 pasting of the Washington Redskins. The Denver Broncos were the victims in the Super Bowl, falling 39–20. Then, just as the rest of the league was getting ready to concede the rest of the decade to Bill Parcells' bad boys, they became eminently beatable.

A good part of their reputation, it turns out, was due to the inspired play of a few outstanding players who could not manage to maintain their collective focus for an entire season. How can a team lose with such stars as Pro Bowlers Lawrence Taylor, Phil Simms, Harry Carson, Joe Morris, Mark Bavaro, Mark Haynes, Carl Banks, Leonard Marshall and Jim Burt?

Well, credit the Giants; they often found a way.

12) New England Patriots

What can you say about the Pats? That they had a .513 winning percentage while playing in one of the NFL's weakest divisions. Or that they had seven winning seasons in the decade and won their division in '85? Probably the best that could be said is that they made the Super Bowl after the '85 season from just a wild card berth, only the second time that has happened.

(Prior to 1978, only one wild card team from each conference qualified for the playoffs, and it was pitted against the club with the best conference record. But beginning in '78, the two best teams after the division champions played one another in the wild card game. Since the new format was introduced, only two wild card teams have made it to the Super Bowl: the 1980 Oakland Raiders, who beat the Philadelphia Eagles 27–10; and the '85 Patriots, who lost to the Chicago Bears 46–10.)

While not exactly dominating the league, the Patriots have been a pretty good football team in the '80s. OK, so '81 was not so hot—they managed only two wins —and they did have a couple of eight- and nine-win seasons. But, they won 11 games twice and made the playoffs three times, posting an overall 3–3 record in the post-season. They also had 17 players who were named to play in the Pro Bowl during the decade, and their coach, Raymond Berry, is in the Hall of Fame. So, overall, they're not great, but good enough to deserve this ranking.

11) Dallas Cowboys

With the second best composite record since the NFL-AFL merger in 1970, 18 playoff and five Super Bowl appearances, six years in a row (1976–81) in which they either won or tied for the NFC East title and the longest streak of winning seasons in NFL history (20), the Cowboys were truly "America's Team," for more than two decades. But in spite of another NFC East title in 1985, the team has been running on fumes since Roger Staubach retired after the 1979 season. Danny White, Gary Hogeboom and Steve Pelleur tried to fill

Staubach's cleats before the team drafted two college superstars, UCLA's Troy Aikman and Miami's Steve Walsh, in 1989.

The Cowboys were 75–45 (.625) in the first eight years of the decade, but closed out with horrendous seasons of 3–13 and 1–15. The past two years prevent a higher ranking than 11th.

10) Seattle Seahawks

No team that plays its home games in a domed stadium has played in a Super Bowl (Minnesota played outdoors during its four Super Bowl seasons). So why are the Seahawks, who joined the league in 1976, rated higher than the Steelers, Giants and Cowboys, who have 10 Super Bowl appearances among them? Well, a .513 winning percentage in the '80s for starters— despite playing in the toughest division in the decade, the AFC West. Also, the Seahawks have five winning seasons and four playoff appearances in the decade, including the 1983 AFC championship game, which they lost to the eventual NFL champion Raiders. Even when the Seahawks were bad (4–12 in 1980), seven of their losses were in the division.

The rest of the time they were pretty competitive. Pretty entertaining, too. Remember the Monday night games with Jim Zorn and Efren Herrera running fake field goals and anything else that might score points?

The Seahawks also get this relatively high ranking because we admire a couple of their personnel decisions —the acquisition of Steve Largent, Dave Kreig and Zorn in particular. Largent, of course, is the lightly regarded wide receiver from Tulsa who led the nation in '74 and '75 with 14 touchdown catches each year. Drafted in the fourth round by Houston in '76, he was traded to Seattle during the pre-season for an eighth round pick in '77 (the Oilers chose another wide receiver, Steven Davis from Georgia, whom they cut). Largent has gone on to become the NFL's all-time leader in receptions, receiving yardage, touchdown catches and consecutive games with at least one reception.

Kreig's story is interesting, too. Signed as a free agent in 1980, the Wisconsin native had played football at tiny Milton College, an NAIA school. (That probably explains why he was not selected in the NFL draft. Scouts don't spend a lot of time in Wisconsin watching NAIA football games.) What makes Kreig's story unusual is that not only did Milton College drop football the year after he graduated—a couple of other NFL players' colleges also dropped the sport—but also the school itself closed in 1983. At least there is no pressure to contribute to the alumni association.

And what can you say about Jim Zorn? He joined the expansion Seahawks in 1976 as a free agent from that football powerhouse California Polytechnic-Pomona. With almost none of the skills of other starting NFL quarterbacks, he scrapped and dazzled his way into the hearts of Seattle-ites for nine seasons before packing up his bag of tricks and taking them to Pittsburgh for a year after Kreig won the position full time. A classic NFL overachiever. Hats off to all three.

9) Cincinnati Bengals

All right, stop whining. Yes, the Bengals played in two Super Bowls. Yes, they won the AFC Central Division twice. Yes, they were one of the best teams in the NFL at the end of the decade. But . . .

They posted a fairly impressive winning percentage of .533, but it came in what, for a while, ranked as one of the NFL's weakest divisions. They made the playoffs only three times—including the '82 strike season, when they lost in the first round—and had only four winning seasons while going 4–11 as late as 1987. They made it to two Super Bowls, but lost both.

8) Oakland/Los Angeles/Irwindale/ Sacramento/Oakland Raiders

With three Super Bowl victories in four appearances and one of the best composite records since the merger in 1970, the Raiders would certainly be a candidate for Team of the Score (20 Years). But a quarterback deficiency in the '80s that included a revolving door that would make anyone's head spin leaves us with serious doubts. Jim Plunkett came in at the beginning of the decade to lead the team into Super Bowl XV. Then out again the former Heisman Trophy winner went as head coach Tom Flores and later Mike Shanahan tried Marc Wilson, Mark Herrmann, Rusty Hilger, Stever Beuerlein and Jay Schroeder.

The Raiders posted a .586 winning percentage, two division titles, two conference titles and five winning records despite playing in the AFC West. They also had the distinction of going to the Super Bowl once during the decade as the Oakland Raiders (1980 season) and once as the L.A. Raiders (1983 season), winning both times. But things went downhill for the bad boys after the '85 season when the team's quarterback roulette caused the offense to frequently misfire. The defense was strong throughout the decade, but the Raiders were truly a team that could not be recognized without a program.

A team with six starting quarterbacks in nine years simply cannot be considered the best team of the decade. Maybe once owner Al Davis drops anchor long enough to let his magazine subscriptions catch up with him the Raiders will return to their former glory. But until then, we'll move on.

7) Los Angeles Rams

And you thought the Raiders were L.A.'s best football team in the '80s. Do not be fooled by Super Bowl appearances alone.

The Rams had a decent winning percentage of .566 and won one NFC West title, with an 11–5 record in 1985. (The 49ers won the division title seven times and in '82 no winner was declared.) L.A. also made six wild card playoff appearances and had seven winning seasons. True, they have not shown great success in the playoffs. Despite winning their first two post-season games in 1989 until losing to the 49ers in the NFC title game, the Rams were only 4–7 in the playoffs in the 1980s. But twice they lost to the eventual Super Bowl champion—the 18–1 Chicago Bears in 1985 and the 17–2 49ers in '89.

They probably would have been even more productive in the decade if not for a serious quarterback problem not unlike that of the Raiders. Head coaches Ray Malavasi and John Robinson had one of the best quarterback rosters in pro football history. The only trouble was, most of them did not play for the Rams at their peak.

How would you like to have had these guys play for you in the same decade: Pat Haden ('80–'81), Vince Ferragamo ('80, '82–'84), Bert Jones ('82), Dieter Brock ('85), Steve Bartkowski ('86), Steve Fuller ('83), Jeff Kemp ('81–'85), Bob Lee ('80), Dan Pastorini ('81) and Jeff Rutledge ('80–'81). That does not include, of course, Joe Namath ('77) and John Hadl ('73–'74). They finally seem to have found their man in Jim Everett, whom they acquired in a trade with the Oilers.

Not the Team of the '80s, but possibly contenders for Team of the '90s. Now if they could only do something about those uniforms . . .

6) Chicago Bears

This was a very touch call. Like the Giants, the Bears' reputation often exceeded their performance and was largely a result of one great season—1985.

The Bears had a very strong winning percentage of .605 in the '80s and a total of five winning seasons. They won the NFC Central title five times and placed 13 players in the Pro Bowl. They went 18–1 in '85, losing only to the powerful Dolphins in the regular season, and crushed New England in the Super Bowl 46–10, the largest margin of victory in the game's history. They had one of the league's best defenses, one of its toughest coaches in Mike Ditka and one of pro football's biggest overachievers in quarterback Jim McMahon. They had the NFL's most prolific running back—Walter Payton—and one of the country's favorite pop icons—William "The Refrigerator" Perry.

But . . .

The NFC Central Division was among the league's weakest in the decade, and more than half of their 92 victories in the '80s came against the Vikings, Packers, Lions and Buccaneers. Their five NFC Central titles came in the only years they had winning records, and they did not even qualify for the playoffs before '84, then won only two of six playoff games—excluding the '85 Super Bowl season—despite having the home-field advantage in three of the losses.

The problem for the Bears in the '80s was offense. Only twice during the decade did they score the most points in their division ('85 and '87), and only once did they lead the NFC ('85). Although McMahon gave the team that intangible of leadership that inspired a sensational winning percentage, he was never able to play regularly because of almost constant injury associated with his aggressive style of play.

Ditka never really found a good replacement for the

former BYU star McMahon though he tried Steve Fuller, Doug Flutie, Mike Tomczak and Jim Harbaugh. Ditka and McMahon ended a turbulent relationship when the quarterback was sent to San Diego in 1989 for a conditional draft choice. The deal is virtually risk-free for the Chargers, who benefited from the "This town ain't big enough for the both of us" attitude that developed between the Windy City's second and third most famous sports figures. (Remember Michael Jordan?)

We had thought the Bears deserved to be considered as a finalist for Team of the Decade. But upon close examination, we determined that the weakness of their division is simply too much of an advantage. When a team can virtually assure itself of five or six victories a year within its division, it is not too hard to finish with one of the best records in the conference and get the home-field advantage for the playoffs. In fact, it is more of a surprise that Chicago did not do better.

But, if you still think they should have finished in the top five, read on.

The Finalists
Officially submitted for your approval:
The Candidates for Team of the Decade

5) Cleveland Browns

It may at first seem odd that three AFC teams are ranked among the finalists, because the NFC dominated the decade with eight Super Bowl victories. The truth is, however, the NFC had only a handful of good teams—the four that won Super Bowls, plus the Rams —while the AFC was far stronger top to bottom.

The NFC, of course, was more consistent at the top. The 49ers, Redskins, Bears, Giants and Rams were the conference leaders throughout the decade, while the AFC had quite a bit of turnover. In fact, three of the

AFC's worst teams in terms of overall record in the '80s —the Bills, Colts and Oilers—were among the conference's strongest clubs at the end of the decade. The NFC's worst teams—the Falcons, Packers, Lions and Bucs (remember the NFC Central?)—maintained their lowly status as the '80s came to a close.

You may also be wondering how a team that never made it to a Super Bowl can be ranked among the NFL's top five for the decade. Well, wonder no more. The Browns earned their ranking by being one of the NFL's most consistent teams in one of the league's toughest divisions—the AFC Central.

Cleveland had a .549 winning percentage in the '80s and won their division title three straight times and five times overall ('80, '85, '86, '87 and '89). The Browns were an AFC wild card team in '88 and '82 for a total of seven playoff appearances—second only to the 49ers' eight. They had a total of six winning seasons, went 8–8 in '85 to win the division and qualified in the '82 strike season as well with only a 4–5 record.

The trouble really was the playoffs. In the Browns' seven appearances, they lost to the eventual AFC champion four times and to the Super Bowl champion Oakland Raiders in 1980. And their heartbreaking back-to-back losses to the Denver Broncos in the '86 and '87 AFC championship games did the most to define the team as the decade's perennial runner-up. Even when they were bad though, they were not really that bad. The Browns posted their worst regular season record (5–11) twice ('81 and '84). But 18 of those 22 losses came at the hands of AFC opponents, and eight of the losses came against their rivals in the AFC Central.

So the next time someone tries to tell you that the Cleveland Browns were terrible in the '80s because they did not play in any Super Bowls, just turn to that person and say: "Yeah, but Tampa Bay never beat 'em. They owned the Bucs."

4) Denver Broncos

The last thing John Elway wanted when he graduated from Stanford in 1983 was to play football in Baltimore. Not that he had anything against the city, mind you. He just did not relish the idea of standing in the Colts' backfield while opposing defenses took turns sacking him. Baltimore had spent the previous two NFL seasons going 2–22–1 and setting league records for yards lost rushing by their quarterbacks.

So, prior to the college draft, Elway made it known that he was not interested in joining the Colts, who held the first pick. Since most NFL teams are happy to accommodate a young man's wishes—especially if he asks real nice—Baltimore drafted him, then traded his rights to Denver for two number-one draft picks and back-up quarterback Mark Herrmann. The Colts did not do too badly, ending up with offensive linemen Chris Hinton and Ron Solt—both of whom became Pro Bowl players.

Elway did better.

While the Colts packed their bags and left Baltimore for Indianapolis, Elway packed his and headed to Denver. He spent a lot of his first pro season just as Joe Montana had—watching Steve DeBerg direct the team — but started ten games and managed to lead the Broncos to their first of four playoff appearances in the '80s. Of course, Denver was not exactly a weak franchise. It had gone to Super Bowl XII in 1978 under head coach Red Miller and was 8–8 and 10–6 in '80 and '81 before going 2–7 in '82—the Broncos' only losing season in the decade.

In fact, consistency was the watchword for the Broncos. They posted a .615 winning percentage for the decade and had eight winning seasons while taking the title in one of football's best divisions, the AFC West, four times. They were 6–2 in playoffs other than the Super

Bowls—where they lost three times: to the Giants, Redskins and 49ers.

Overall in the decade, the Broncos had five playoff berths, three Super Bowls and only one losing season. Most NFL experts will say that all great NFL teams must have a truly great quarterback. The Packers had Starr; the Colts had Unitas; the Cowboys had Staubach; and the Steelers had Bradshaw. The 49ers may have had the best one of all in Montana. But the Broncos had Elway, which is the primary reason they made it to the championship three times. Now all they have to do is win one.

3) Miami Dolphins

Speaking of great quarterbacks, the Dolphins fared pretty well in that 1983 college draft themselves. Drafting in the 27th position because of their appearance earlier in the year in Super Bowl XVII, Miami could not believe its good fortune when Dan Marino was still available at the end of the first round. As he was completing a brilliant career at the University of Pittsburgh, Marino's NFL stock dropped suddenly when he suffered a serious knee injury in a game against West Virginia his senior year. But after he joined the Dolphins, the only things that dropped were NFL passing records.

Close your eyes and pretend you are an NFL quarterback. Now try and imagine having a really great season. What would it be like? You would probably throw a lot of passes. And complete a lot, too. You would get a lot of yardage; that certainly follows. And a lot of touchdowns, too. Definitely a lot of touchdowns. And your team would score a lot of points and have the best record in your conference.

OK, how about the numbers? Shall we say 362 completions in 564 attempts for 5,084 yards and 48 touchdowns? All except the attempts would be NFL records by the way. And how about a 14–2 regular season record? After all, nobody would believe it if we went undefeated. And 513 points, that would be a record, too. Naturally we would breeze through the playoffs and end up in the Super Bowl.

All right, now open your eyes. That dream was the season Dan Marino had in 1984. You can open your eyes because the dream ended with the Super Bowl that season when the Dolphins met up with Freddy Krueger in a San Francisco 49ers uniform. The NFC champs turned the game into a Nightmare in Palo Alto by drubbing the Floridians 38–16, but that's another story for another chapter.

The Miami Dolphins were one of the best teams in the NFL in the 1980s. Third best, actually. If that surprises you, consider this: They posted a .622 regular season winning percentage, won the AFC East title four times, and made five playoff appearances (going 6–3 in games other than the Super Bowl), had six winning seasons and went to two Super Bowls.

You may be thinking: "Gee, but aren't the Dolphins the team that stinks? The team that went 8–8, 8–7 and 6–10 in '86, '87 and '88 while giving up the most points in the NFL and not even making the playoffs?"

Well . . . yes, technically.

"And aren't they the team that almost got Don Shula fired, even though he's the second-winningest head coach in NFL history?"

OK, OK, hold it right there. We did not say they were the Team of the Decade. Only third best, remember? Maybe you need to be reminded of the Miami Dolphins earlier in the '80s?

With the best composite record since the NFL-AFL merger in 1970 (.702) and the most AFC East titles (nine; New England is second with two), the Dolphins were the NFL's best team for the first half of the decade. They followed an 8–8 season in 1980 with regular season records of 11–4–1, 12–4, 14–2 and 12–4 in '81, '83, '84 and '85. Why they were even 7–2 in the '82 strike year when everyone had a good excuse to be terrible. Well heck, they only had one losing season in the decade ('88).

The key thing to remember about this whole Team of the Decade deal is that you have to be good over the entire period. It may be stretching it a little to say the Dolphins were really a good team late in the decade, but they were not really bad. You want bad? Try Tampa Bay: 2–14, 2–14, 4–11 and 5–11 in '85, '86, '87 and '88. The Dolphins, on the other hand, were a very good football team on balance in the '80s. And with a defense, they would have been even better. Don't forget: They tied their own NFL record, originally set in 1972 with 16 straight regular season victories in 1983 and '84 (five in '83, 11 in '84).

And after all, look on the bright side: Don Johnson left town in 1989, and they still have Marino and Shula.

2) Washington Redskins

In many ways, the Washington Redskins were the overachievers of the decade. Three different quarterbacks led the team into the playoffs in the '80s, and that is not supposed to happen. Great teams should have great quarterbacks to lead them. And great quarterbacks should lead their teams for many years. Well, that is the conventional wisdom anyway. We will have to look a little deeper to explain the Redskins' extraordinary success in the '80s.

Ironically, not one of the three starting quarterbacks who led the Redskins in the '80s was on the active roster at the close of the decade. Joe Theismann, who bravely and capably guided the franchise through the late '70s and early '80s and into Super Bowl XVII, retired in '85 after a devastating broken leg. His archnemesis, the angelic-looking former back-up to Tom Ramsey (Tom Ramsey?) at UCLA, Jay Schroeder, who won the starting battle over Theismann only to lose it two years later, was traded to the Raiders in '88. And Doug Williams, who beat out Schroeder for the top spot and took the 'Skins to Super Bowl XXII, where he thrashed the Broncos and earned the MVP award, opened the '89 season on injured reserve after major back surgery during the off-season.

So how do the Redskins figure to be the second-best team in the decade? In a word: defense. And a strong supporting cast on offense. And Joe Gibbs and Bobby Beathard. OK, so it's several words.

The Washington Redskins were a remarkable football team in the 1980s and a heartbeat away from being the Team of the Decade. In fact, if for any reason the 49ers are unable to execute their official duties as Team of the Decade, the Redskins will be required to step in and finish out the reign. A .638 regular season winning percentage, three NFC East titles, two conference championships, seven winning seasons—including six in a row—and only two losing seasons ('80 and '88) were the credentials the 'Skins brought to the table in the decade. And, of course, two Super Bowl victories.

The team that General Manager Bobby Beathard put together and Joe Gibbs coached was a model of success in a division that was often paradoxical. On paper —and in the minds of many—the NFC East was the best, or at least second-best, division in pro football. The Giants, Cowboys, Eagles and Redskins were long considered some of the best franchises in the league. And in the '80s, they each took turns being good—the Cowboys at the beginning of the decade, the Giants in the middle, the Eagles at the end and the Redskins throughout. Don't even ask about the Cardinals.

Seventeen Redskins were named to the Pro Bowl in

the '80s, most of them on defense. Washington also showed great skill in bringing in situation players on offense and, of course, tremendous talent at wide receiver. In the former category, include four running backs—John Riggins, who is the franchise's all-time rushing leader; George Rogers, the former Heisman Trophy winner acquired in a trade with the Saints; Kelvin Bryant, the former North Carolina star who led his USFL team to a couple of titles before joining the 'Skins; and Timmy Smith, the Super Bowl record-setter who was a fourth-round draft choice after missing most of his junior and senior seasons at Texas Tech. In the latter group, Beathard drafted All-Pro Art Monk ('80) and Charlie Brown ('81) and acquired Gary Clark ('84) and Ricky Sanders ('86). Remember "the Smurfs"?

It all added up to a 97–55 regular season record and two Super Bowl championships in the '80s. And they didn't even have to use any of those plays Richard Nixon drew up for George Allen in the '70s.

And now for the finale. Drum roll, please.

1) San Francisco 49ers

Why don't we get the hard facts out of the way first so we can focus on the real reasons this team was the best in the decade?

The 49ers had pro football's best overall regular season record in the '80s: 104–47–1, a .687 winning percentage, eight winning seasons, seven NFC West titles, four conference championships and four Super Bowls. They had eight seasons in which they won at least 10 regular season games, four seasons in which they won at least 13 regular season games and a season (1984) in which they won 18 games. But the Niners were much more than just statistics in the '80s.

Every championship team is a product of superior organization, strategic planning and exceptional personnel both on and off the field. With the Niners, it began at the top with owner Eddie DeBartolo. "Eddie wants to play the game," cornerback Eric Wright said. "He's the man with the money, but I think he'd rather be on the field with us with a helmet on."

DeBartolo spent his money wisely. He hired Bill Walsh as coach and paid his players the highest salaries in the league. Walsh hired guys such as George Seifert, Bill McPherson and Bobb McKittrick to coach the athletes as they executed the most innovative game plans in pro football. It was Walsh's offense that got it going for the Niners and Seifert's defense that kept them competitive. But the real key to the 49ers' success from 1980 to '88 was stability. One owner. One head coach. One starting quarterback. No other team in professional football can make that claim.

The stability in the organization bred an atmosphere of confidence and pride. Linebacker Bill Romanowski joined the team in the college draft of 1988 and noticed the feeling immediately. "Winning is an attitude," he said. "Right away when I came here it was taken very seriously that we were supposed to win. When you approach a game, you just feel like you're going to win going in. Everybody does on this team. We go into every game knowing we can win. It's an attitude that coach Walsh and the rest of the staff has given everybody."

Well, we have all heard that before. Every championship team says the same sort of thing. So why does it sound so believable when the 49ers say it? Because they have been saying it since 1981.

Five of the 28 NFL teams won Super Bowls in the 1980 seasons: the Raiders, Redskins, Giants, Bears and 49ers. The 49ers won four Super Bowls with decidedly different teams. Only three players started all three games, but look who they were: Joe Montana, Keena Turner and Ronnie Lott. All three were Pro Bowl players, but really they were more than that. They were leaders and role models at their respective positions. And not the boisterous rah-rah "let's make a video" kind of leaders. They led quietly, by example.

That was what really set this team apart from the rest of the NFL. No gimmicks. No Gatorade showers for Bill Walsh at the end of games. No MTV VJs. No rap songs. No cute slogans (Who Dey?, Welcome to the Jungle, Just Win Baby, Super Bowl Shuffle). Just an attitude that every time they walked onto the field they could win. And not just for a year or two; that was easy. Remember how the Bears looked so invincible for a couple of years? Or the Giants; remember how unbeatable they looked after winning the Super Bowl?

The 49ers evolved. Walsh put together a solid plan in 1981, and they won 13 regular season games and the Super Bowl. They did it largely with proven veterans such as Fred Dean and Hacksaw Reynolds and the great rookies they drafted: Lott, Wright and Carlton Williamson. Three years later, Walsh did it again with an almost entirely different group. In fact, the '84 49ers may have been the NFL's greatest team. But they were also good in '85. The Bears were just better. And the 49ers were good in '86, too. The Giants, though, were better. Many people thought the 49ers were the best team in the league in '87, but the Vikings surprised them in the playoffs, and the Redskins won the Super Bowl. The Niners came back in '88 to win it all, a resurgence that is the mark of a truly great franchise.

The Steelers once won four Super Bowls in six seasons. But they did it with pretty much the same team. Not to diminish their accomplishment, but Pittsburgh had several years of bad teams in the early '70s, which meant high draft choices. After five or six years, those draft choices paid off with the NFL championship. But the nucleus—Bradshaw, Harris, Swann, Greene, Lambert, Blount, Bleier and Stallworth—was all there together. When they retired or left, the team was not the same. And has not been close since.

But the 49ers have replaced veterans with capable rookies without the benefit of a high draft choice. Why, the highest pick they have had since '81, other than through trades, was when they took offensive lineman Harris Barton with the 22nd pick in the '87 draft. Four times in the '80s they did not even have a first-round pick. Yet, the 49ers stayed competitive.

Of course, scouting had a lot to do with it. They found Roger Craig in the second round after he spent his college career blocking for guys such as Heisman Trophy winner Mike Rozier and Jarvis Redwine at Nebraska. And Jerry Rice, whom no one thought could catch passes in the pros the way he did at Mississippi Valley State. And Michael Carter, who was overlooked because of his commitment to track and field. But what it really came down to for the 49ers in the '80s was three very special people who contributed their unique skills to the winning effort: Eddie DeBartolo, Bill Walsh and Joe Montana. The owner, the coach and the quarterback.

All that could be asked of an owner was provided by Eddie. He came to town with his checkbook in hand and hired the right people. He did not diagram plays on cocktail napkins from the owner's box and demand Walsh use them. He did not call the sideline during games and tell Walsh to play Steve Young. He did not show up on draft day and tell the coaches whom to pick. He simply let his people do their jobs and bring in the personnel they wanted, and then he picked up the check. He rewarded commitment and provided support. No other owner in NFL history traveled as much to support his team. Forty trips a year to the Bay Area, plus exhibition games in London and Tokyo.

And parties, too. After Super Bowl XXIII, he flew the entire team with their wives and girlfriends to

Youngstown, Ohio, for a dinner celebration. And don't forget the Super Bowl rings. That was a real nice touch. And the new headquarters. And about a million other things. "I just felt lucky and fortunate to play for Mr. D.," Keena Turner said. "He treats you with respect and always lets you know you're appreciated. I think if he could, he'd be out there with us. He's definitely one of us."

Bill Walsh made his contribution from the coach's box. Sure, we all know by now that Walsh was an offensive genius. That he took a team that was the NFL's worst and turned it into a champion faster than had been done with any other team in history. We know that the rest of the league imitated his wide-open passing style when it was beginning to look as if pro football was reverting to the "three yards and a cloud of dust" style of Earl Campbell and the Houston Oilers. We heard about Walsh's lighter side. The bellboy incident at the first Super Bowl. And the time he came to a meeting dressed like a cab driver because that was going to be his next job after he got fired from coaching. But Walsh was much more than that. He was a leader. A role model. A motivator.

In the wake of his retirement to the broadcast booth, several players were quoted as saying they felt that a huge weight was lifted by his departure. That his brooding, stoic, autocratic style would not be missed. But Roger Craig aptly described his coach's contribution by saying: "Bill had a great presence. Great charisma. He would walk into the locker room and the whole atmosphere would change. He had that glow about him, the glow of a champion."

And Joe Montana? Well, if you were going to start a professional basketball team you would probably start with Magic Johnson, not necessarily because he is the best player, but because he has that overwhelming desire to win that infects everyone around him. The pride and poise that make him a winner year-in and year-out. In pro football, Joe Montana is your man.

On paper, it is hard to figure Joe out. Skinny legs, wiry frame, average throwing ability, bad back. All he does is get the job done. Sure, he is the NFL's all-time top-rated quarterback, but that does not even begin to explain his accomplishments. John Madden said Montana was the only quarterback he would want in the last two minutes of a Super Bowl with the game on the line. Hank Stram thinks he is the best quarterback who ever played. We already know what Tony Razzano, Bill Walsh and Eddie DeBartolo think. Joe's teammates would follow him anywhere. Not because he is the loudest, but because he is the coolest.

Many good quarterbacks have played in the NFL in the 1980s: John Elway, Dan Marino, Boomer Esiason, Phil Simms, Bernie Kosar. All had good seasons. Once, or maybe two or three times. But no one led his team to more victories over a longer period of time and through greater adversity than Joe Montana. And no one has performed better when a game was on the line.

Just ask the Cowboys and the Bengals and about a dozen other teams he beat in the final seconds of NFL games.

Team of the Sixties? Uh-uh.

Team of the Seventies? No way.

Team of the Eighties? Yes indeed.

Team of the Nineties? Well, we would not be a bit surprised.

Appendix

Club Career Leaders

RUSHING
(Yards)

Player	No.	Yds.	Avg.	Long.	TD
1. Perry, Joe (1950-60, 1963)	1,475	7,344	4.9	78t	50
2. Craig, Roger (1983- —)	1,545	6,625	4.29	71	49
3. Willard, Ken (1965-73)	1,582	5,930	3.7	69t	45
4. Smith, J.D. (1956-64)	1,007	4,370	4.3	80t	37
5. McElhenny, Hugh (1952-60)	877	4,288	4.9	89t	35
6. Tyler, Wendell (1983-86)	624	3,112	5.0	40	17
7. Williams, Delvin (1974-77)	669	2,966	4.4	80t	20
8. Jackson, Wilbur (1974-79)	745	2,955	3.9	80	10
9. Washington, Vic (1971-73)	483	1,813	3.8	42	14
10. Hofer, Paul (1976-81)	416	1,746	4.2	47	16

PASSING
(Completions)

Player	Att.	Comp.	Pct.	Yds.	TD	Int.
1. Montana, Joe (1979- —)	4,059	2,593	.639	31,054	216	107
2. Brodie, John (1957-73)	4,491	2,469	.550	31,548	214	224
3. Tittle, Y.A. (1951-60)	2,194	1,226	.559	16,016	108	134
4. DeBerg, Steve (1977-80)	1,201	670	.558	7,220	37	60
5. Spurrier, Steve (1967-75)	840	441	.525	5,250	33	48
6. Albert, Frank (1946-52)	601	316	.526	3,847	27	43
7. Plunkett, Jim (1976-77)	491	254	.517	3,285	22	30
8. Young, Steve (1987- —)	262	155	.592	2,251	21	6
9. Snead, Norman (1974-75)	237	138	.582	1,705	11	11
10. Kemp, Jeff (1986)	200	119	.595	1,554	11	8

RECEIVING
(Catches)

Player	No.	Yds.	Avg.	Long.	TD
1. Clark, Dwight (1979-87)	506	6,750	13.3	80t	48
2. Craig, Roger (1983- —)	483	4,241	8.8	73	16
3. Wilson, Billy (1951-60)	407	5,902	14.5	77t	49
4. Washington, Gene (1969-77)	371	6,664	17.9	79t	59
5. Rice, Jerry (1985- —)	346	6,364	18.4	96t	66
6. Solomon, Freddie (1978-85)	310	4,873	15.7	93t	42
7. Casey, Bernie (1961-66)	277	4,008	14.5	68t	27
8. Willard, Ken (1965-73)	273	2,156	7.8	62	16
9. Soltau, Gordy (1950-58)	249	3,487	14.0	54t	25
10. Cooper, Earl (1980-85)	213	1,908	9.0	73t	12

RECEIVING
(Yards)

Player	No.	Yds.	Avg.	Long.	TD
1. Clark, Dwight (1979-87)	506	6,750	13.3	80t	48
2. Washington, Gene (1969-77)	371	6,664	17.9	79t	59
3. Rice, Jerry (1985-)	346	6,364	18.4	96t	66
4. Wilson, Billy (1951-60)	407	5,902	14.5	77t	49
5. Solomon, Freddie (1978-85)	310	4,873	15.7	93t	42
6. Craig, Roger (1983-)	483	4,241	8.8	73	16
7. Casey, Bernie (1961-66)	277	4,008	14.5	68t	27
8. Soltau, Gordy (1950-58)	249	3,487	14.0	54t	25
9. Parks, Dave (1964-67)	208	3,334	16.0	83t	27
10. Stickles, Monty (1960-67)	207	2,993	14.5	54	14

SCORING
(Total Points)

Player	TD	PAT	FG	TOTAL
1. Wersching, Ray (1977-87)	—	409	190	979
2. Davis, Tommy (1959-69)	—	348	130	738
3. Soltau, Gordy (1950-58)	25	284	70	644
4. Gossett, Bruce (1970-74)	—	163	99	460
5. Rice, Jerry (1985-)	70	—	—	420
6. Craig, Roger (1983-)	65	—	—	390
7. Willard, Ken (1965-73)	61	—	—	366
8. Washington, Gene (1969-77)	59	—	—	354
9. Perry, Joe (1950-60, 1963)	57	6	1	351
10. McElhenny, Hugh (1952-60)	51	—	—	306

FIELD GOALS
(Made)

Player	Att.	Made	Pct.	Long
1. Wersching, Ray (1977-87)	261	190	.727	53
2. Davis, Tommy (1959-69)	276	130	.471	53
3. Gossett, Bruce (1970-74)	153	99	.641	54
4. Soltau, Gordy (1950-58)	138	70	.507	43
5. Cofer, Mike (1988-)	74	56	.757	52
6. Mike-Mayer, Steve (1975-76)	56	30	.536	54
7. Gavric, Momcilo (1969)	11	3	.273	32
8. Bahr, Matt (1981)	6	2	.333	47
Patera, Dennis (1968)	8	2	.250	21
10. Wittum, Tom (1977)	2	1	.500	28
Perry, Joe (1950-60, 1963)	6	1	.167	14

Super Bowl Seasons

1981 (13-3/16-3)
Bill Walsh, Coach

L	17 At Detroit (62,123)/S-6	24
W	28 Chicago (49,520)/S-13	17
L	17 At Atlanta (56,653)/S-20	34
W	21 New Orleans (44,433)/S-27	14
W	30 At Washington (51,843)/0-4	17
W	45 Dallas (57,574)/0-11	14
W	13 At. G.B. in Milwaukee (50,171)/0-18	3
W	20 Los Angeles Rams (59,190)/0-25	17
W	17 At Pittsburgh (52,878)/N-1	14
W	17 Atlanta (59,127)/N-8	14
L	12 Cleveland (52,445)/N-15	15
W	33 At Los Angeles Rams (63,456)/N-22	31
W	17 New York Giants (57,186)/N-29	10
W	21 At Cincinnati (56,796)/D-6	3
W	28 Houston (55,707)/D-13	6
W	21 At New Orleans (43,639)/D-20	17
	357	250

NFC PLAYOFF—JAN. 3
(At San Francisco-Candlestick)

W	38 New York Giants (58,360)	24

NFC CHAMPIONSHIP—JAN. 10
(At San Francisco-Candlestick)

W	28 Dallas (60,525)	27

SUPER BOWL XVI—JAN. 24
(At Pontiac, Michigan-Silverdome)

W	26 Cincinnati (81,270)	21

1984 (15-1/18-1)
Bill Walsh, Coach

W	30 At Detroit (56,782)/S-2	27
W	37 Washington (59,707)-MN/S-10	31
W	30 New Orleans (57,611)/S-16	20
W	21 At Philadelphia (62,771)/S-23	9
W	14 Atlanta (57,990)/S-30	5
W	31 At New York Giants (76,112)-MN/0-8	10
L	17 Pittsburgh (59,110)/0-14	20
W	34 At Houston (39,900)/0-21	21
W	33 At Los Angeles Rams (65,481)/0-28	0
W	23 Cincinnati (58,234)/N-4	17
W	41 At Cleveland (60,092)/N-11	7
W	24 Tampa Bay (57,704)/N-18	17
W	35 At New Orleans (65,177)/N-25	3
W	35 At Atlanta (29,644)/D-2	17
W	51 Minnesota (56,670)-SA/D-8	7
W	19 Los Angeles Rams (59,743)-FN/D14	16
	475	227

NFC PLAYOFF—DEC.29
(At San Francisco-Candlestick)

W	21 New York Giants (60,303)-SA	10

NFC CHAMPIONSHIP—JAN. 6
(At San Francisco-Candlestick)

W	23 Chicago (61,040)	0

SUPER BOWL XIX—JAN. 20
(At Palo Alto, California-Stanford Stadium)

W	38 Miami (84,059)	16

MN-Monday Night
SA-Saturday

1988 (10-6/13-6)
Bill Walsh, Coach

W	34 At New Orleans (66,357)/S-4	33
W	20 At New York Giants (75,948)/S-11	17
L	17 Atlanta (60,168)/S-18	34
W	38 At Seattle (62,382)/S-25	7
W	20 Detroit (58,285)/0-2	13
L	13 Denver (61,711)/0-9	(OT) 16
W	24 At L.A. Rams (65,450)/0-16	21
L	9 At Chicago (65,293)MN/0-24	10
W	24 Minnesota (60,738)/0-30	21
L	23 At Phoenix (64,544)/N-6	24
L	3 L.A. Raiders (54,448)/N-13	9
W	37 Washington (59,268)MN/N-21	21
W	48 At San Diego (51,484)/N-27	10
W	13 At Atlanta (44,048)/D-4	3
W	30 New Orleans (62,977)/D-11	17
L	16 Rams (62,444)MN/D-18	38
	369	294

NFC PLAYOFF—JAN. 1
(At San Francisco-Candlestick)

W	34 Minnesota (61,848)	9

NFC CHAMPIONSHIP—JAN. 8
(At Chicago-Soldier Field)

W	28 At Chicago (66,946)	3

SUPER BOWL XXII—JAN. 22
(At Miami-Joe Robbie Stadium)

W	20 Cincinnati (75,129)	16

1989 (14-2/17-2)
George Seifert, Coach

W	30 At Indianapolis (60,111)/S-10	24
W	20 At Tampa Bay (64,087)/S-17	16
W	38 At Philadelphia (66,042)/S-24	28
L	12 At Los Angeles Rams (64,250)/0-1	13
W	24 At New Orleans (60,488)MN/0-8	20
W	31 At Dallas (61,077)/0-15	14
W	37 At New England (70,000)/0-22	20
W	23 At New York Jets (62,805)/0-29	10
W	31 At New Orleans (60,667)/N-6	13
W	45 At Atlanta (59,914)/N-12	3
L	17 At Green Bay (62,219)/N-19	21
W	34 At N.Y. Giants (63,461)MN/N-27	24
W	23 At Atlanta (43,128)/D-3	10
W	30 At Los Angeles Rams (67,959)MN/D-11	27
W	21 At Buffalo (60,927)/D-17	10
W	26 At Chicago (60,207)/D-24	0
	442	253

NFC PLAYOFF—JAN. 1
(At San Francisco-Candlestick)

W	41 Minnesota (64,585)/SA	13

NFC CHAMPIONSHIP—JAN. 14
(At San Francisco-Candlestick)

W	30 L.A. Rams (64,769)	3

SUPER BOWL XXIV—JAN. 28
(At New Orleans-Superdome)

W	55 Denver (72,919)	10

INDEX